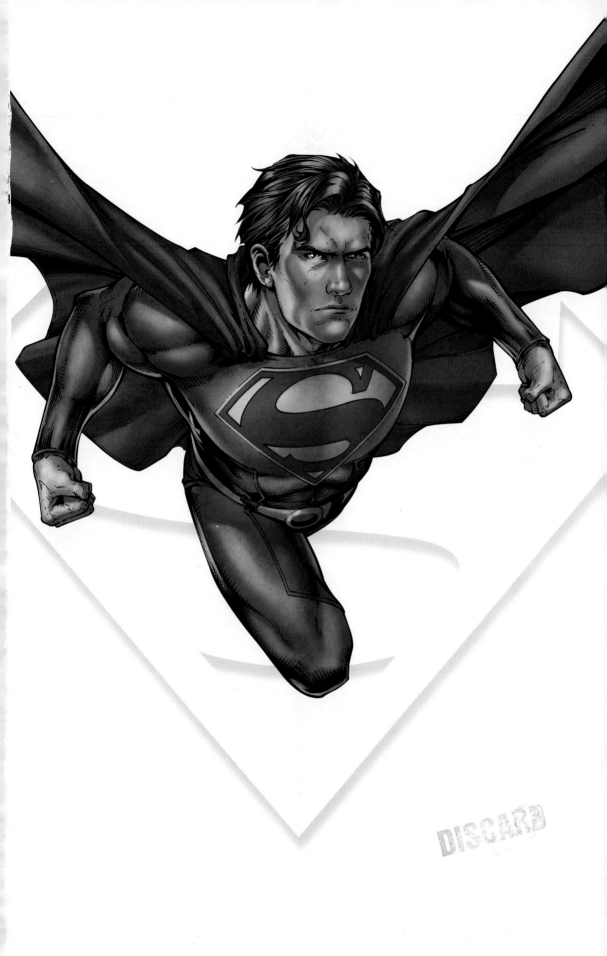

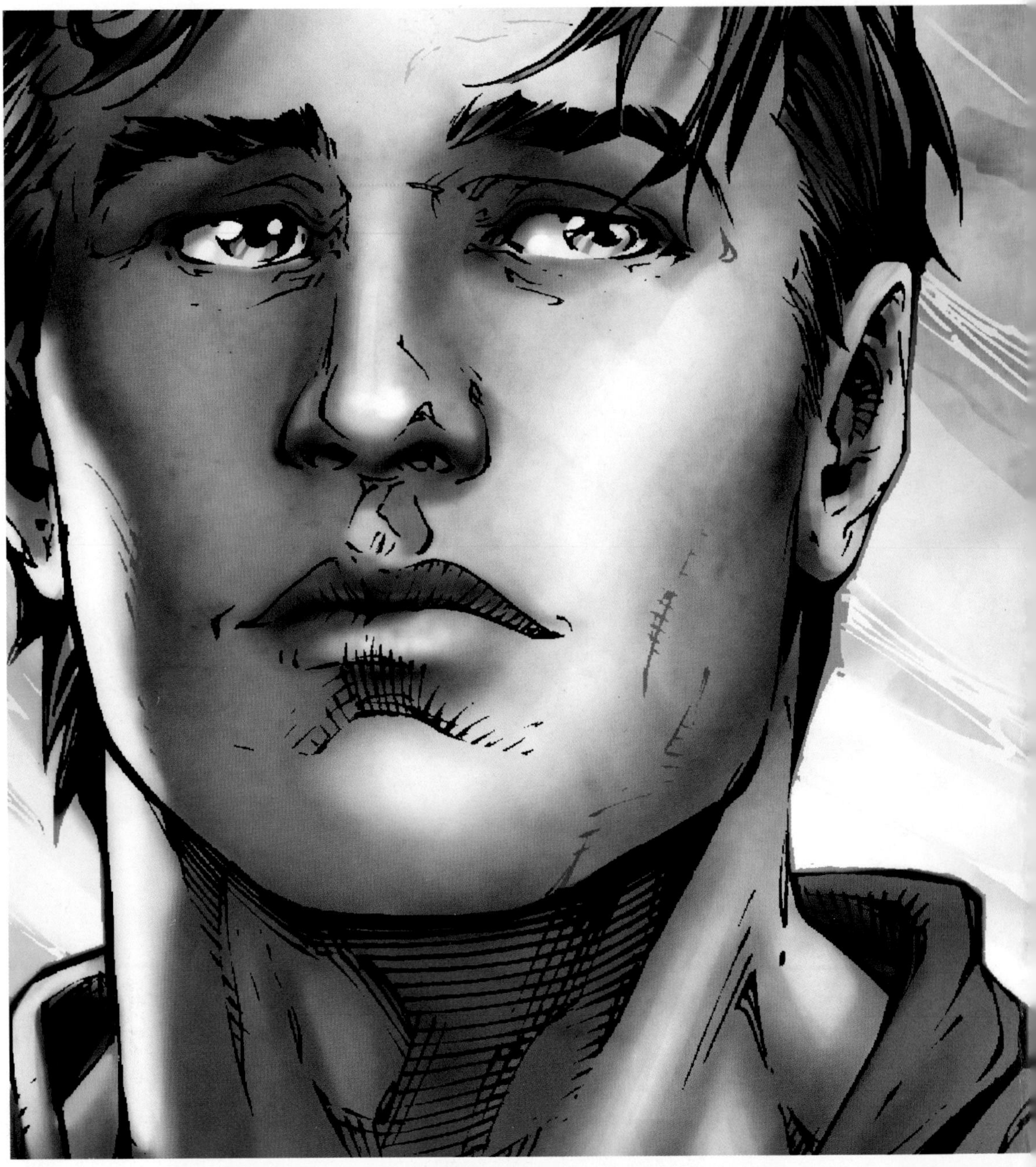
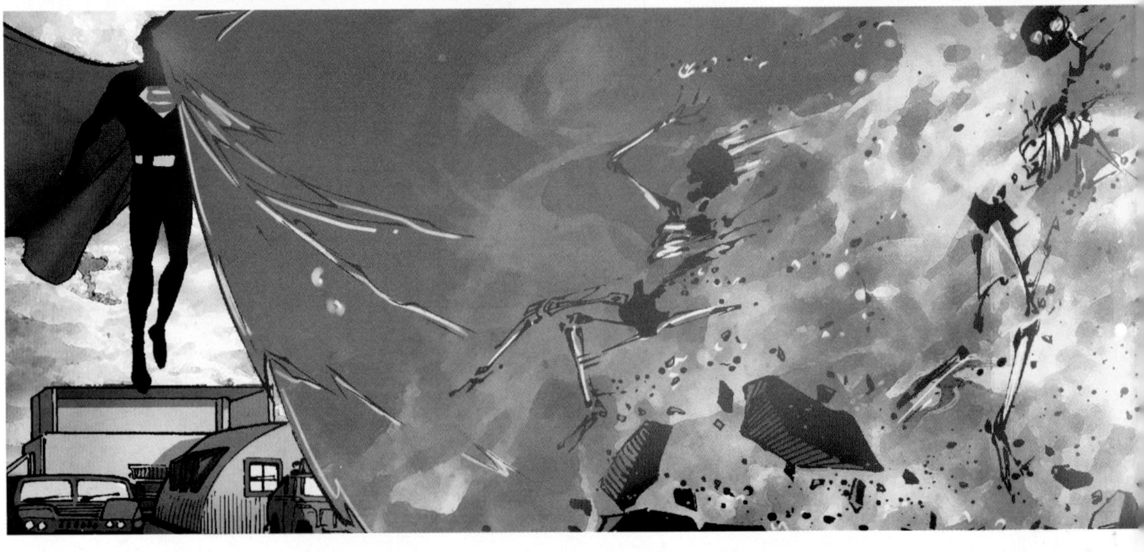

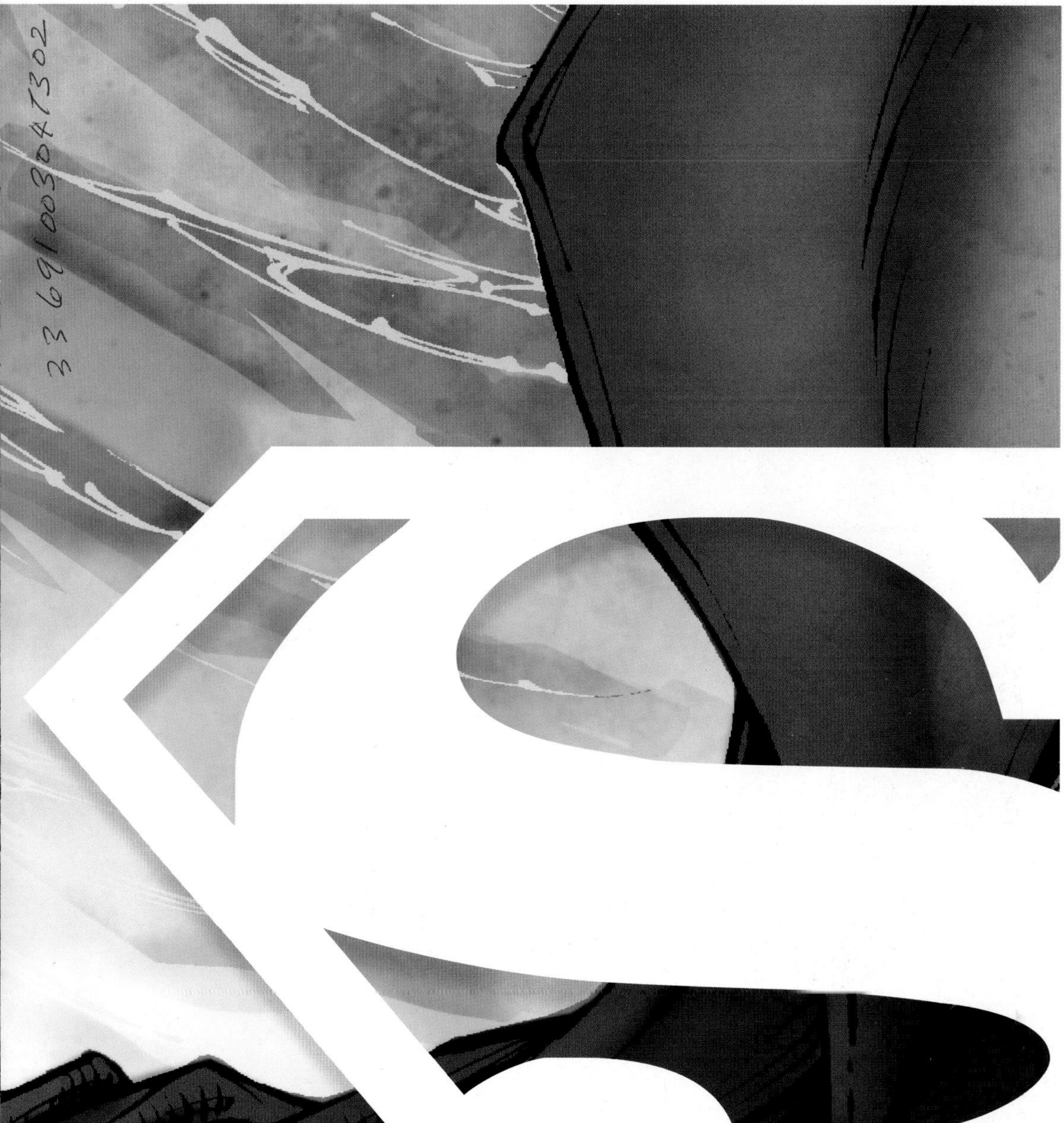

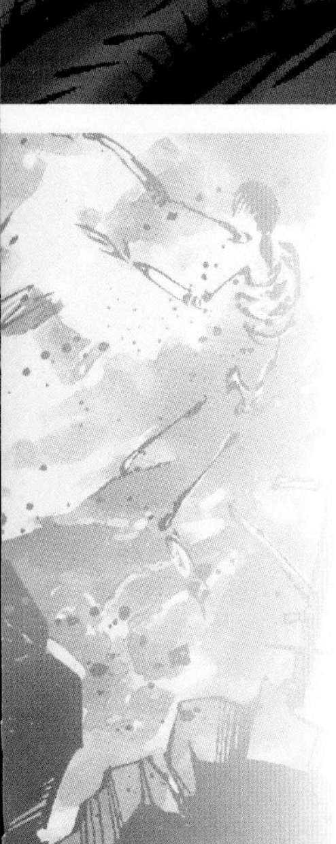

EARTH ONE

Written by J. Michael Straczynski
Pencils by Shane Davis
Inks by Sandra Hope
Colors by Barbara Ciardo
Lettered by Rob Leigh
Superman created by Jerry Siegel and Joe Shuster.

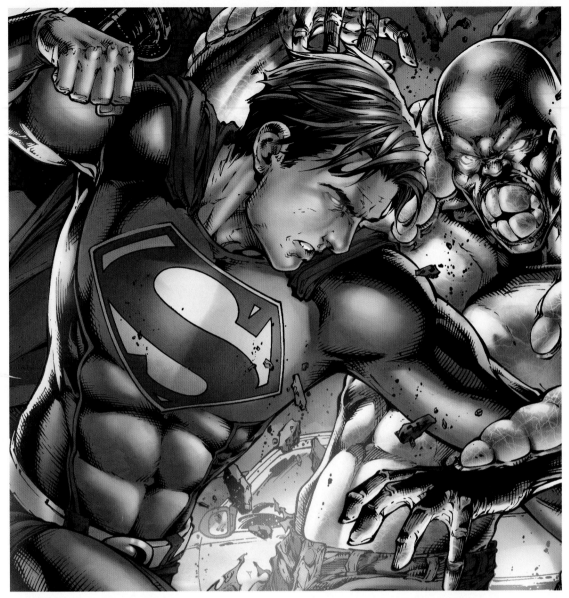

Eddie Berganza Editor
Darren Shan Assistant Editor
Robbin Brosterman Design Director – Books
Louis Prandi Art Director

Bob Harras VP – Editor-in-Chief

Diane Nelson President
Dan DiDio and **Jim Lee** Co-Publishers
Geoff Johns Chief Creative Officer
John Rood Executive VP – Sales, Marketing and Business Development
Amy Genkins Senior VP – Business and Legal Affairs
Nairi Gardiner Senior VP – Finance
Jeff Boison VP – Publishing Operations
Mark Chiarello VP – Art Direction and Design
John Cunningham VP – Marketing
Terri Cunningham VP – Talent Relations and Services
Alison Gill Senior VP – Manufacturing and Operations
Hank Kanalz Senior VP – Digital
Jay Kogan VP – Business and Legal Affairs, Publishing
Jack Mahan VP – Business Affairs, Talent
Nick Napolitano VP – Manufacturing Administration
Sue Pohja VP – Book Sales
Courtney Simmons Senior VP – Publicity
Bob Wayne Senior VP – Sales

 SUPERMAN:EARTH ONE VOLUME TWO

Published by DC Comics, 1700 Broadway, New York, NY 10019.
Copyright © 2012 DC Comics. All rights reserved. All characters featured
in this publication, the distinctive likenesses thereof and related elements
are trademarks of DC Comics. Printed by RR Donnelley, Salem, VA, USA.
9/5/12 First Printing. DC Comics, a Warner Bros. Entertainment Company.

IT'S ALRIGHT , MA (I'M ONLY BLEEDING), Author, BOB DYLAN, Copyright
© 1965 by Warner Bros. Inc.; renewed 1993 by Special Rider Music. All
rights reserved. International copyright secured. Reprinted by permission.
HC ISBN: 978-1-4012-3196-5   SC ISBN: 978-1-4012-3559-8

Library of Congress Cataloging-in-Publication Data

Straczynski, J. Michael, 1954-
  Superman earth one volume 2 / J. Michael Straczynski, Shane Davis.
    p. cm.
  ISBN 978-1-4012-3196-5
  1. Graphic novels. I. Davis, Shane. II. Title.
PN6728.S9S773 2012
741.5'973--dc23
                                2012023698

SUSTAINABLE
FORESTRY
INITIATIVE
Certified Chain of Custody
Promoting Sustainable
Forest Management
www.sfiprogram.org
Fiber used in this product line meets the
sourcing requirements of the SFI program.
www.sfiprogram.org NFS-SPIC0C-C0001801

DEDICATIONS

To the writers who lit the fire and led the way
ROD SERLING, HARLAN ELLISON
and NORMAN CORWIN
And the high school teachers
who set me safely on the path
JO ANN SEIPLE and ROCHELLE TERRY
Thank you
I would not be here without you

J. Michael Straczynski

I would like to dedicate this book to Shannon
and the dreams that kept him up at night. I would
also like to thank Dan, Larry, John and Michelle
for their support.

Shane Davis

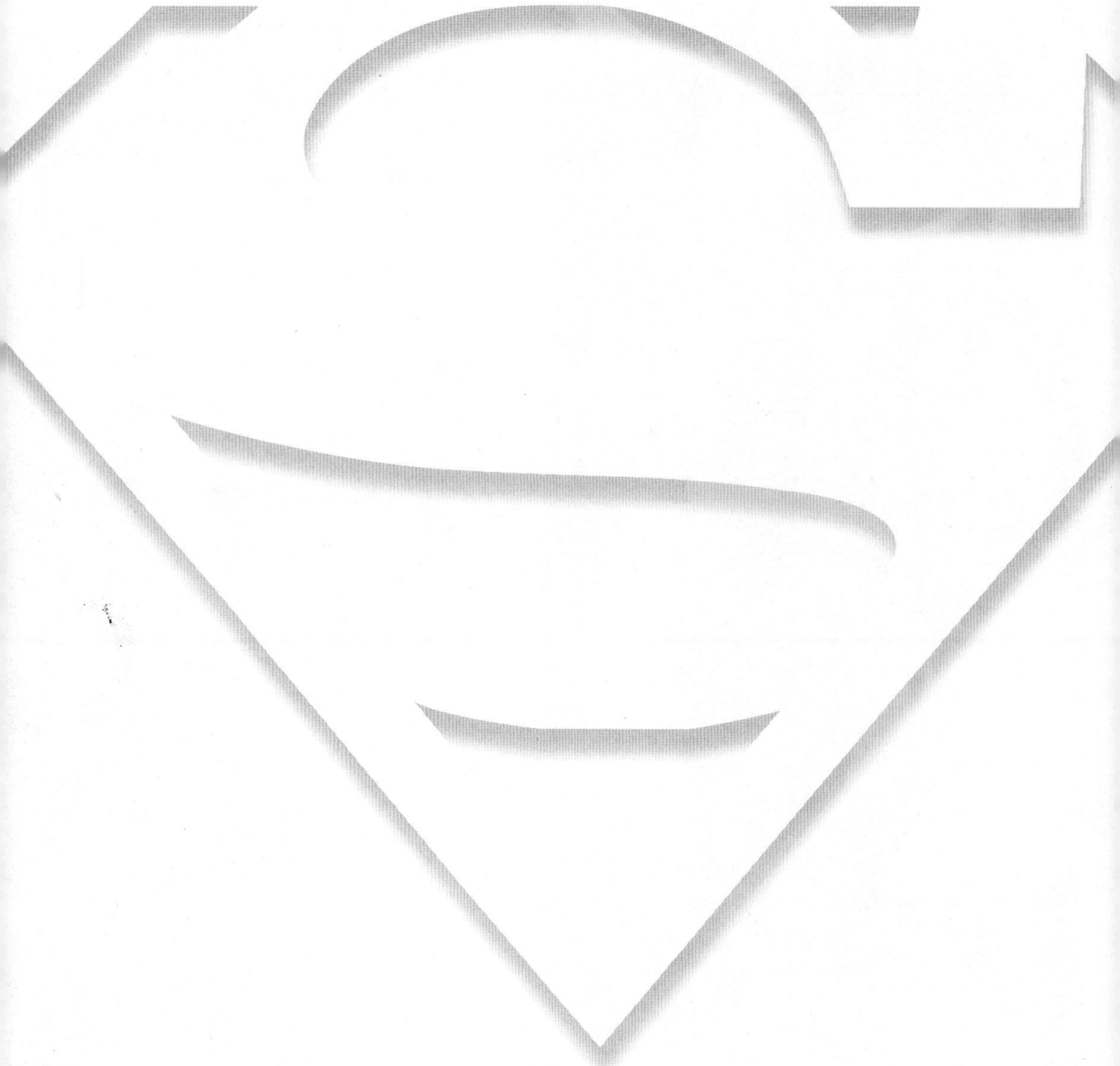

DAILY PLANET

"S" IS FOR...

...SUPERMAN. At least that's how he identified himself when he sat down for this exclusive interview with the *Daily Planet*, conducted in the aftermath of the...

himself whe
Daily Planet

By Clark Kent
Daily Planet
Staff Reporter

YOU KNOW WHY THAT'S ON THE WALL, KENT?

SORRY...?

I SAID DO YOU KNOW WHY THAT'S ON THE WALL?

BECAUSE PUTTING IT ON THE FLOOR WOULD SMEAR THE INK?

IT'S BEHIND GLASS.

BECAUSE PUTTING IT ON THE FLOOR WOULD BREAK THE GLASS?

A LOT OF FOLKS THINK I HAVE THEIR ARTICLES FRAMED TO COMMEMORATE HIGH POINTS IN THE HISTORY OF THE *DAILY PLANET*.

IT'S NOT?

WELL... YES, IN A WAY. BUT THAT'S NOT THE *MAIN* REASON.

I FRAMED THEM TO MAKE THE POINT THAT THEY'RE OLD NEWS, KENT.

FROZEN IN TIME. DEAD.

MUMMIFIED BEHIND GLASS, LIKE BUTTERFLIES ON PINS.

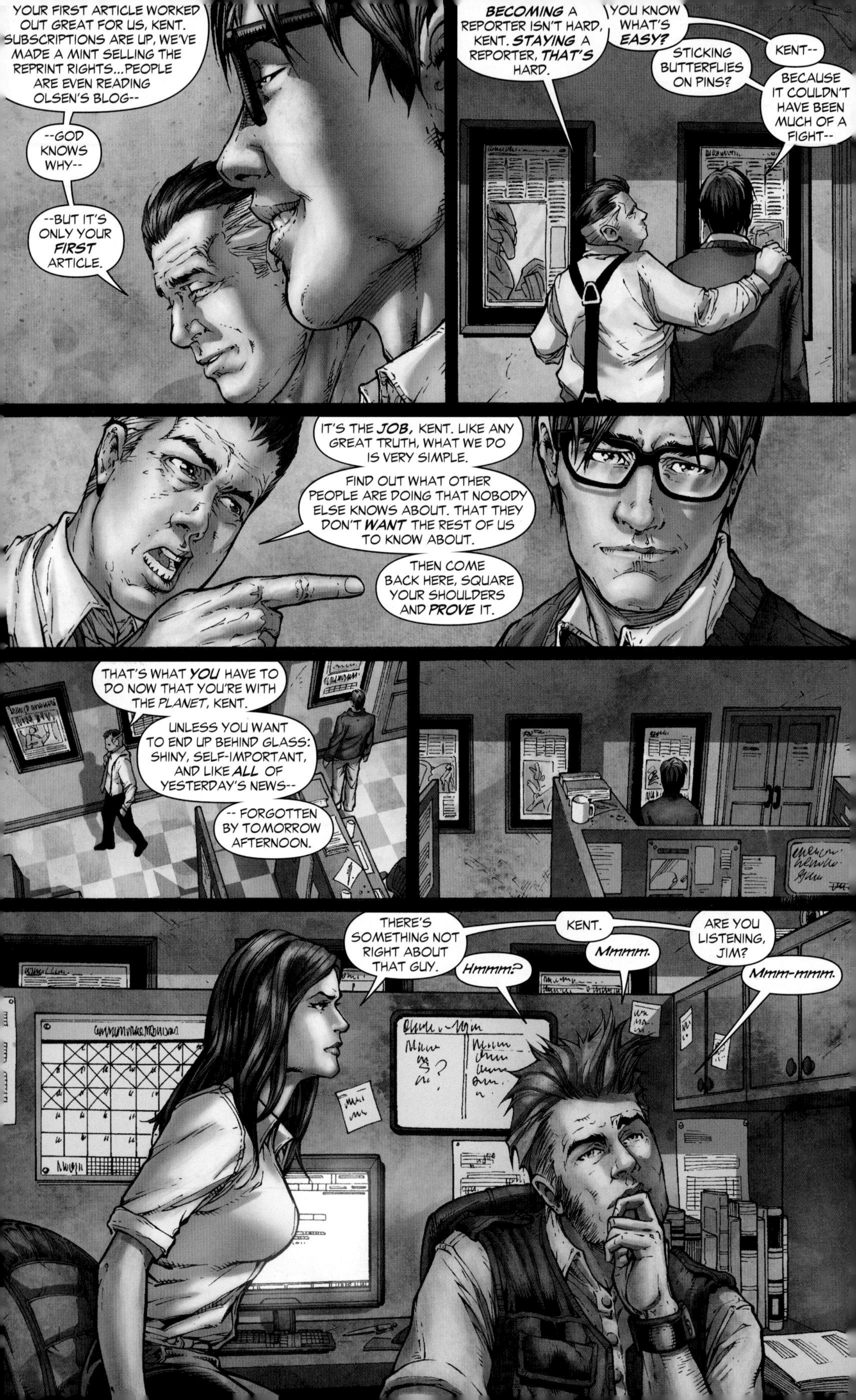
YOUR FIRST ARTICLE WORKED OUT GREAT FOR US, KENT. SUBSCRIPTIONS ARE UP, WE'VE MADE A MINT SELLING THE REPRINT RIGHTS...PEOPLE ARE EVEN READING OLSEN'S BLOG--
--GOD KNOWS WHY--
--BUT IT'S ONLY YOUR *FIRST* ARTICLE.
BECOMING A REPORTER ISN'T HARD, KENT. *STAYING* A REPORTER, *THAT'S* HARD.
YOU KNOW WHAT'S *EASY?*
STICKING BUTTERFLIES ON PINS?
KENT--
BECAUSE IT COULDN'T HAVE BEEN MUCH OF A FIGHT--
IT'S THE *JOB,* KENT. LIKE ANY GREAT TRUTH, WHAT WE DO IS VERY SIMPLE.
FIND OUT WHAT OTHER PEOPLE ARE DOING THAT NOBODY ELSE KNOWS ABOUT. THAT THEY DON'T *WANT* THE REST OF US TO KNOW ABOUT.
THEN COME BACK HERE, SQUARE YOUR SHOULDERS AND *PROVE* IT.
THAT'S WHAT *YOU* HAVE TO DO NOW THAT YOU'RE WITH THE *PLANET*, KENT.
UNLESS YOU WANT TO END UP BEHIND GLASS: SHINY, SELF-IMPORTANT, AND LIKE *ALL* OF YESTERDAY'S NEWS--
-- FORGOTTEN BY TOMORROW AFTERNOON.
THERE'S SOMETHING NOT RIGHT ABOUT THAT GUY.
Hmmm?
KENT.
Mmmm.
ARE YOU LISTENING, JIM?
Mmm-mmm.

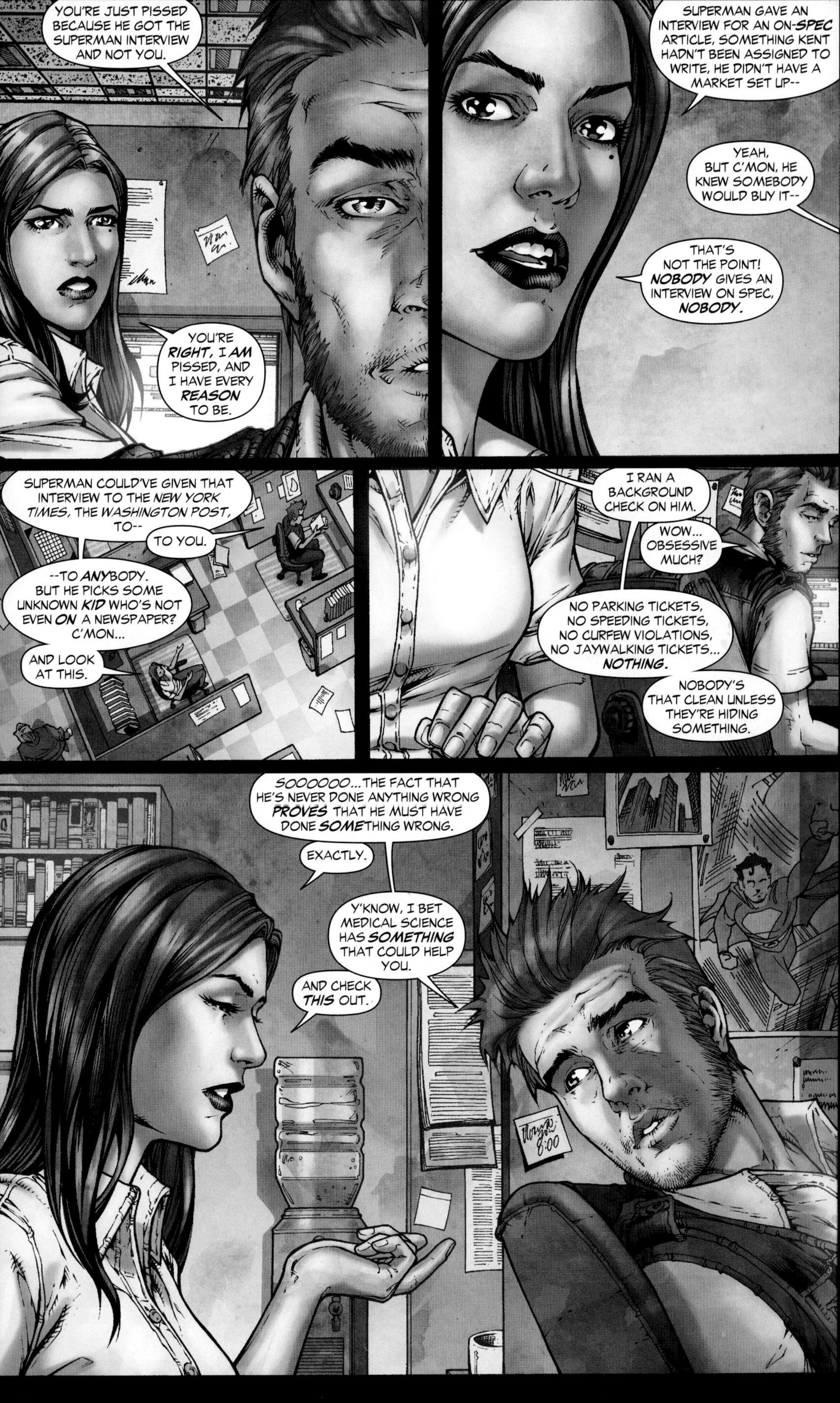
YOU'RE JUST PISSED BECAUSE HE GOT THE SUPERMAN INTERVIEW AND NOT YOU.
YOU'RE RIGHT, I AM PISSED, AND I HAVE EVERY REASON TO BE.
SUPERMAN GAVE AN INTERVIEW FOR AN ON-SPEC ARTICLE, SOMETHING KENT HADN'T BEEN ASSIGNED TO WRITE, HE DIDN'T HAVE A MARKET SET UP--
YEAH, BUT C'MON, HE KNEW SOMEBODY WOULD BUY IT--
THAT'S NOT THE POINT! NOBODY GIVES AN INTERVIEW ON SPEC, NOBODY.
SUPERMAN COULD'VE GIVEN THAT INTERVIEW TO THE NEW YORK TIMES, THE WASHINGTON POST, TO--
TO YOU.
--TO ANYBODY. BUT HE PICKS SOME UNKNOWN KID WHO'S NOT EVEN ON A NEWSPAPER? C'MON...
AND LOOK AT THIS.
I RAN A BACKGROUND CHECK ON HIM.
WOW... OBSESSIVE MUCH?
NO PARKING TICKETS, NO SPEEDING TICKETS, NO CURFEW VIOLATIONS, NO JAYWALKING TICKETS... NOTHING.
NOBODY'S THAT CLEAN UNLESS THEY'RE HIDING SOMETHING.
SOOOOOO... THE FACT THAT HE'S NEVER DONE ANYTHING WRONG PROVES THAT HE MUST HAVE DONE SOMETHING WRONG.
EXACTLY.
Y'KNOW, I BET MEDICAL SCIENCE HAS SOMETHING THAT COULD HELP YOU.
AND CHECK THIS OUT.

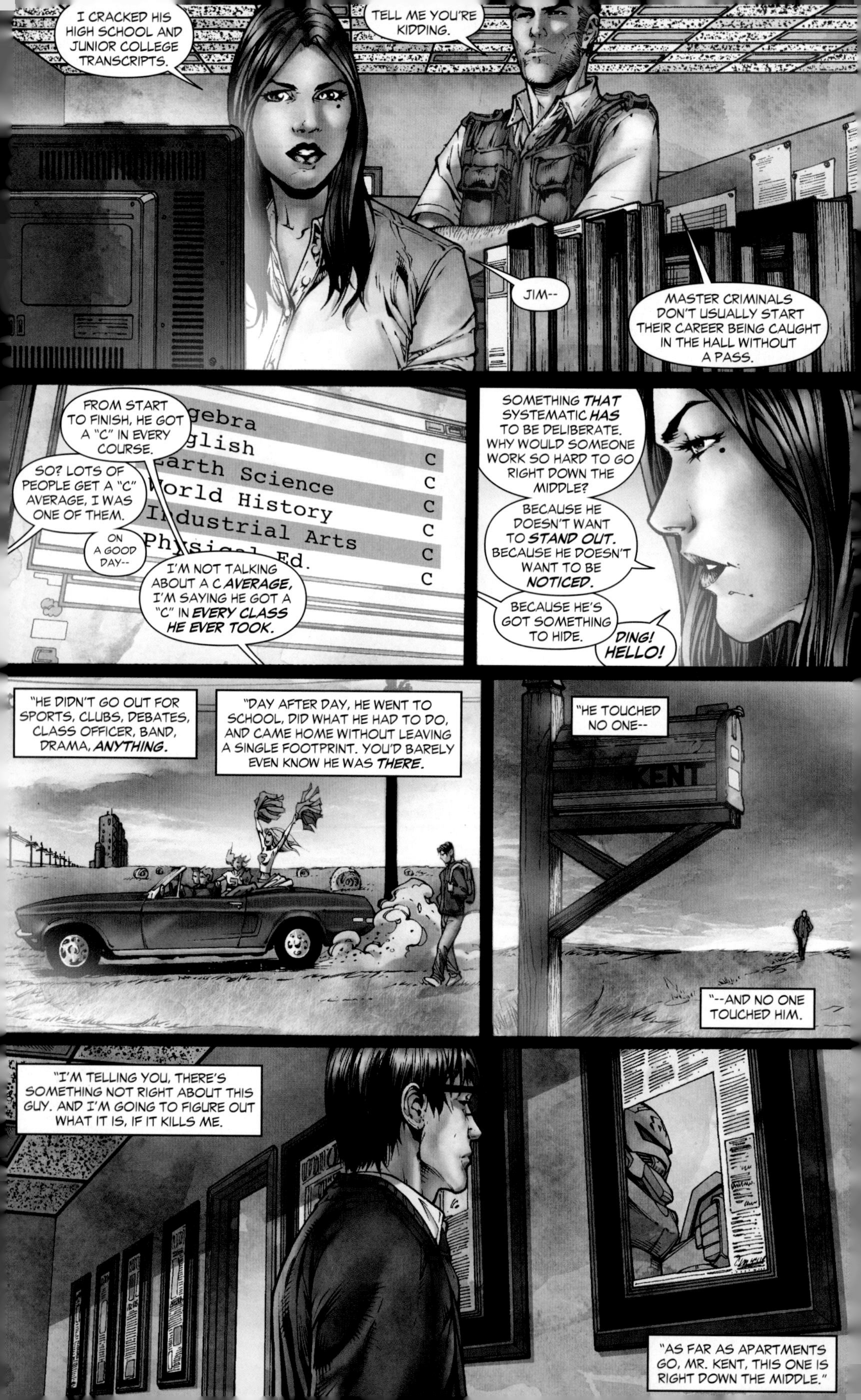
I CRACKED HIS HIGH SCHOOL AND JUNIOR COLLEGE TRANSCRIPTS.
TELL ME YOU'RE KIDDING.
JIM--
MASTER CRIMINALS DON'T USUALLY START THEIR CAREER BEING CAUGHT IN THE HALL WITHOUT A PASS.
gebra
glish
Earth Science C
World History C
Industrial Arts C
FROM START TO FINISH, HE GOT A "C" IN EVERY COURSE.
SO? LOTS OF PEOPLE GET A "C" AVERAGE, I WAS ONE OF THEM.
ON A GOOD DAY--
I'M NOT TALKING ABOUT A C AVERAGE, I'M SAYING HE GOT A "C" IN EVERY CLASS HE EVER TOOK.
SOMETHING THAT SYSTEMATIC HAS TO BE DELIBERATE. WHY WOULD SOMEONE WORK SO HARD TO GO RIGHT DOWN THE MIDDLE?
BECAUSE HE DOESN'T WANT TO STAND OUT. BECAUSE HE DOESN'T WANT TO BE NOTICED.
BECAUSE HE'S GOT SOMETHING TO HIDE.
DING! HELLO!
"HE DIDN'T GO OUT FOR SPORTS, CLUBS, DEBATES, CLASS OFFICER, BAND, DRAMA, ANYTHING.
"DAY AFTER DAY, HE WENT TO SCHOOL, DID WHAT HE HAD TO DO, AND CAME HOME WITHOUT LEAVING A SINGLE FOOTPRINT. YOU'D BARELY EVEN KNOW HE WAS THERE.
"HE TOUCHED NO ONE--
KENT
"--AND NO ONE TOUCHED HIM.
"I'M TELLING YOU, THERE'S SOMETHING NOT RIGHT ABOUT THIS GUY. AND I'M GOING TO FIGURE OUT WHAT IT IS, IF IT KILLS ME.
"AS FAR AS APARTMENTS GO, MR. KENT, THIS ONE IS RIGHT DOWN THE MIDDLE."

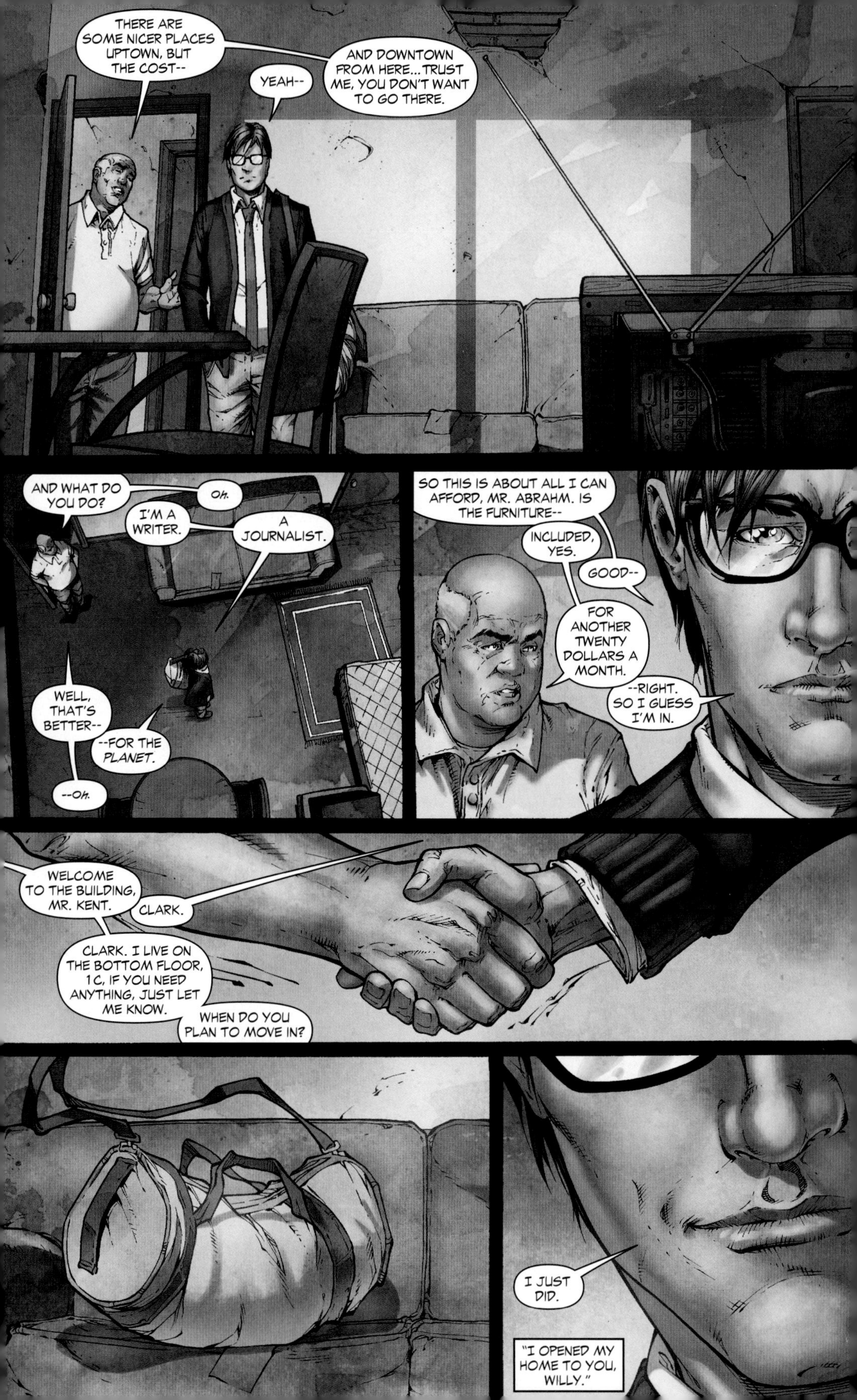
THERE ARE SOME NICER PLACES UPTOWN, BUT THE COST--
YEAH--
AND DOWNTOWN FROM HERE...TRUST ME, YOU DON'T WANT TO GO THERE.
AND WHAT DO YOU DO?
Oh.
I'M A WRITER.
A JOURNALIST.
WELL, THAT'S BETTER--
--FOR THE PLANET.
--Oh.
SO THIS IS ABOUT ALL I CAN AFFORD, MR. ABRAHM. IS THE FURNITURE--
INCLUDED, YES.
GOOD--
FOR ANOTHER TWENTY DOLLARS A MONTH.
--RIGHT. SO I GUESS I'M IN.
WELCOME TO THE BUILDING, MR. KENT.
CLARK.
CLARK. I LIVE ON THE BOTTOM FLOOR, 1C, IF YOU NEED ANYTHING, JUST LET ME KNOW.
WHEN DO YOU PLAN TO MOVE IN?
I JUST DID.
"I OPENED MY HOME TO YOU, WILLY."

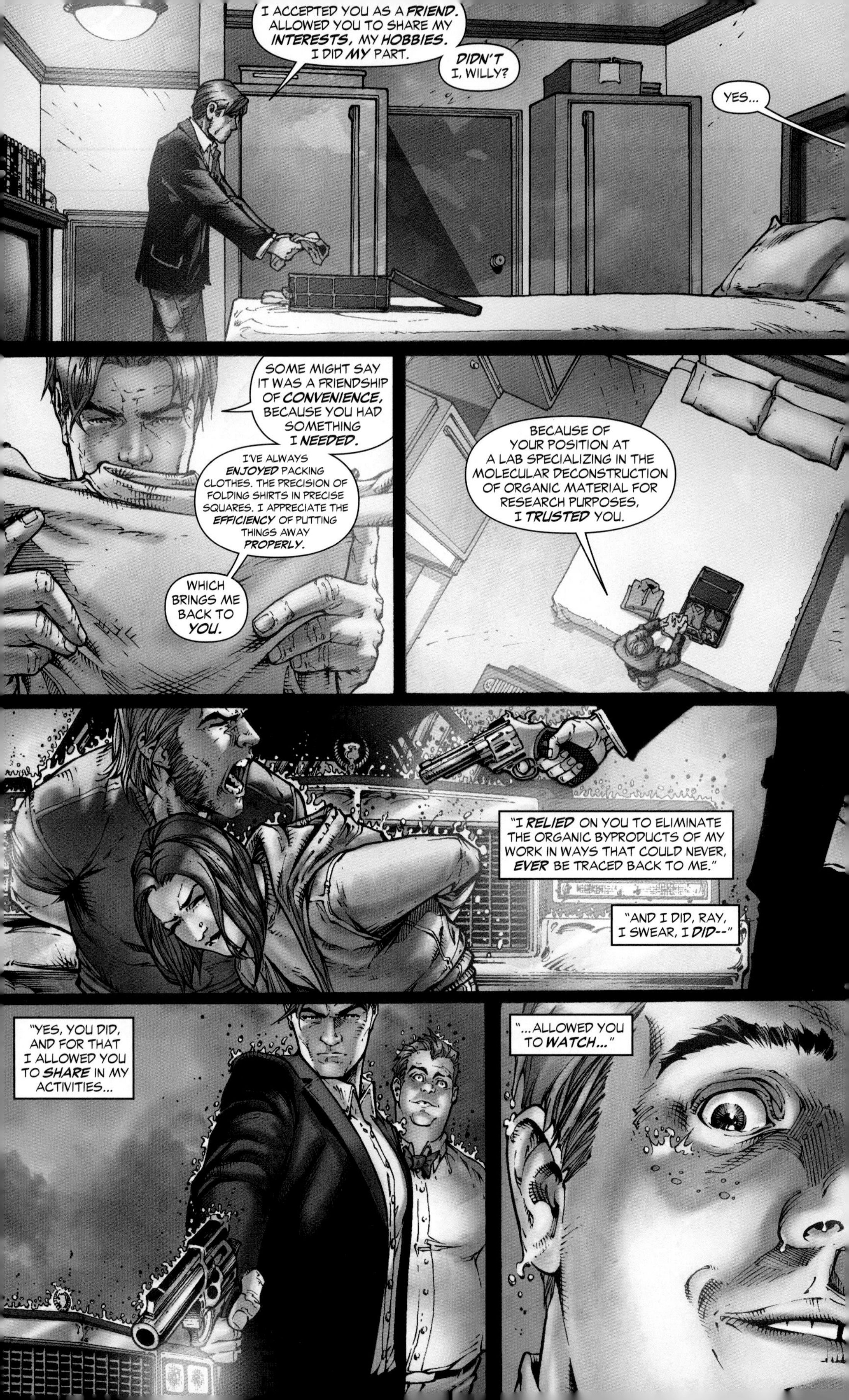
I ACCEPTED YOU AS A FRIEND. ALLOWED YOU TO SHARE MY INTERESTS, MY HOBBIES. I DID MY PART.
DIDN'T I, WILLY?
YES...
SOME MIGHT SAY IT WAS A FRIENDSHIP OF CONVENIENCE, BECAUSE YOU HAD SOMETHING I NEEDED.
I'VE ALWAYS ENJOYED PACKING CLOTHES. THE PRECISION OF FOLDING SHIRTS IN PRECISE SQUARES. I APPRECIATE THE EFFICIENCY OF PUTTING THINGS AWAY PROPERLY.
WHICH BRINGS ME BACK TO YOU.
BECAUSE OF YOUR POSITION AT A LAB SPECIALIZING IN THE MOLECULAR DECONSTRUCTION OF ORGANIC MATERIAL FOR RESEARCH PURPOSES, I TRUSTED YOU.
"I RELIED ON YOU TO ELIMINATE THE ORGANIC BYPRODUCTS OF MY WORK IN WAYS THAT COULD NEVER, EVER BE TRACED BACK TO ME."
"AND I DID, RAY, I SWEAR, I DID--"
"YES, YOU DID, AND FOR THAT I ALLOWED YOU TO SHARE IN MY ACTIVITIES...
"...ALLOWED YOU TO WATCH..."

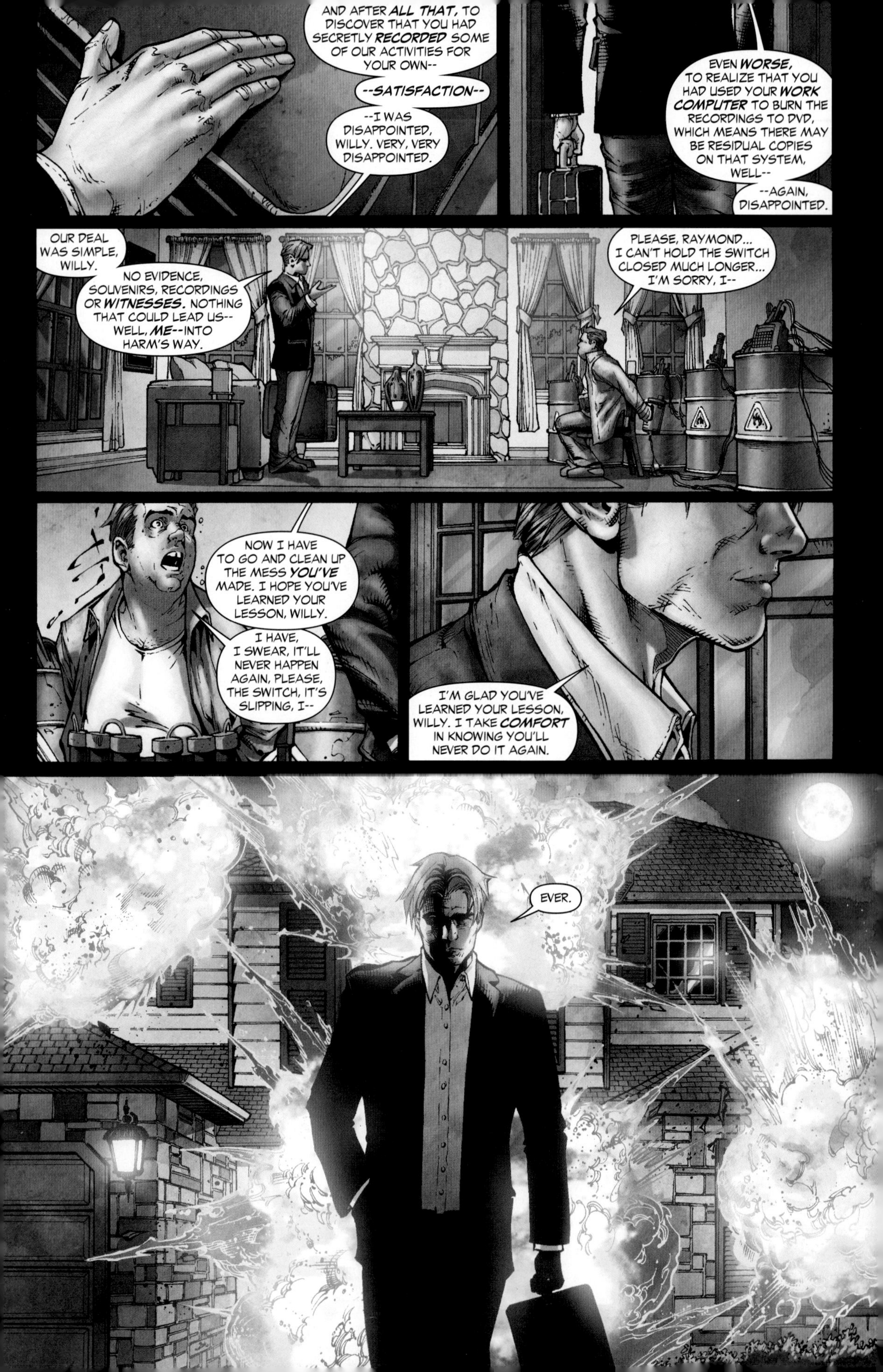
AND AFTER ALL THAT, TO DISCOVER THAT YOU HAD SECRETLY RECORDED SOME OF OUR ACTIVITIES FOR YOUR OWN--
--SATISFACTION--
--I WAS DISAPPOINTED, WILLY. VERY, VERY DISAPPOINTED.
EVEN WORSE, TO REALIZE THAT YOU HAD USED YOUR WORK COMPUTER TO BURN THE RECORDINGS TO DVD, WHICH MEANS THERE MAY BE RESIDUAL COPIES ON THAT SYSTEM, WELL--
--AGAIN, DISAPPOINTED.
OUR DEAL WAS SIMPLE, WILLY.
NO EVIDENCE, SOUVENIRS, RECORDINGS OR WITNESSES. NOTHING THAT COULD LEAD US--WELL, ME--INTO HARM'S WAY.
PLEASE, RAYMOND... I CAN'T HOLD THE SWITCH CLOSED MUCH LONGER... I'M SORRY, I--
NOW I HAVE TO GO AND CLEAN UP THE MESS YOU'VE MADE. I HOPE YOU'VE LEARNED YOUR LESSON, WILLY.
I HAVE, I SWEAR, IT'LL NEVER HAPPEN AGAIN, PLEASE, THE SWITCH, IT'S SLIPPING, I--
I'M GLAD YOU'VE LEARNED YOUR LESSON, WILLY. I TAKE COMFORT IN KNOWING YOU'LL NEVER DO IT AGAIN.
EVER.

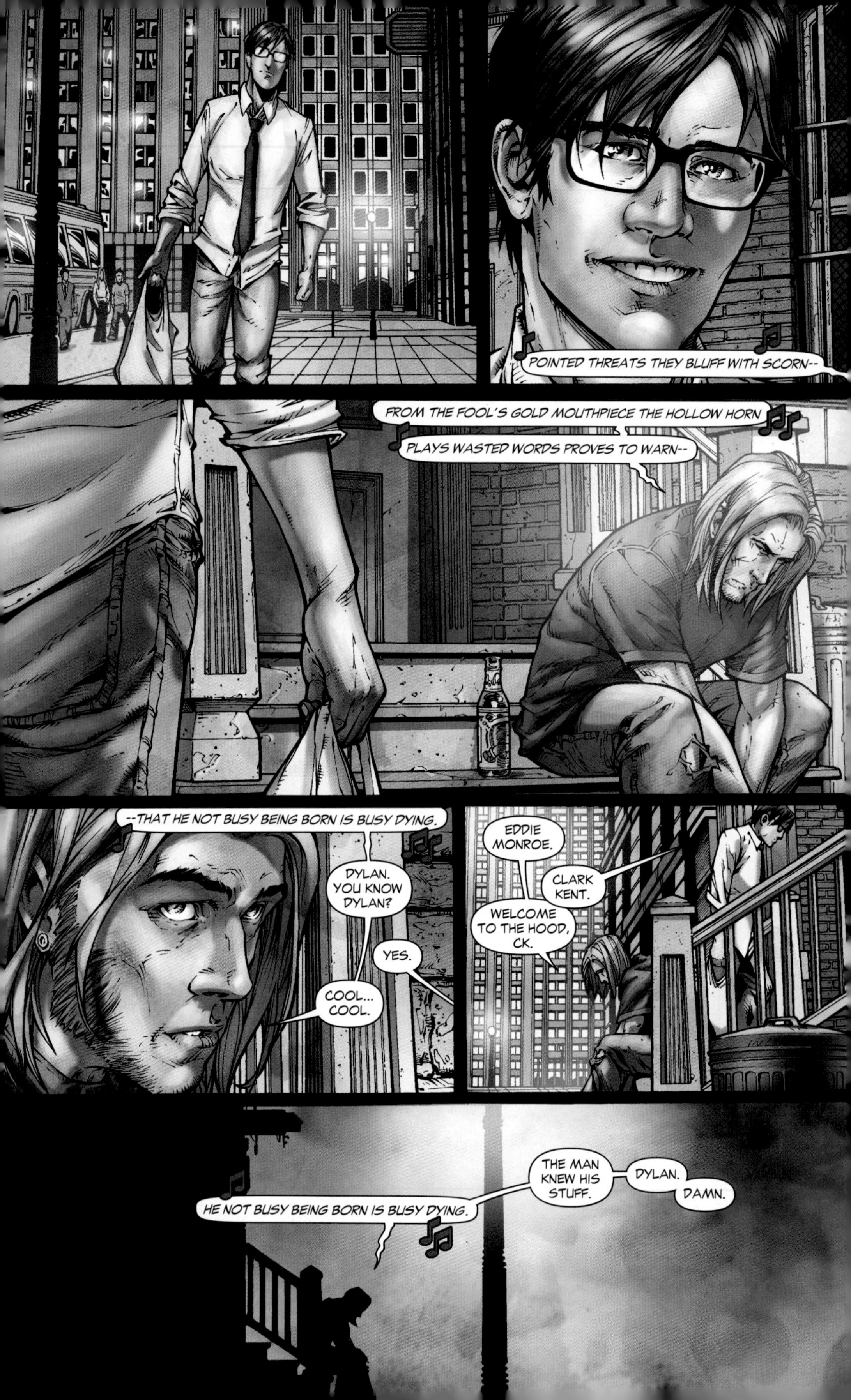
POINTED THREATS THEY BLUFF WITH SCORN--
FROM THE FOOL'S GOLD MOUTHPIECE THE HOLLOW HORN
PLAYS WASTED WORDS PROVES TO WARN--
--THAT HE NOT BUSY BEING BORN IS BUSY DYING.
DYLAN. YOU KNOW DYLAN?
YES.
COOL... COOL.
EDDIE MONROE.
CLARK KENT.
WELCOME TO THE HOOD, CK.
HE NOT BUSY BEING BORN IS BUSY DYING.
THE MAN KNEW HIS STUFF.
DYLAN.
DAMN.

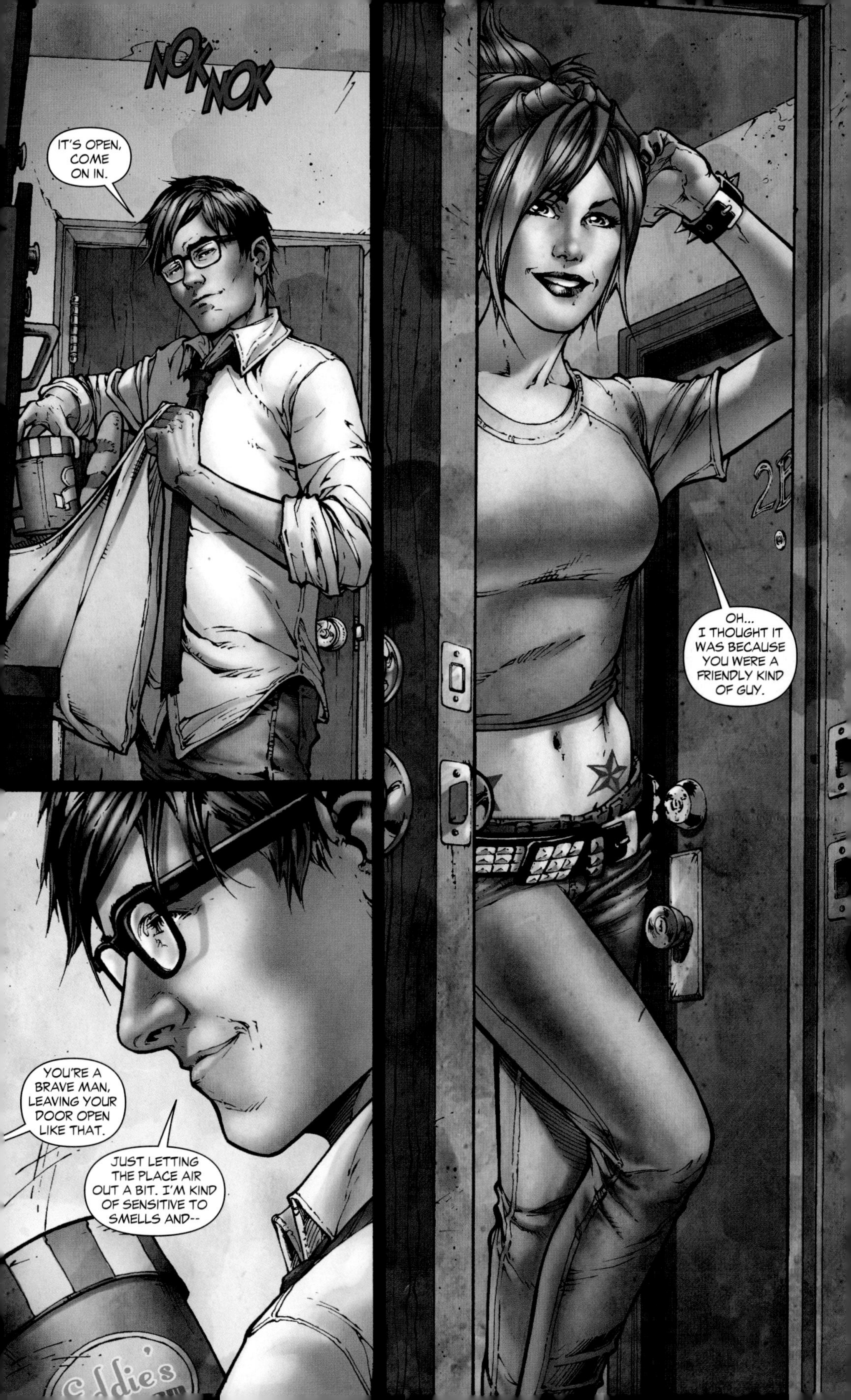
NOK NOK
IT'S OPEN, COME ON IN.
YOU'RE A BRAVE MAN, LEAVING YOUR DOOR OPEN LIKE THAT.
JUST LETTING THE PLACE AIR OUT A BIT. I'M KIND OF SENSITIVE TO SMELLS AND--
OH... I THOUGHT IT WAS BECAUSE YOU WERE A FRIENDLY KIND OF GUY.
2B

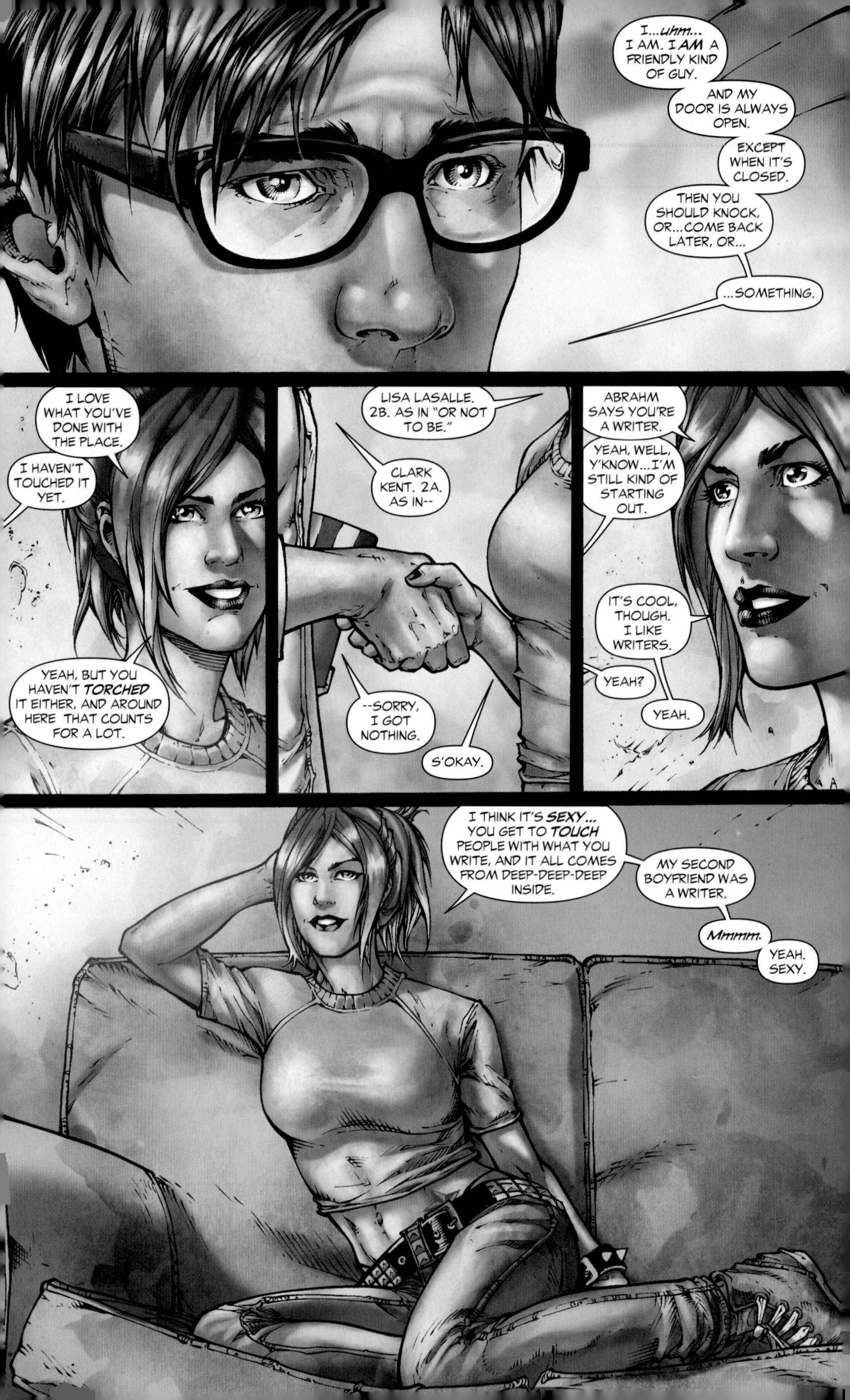
I...uhm... I AM. I AM A FRIENDLY KIND OF GUY.
AND MY DOOR IS ALWAYS OPEN.
EXCEPT WHEN IT'S CLOSED.
THEN YOU SHOULD KNOCK, OR...COME BACK LATER, OR...
...SOMETHING.
I LOVE WHAT YOU'VE DONE WITH THE PLACE.
I HAVEN'T TOUCHED IT YET.
YEAH, BUT YOU HAVEN'T TORCHED IT EITHER, AND AROUND HERE THAT COUNTS FOR A LOT.
LISA LASALLE. 2B. AS IN "OR NOT TO BE."
CLARK KENT. 2A. AS IN--
--SORRY, I GOT NOTHING.
S'OKAY.
ABRAHM SAYS YOU'RE A WRITER.
YEAH, WELL, Y'KNOW...I'M STILL KIND OF STARTING OUT.
IT'S COOL, THOUGH. I LIKE WRITERS.
YEAH?
YEAH.
I THINK IT'S SEXY... YOU GET TO TOUCH PEOPLE WITH WHAT YOU WRITE, AND IT ALL COMES FROM DEEP-DEEP-DEEP INSIDE.
MY SECOND BOYFRIEND WAS A WRITER.
Mmmm.
YEAH. SEXY.

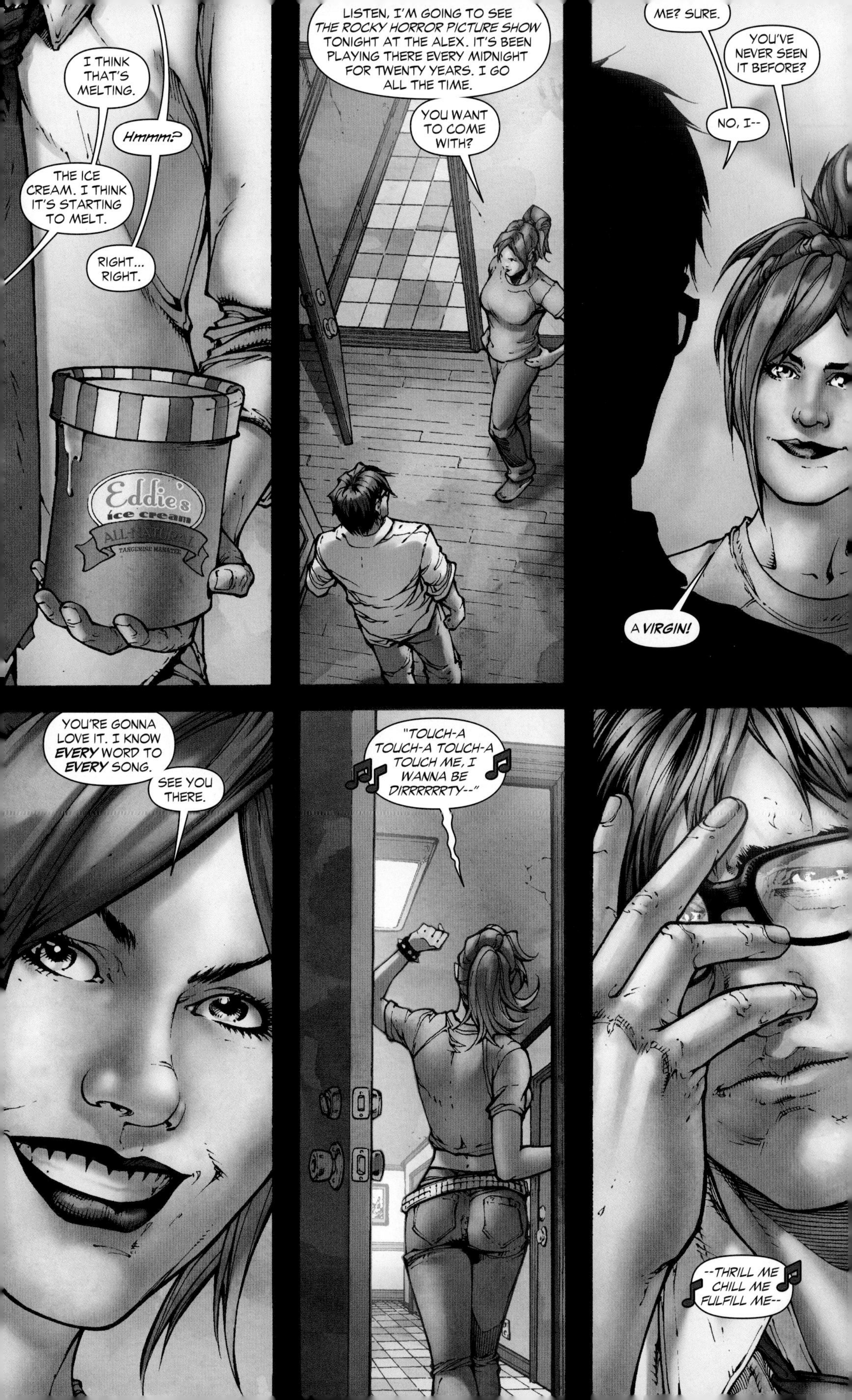
I THINK THAT'S MELTING.
Hmmm?
THE ICE CREAM. I THINK IT'S STARTING TO MELT.
RIGHT... RIGHT.
Eddie's ice cream
ALL-NATURAL
LISTEN, I'M GOING TO SEE THE ROCKY HORROR PICTURE SHOW TONIGHT AT THE ALEX. IT'S BEEN PLAYING THERE EVERY MIDNIGHT FOR TWENTY YEARS. I GO ALL THE TIME.
YOU WANT TO COME WITH?
ME? SURE.
YOU'VE NEVER SEEN IT BEFORE?
NO, I--
A VIRGIN!
YOU'RE GONNA LOVE IT. I KNOW EVERY WORD TO EVERY SONG.
SEE YOU THERE.
"TOUCH-A TOUCH-A TOUCH-A TOUCH ME, I WANNA BE DIRRRRRRTY--"
--THRILL ME CHILL ME FULFILL ME--

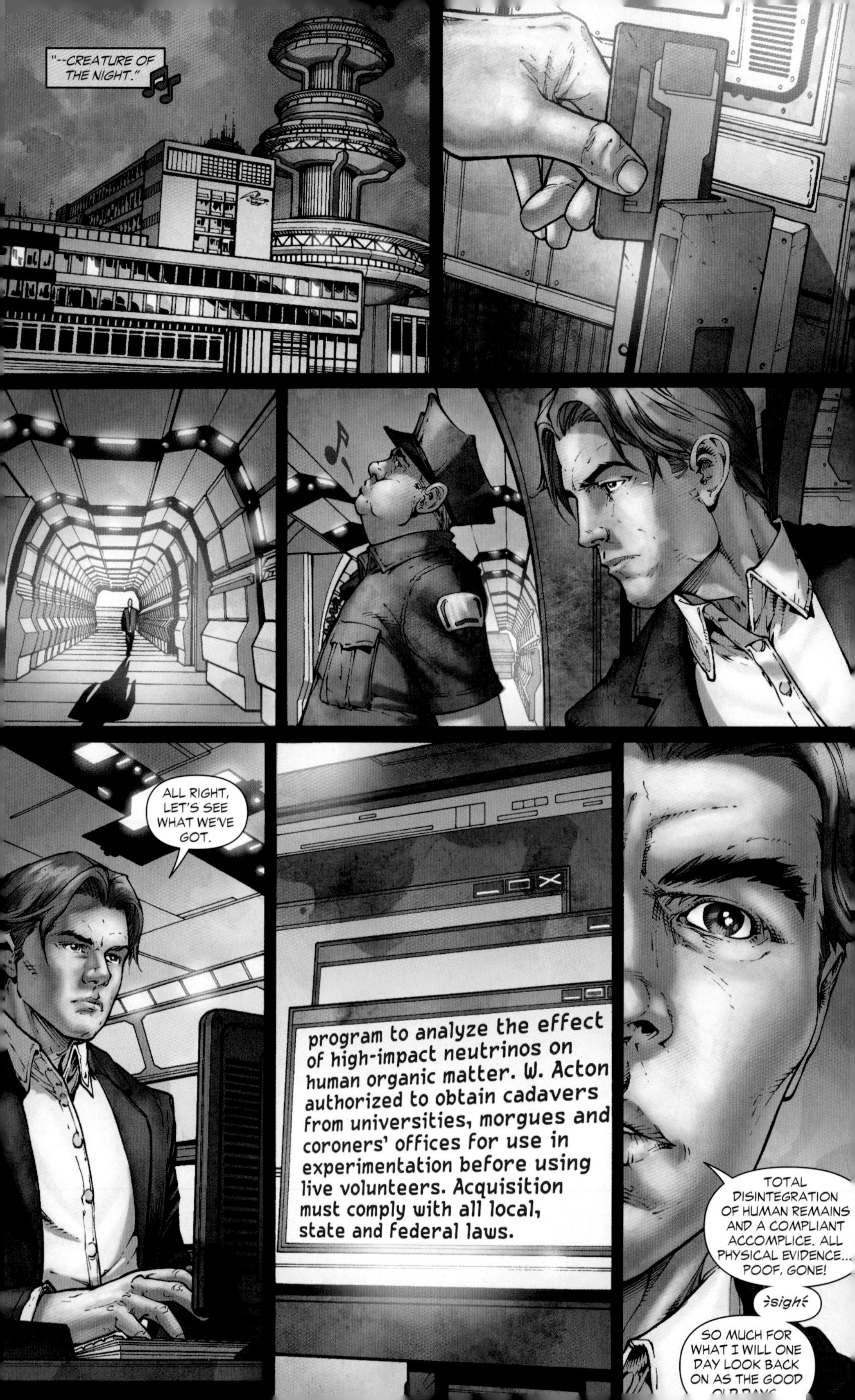
"--CREATURE OF THE NIGHT."
ALL RIGHT, LET'S SEE WHAT WE'VE GOT.
program to analyze the effect of high-impact neutrinos on human organic matter. W. Acton authorized to obtain cadavers from universities, morgues and coroners' offices for use in experimentation before using live volunteers. Acquisition must comply with all local, state and federal laws.
TOTAL DISINTEGRATION OF HUMAN REMAINS AND A COMPLIANT ACCOMPLICE. ALL PHYSICAL EVIDENCE... POOF, GONE!
sigh
SO MUCH FOR WHAT I WILL ONE DAY LOOK BACK ON AS THE GOOD

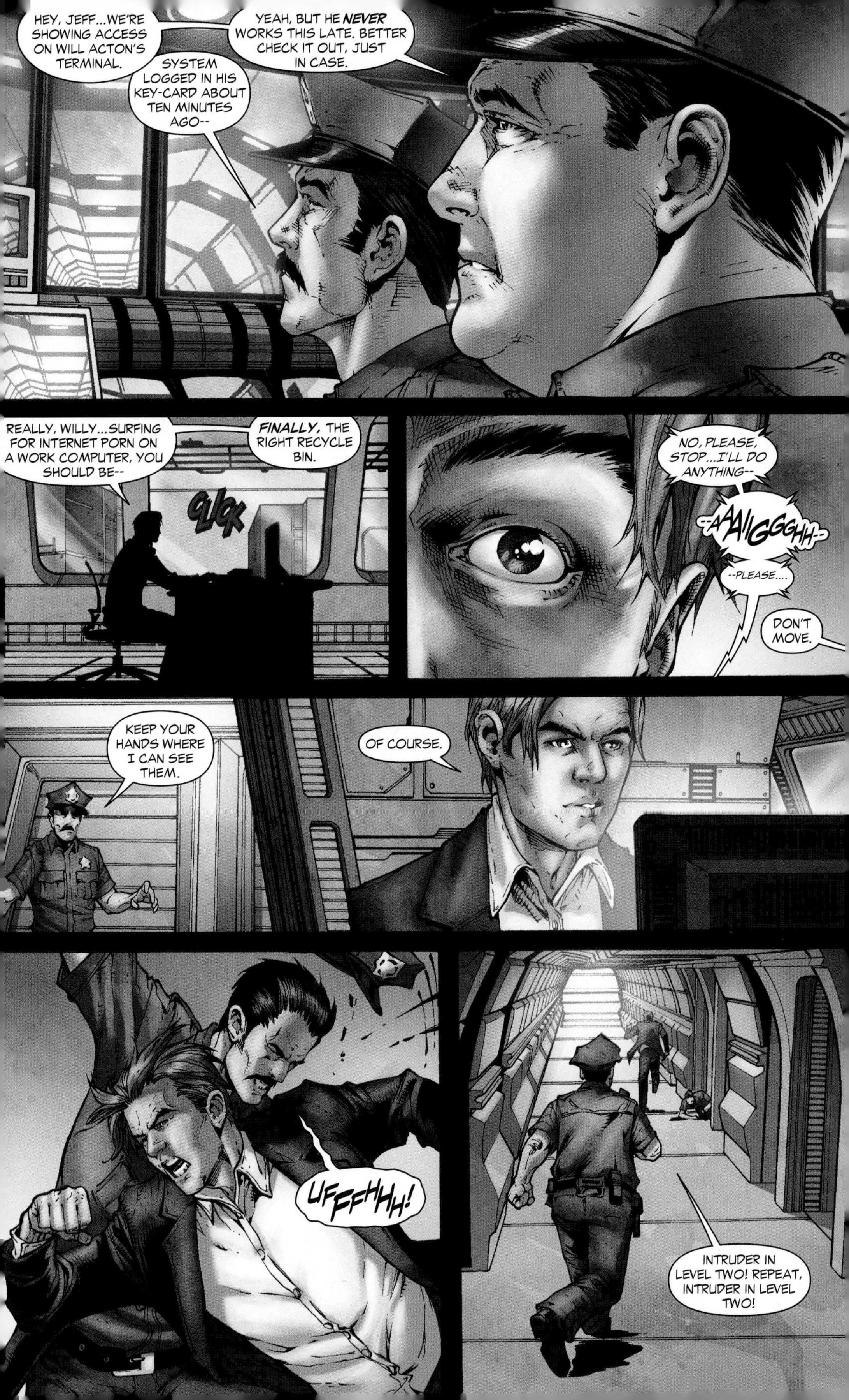
HEY, JEFF...WE'RE SHOWING ACCESS ON WILL ACTON'S TERMINAL.
YEAH, BUT HE NEVER WORKS THIS LATE. BETTER CHECK IT OUT, JUST IN CASE.
SYSTEM LOGGED IN HIS KEY-CARD ABOUT TEN MINUTES AGO--
REALLY, WILLY...SURFING FOR INTERNET PORN ON A WORK COMPUTER, YOU SHOULD BE--
FINALLY, THE RIGHT RECYCLE BIN.
CLICK
NO, PLEASE, STOP...I'LL DO ANYTHING--
-AAAIIGGGHH-
--PLEASE....
DON'T MOVE.
KEEP YOUR HANDS WHERE I CAN SEE THEM.
OF COURSE.
UFFFHHH!
INTRUDER IN LEVEL TWO! REPEAT, INTRUDER IN LEVEL TWO!

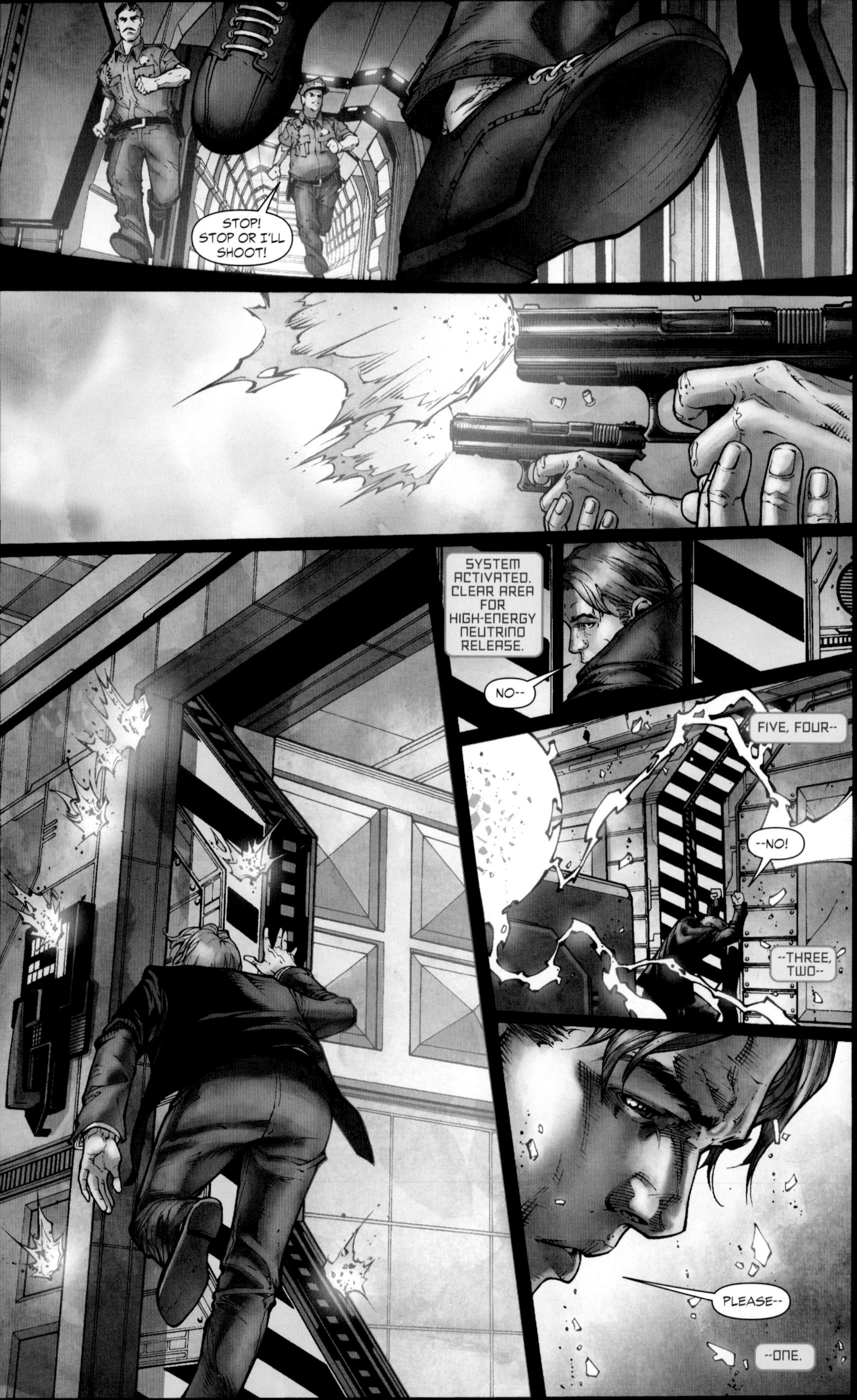
STOP! STOP OR I'LL SHOOT!
SYSTEM ACTIVATED. CLEAR AREA FOR HIGH-ENERGY NEUTRINO RELEASE.
NO--
FIVE, FOUR--
--NO!
--THREE, TWO--
PLEASE--
--ONE.

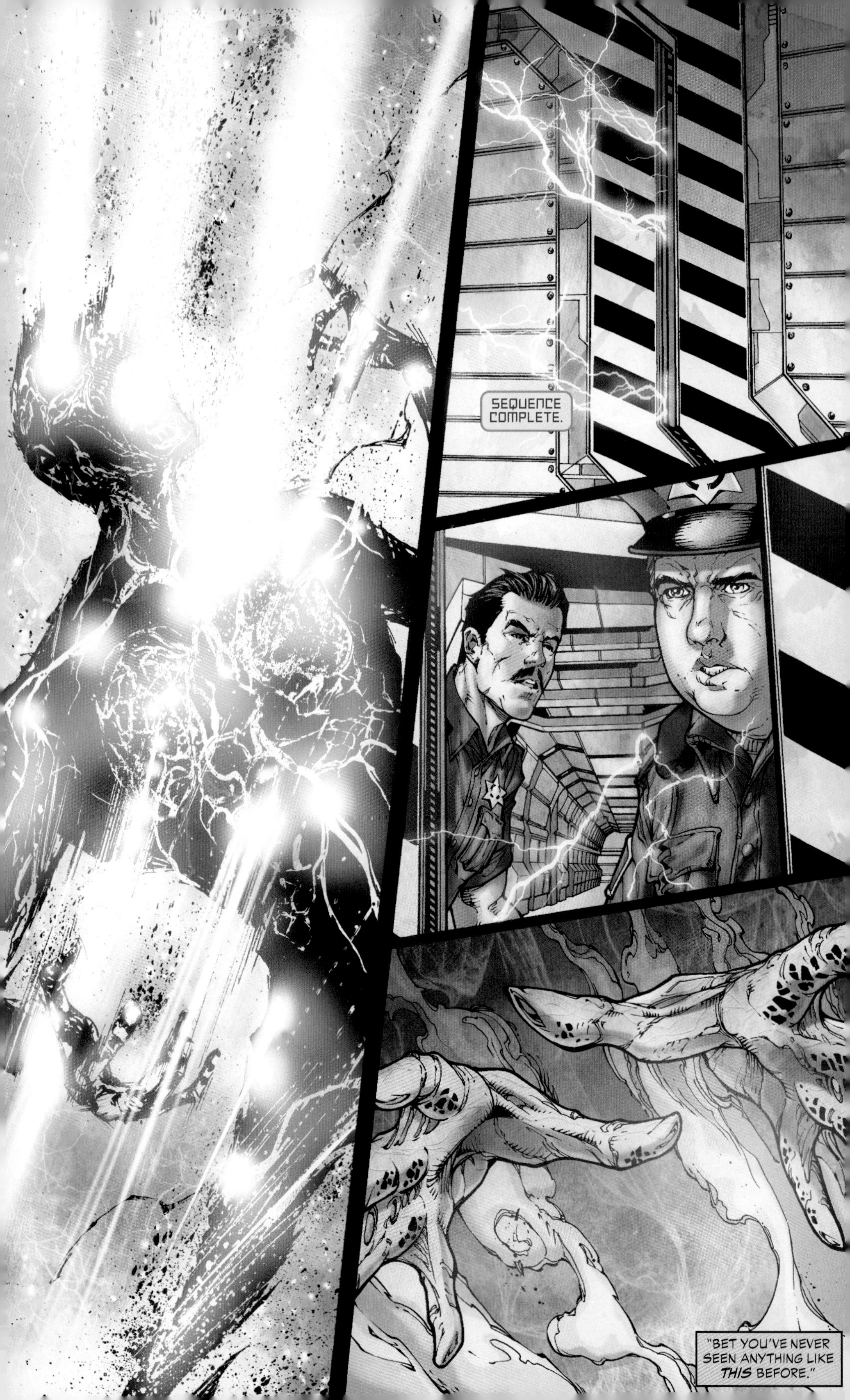
SEQUENCE COMPLETE.
"BET YOU'VE NEVER SEEN ANYTHING LIKE *THIS* BEFORE."

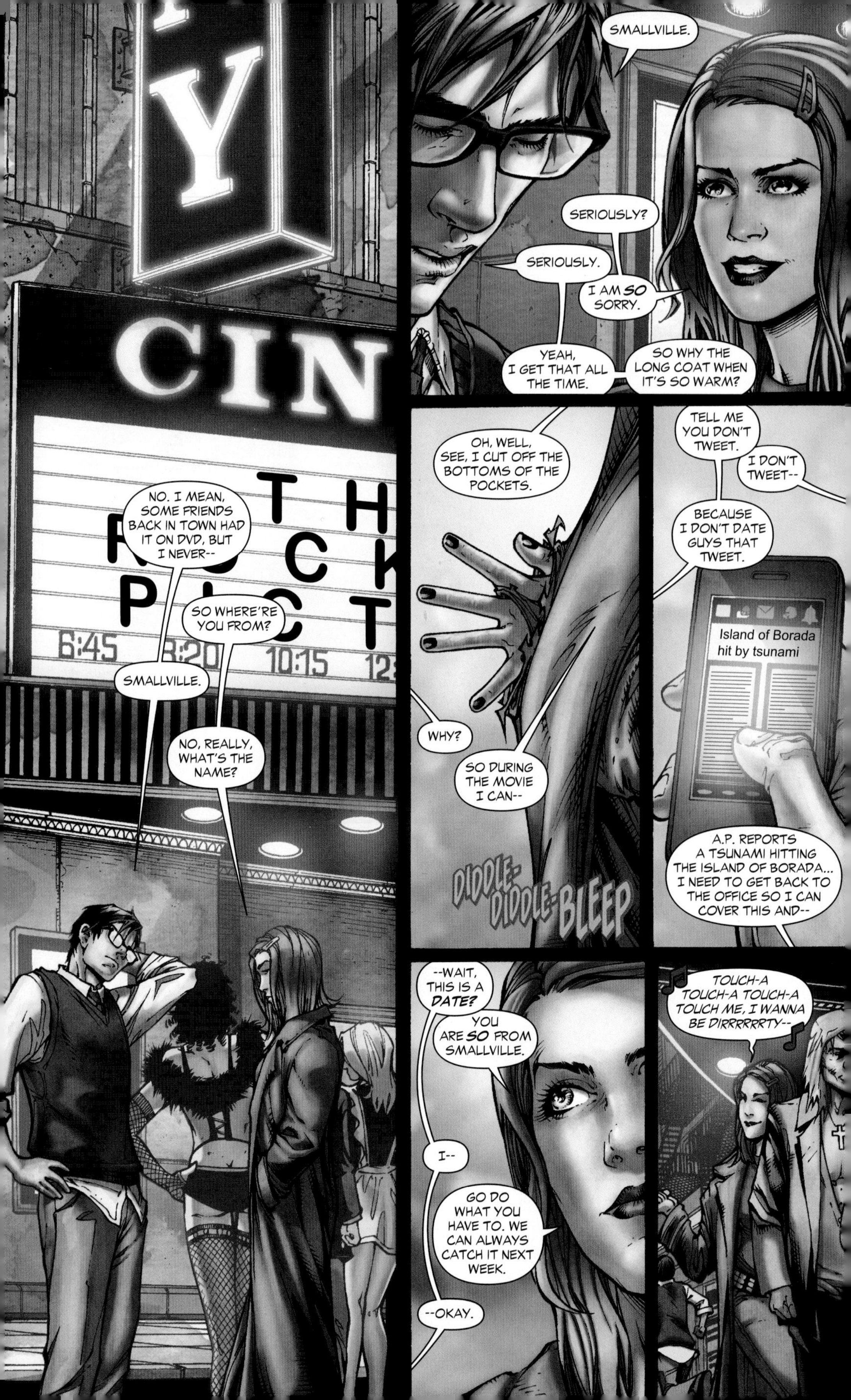
Y
CIN
6:45
10:15
NO. I MEAN, SOME FRIENDS BACK IN TOWN HAD IT ON DVD, BUT I NEVER--
SO WHERE'RE YOU FROM?
SMALLVILLE.
NO, REALLY, WHAT'S THE NAME?
SMALLVILLE.
SERIOUSLY?
SERIOUSLY.
I AM *SO* SORRY.
YEAH, I GET THAT ALL THE TIME.
SO WHY THE LONG COAT WHEN IT'S SO WARM?
OH, WELL, SEE, I CUT OFF THE BOTTOMS OF THE POCKETS.
WHY?
SO DURING THE MOVIE I CAN--
DIDDLE-DIDDLE-BLEEP
TELL ME YOU DON'T TWEET.
I DON'T TWEET--
BECAUSE I DON'T DATE GUYS THAT TWEET.
Island of Borada hit by tsunami
A.P. REPORTS A TSUNAMI HITTING THE ISLAND OF BORADA... I NEED TO GET BACK TO THE OFFICE SO I CAN COVER THIS AND--
--WAIT, THIS IS A *DATE?*
YOU ARE *SO* FROM SMALLVILLE.
I--
GO DO WHAT YOU HAVE TO. WE CAN ALWAYS CATCH IT NEXT WEEK.
--OKAY.
TOUCH-A TOUCH-A TOUCH-A TOUCH ME, I WANNA BE DIRRRRRTY--

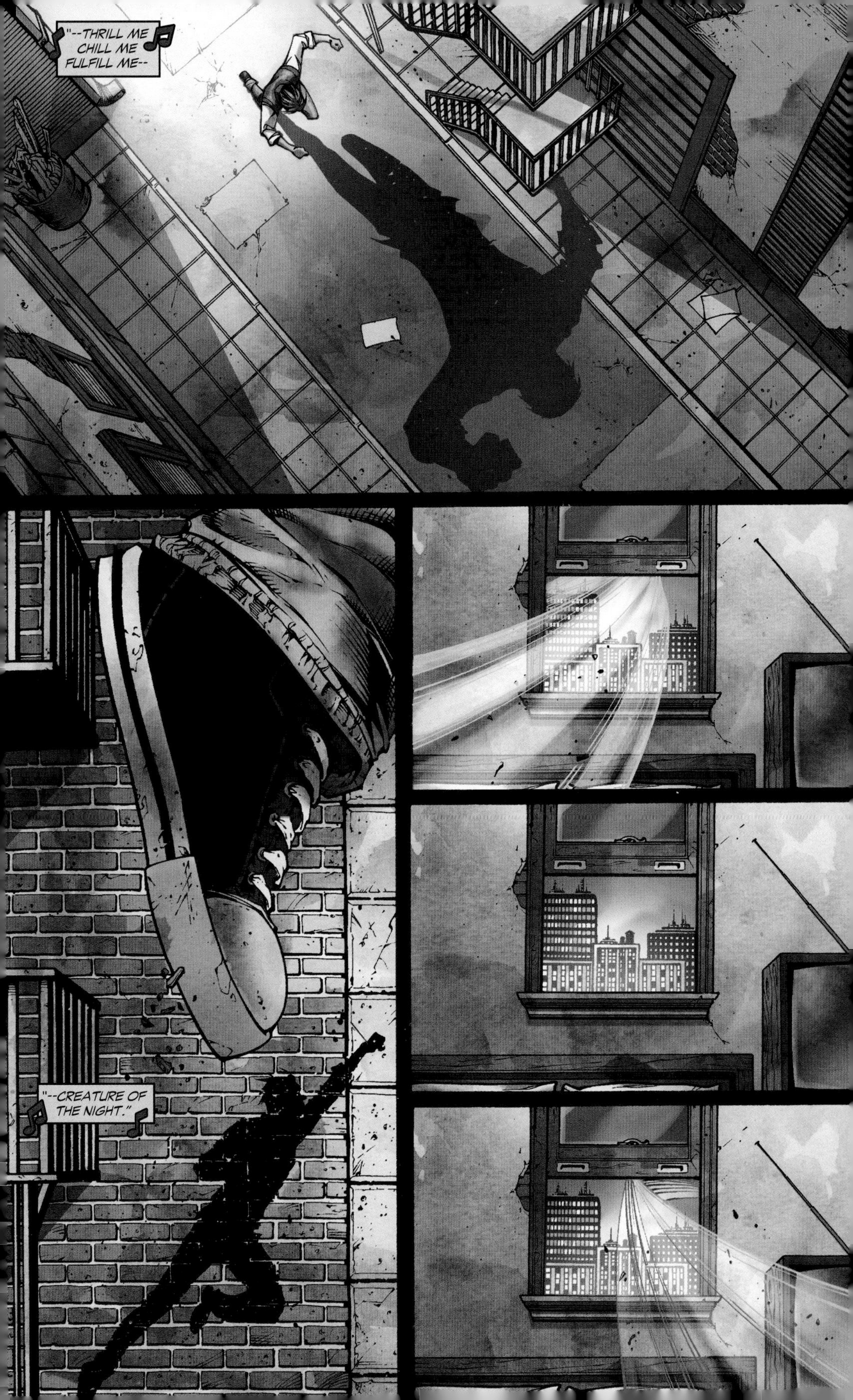
"--THRILL ME CHILL ME FULFILL ME--
"--CREATURE OF THE NIGHT."

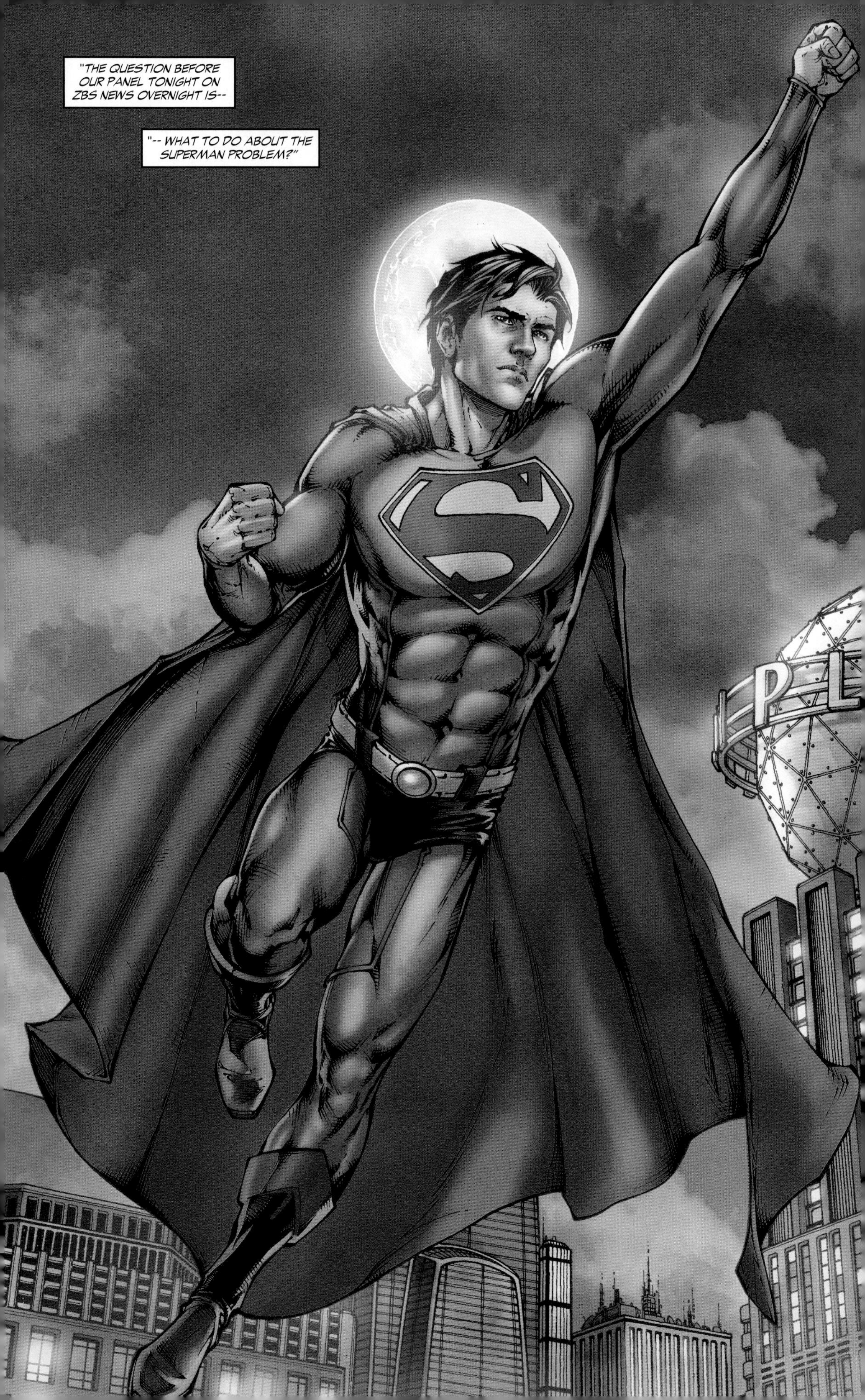
"THE QUESTION BEFORE OUR PANEL TONIGHT ON ZBS NEWS OVERNIGHT IS--
"-- WHAT TO DO ABOUT THE SUPERMAN PROBLEM?"

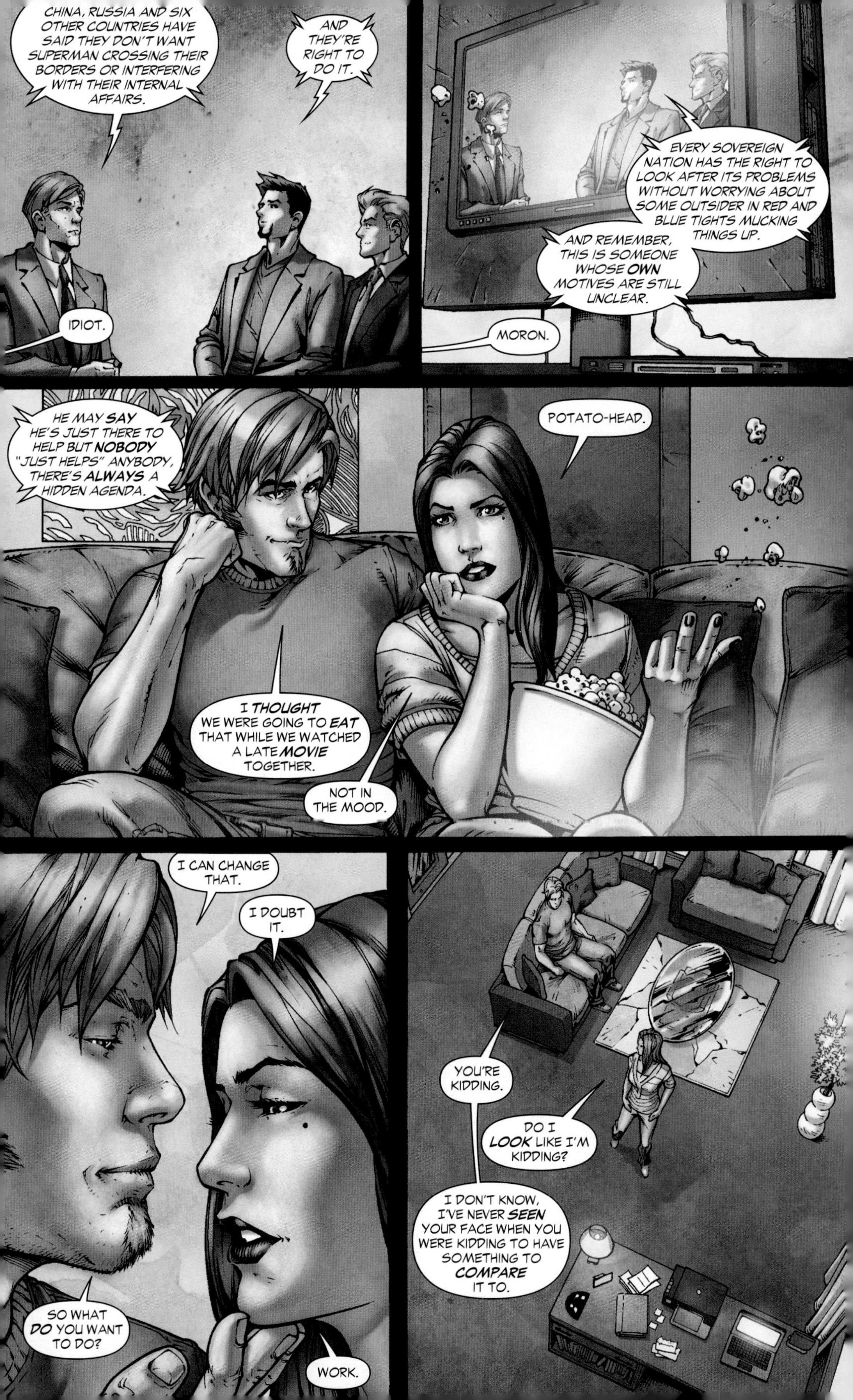
CHINA, RUSSIA AND SIX OTHER COUNTRIES HAVE SAID THEY DON'T WANT SUPERMAN CROSSING THEIR BORDERS OR INTERFERING WITH THEIR INTERNAL AFFAIRS.
AND THEY'RE RIGHT TO DO IT.
IDIOT.
EVERY SOVEREIGN NATION HAS THE RIGHT TO LOOK AFTER ITS PROBLEMS WITHOUT WORRYING ABOUT SOME OUTSIDER IN RED AND BLUE TIGHTS MUCKING THINGS UP.
AND REMEMBER, THIS IS SOMEONE WHOSE OWN MOTIVES ARE STILL UNCLEAR.
MORON.
HE MAY SAY HE'S JUST THERE TO HELP BUT NOBODY "JUST HELPS" ANYBODY, THERE'S ALWAYS A HIDDEN AGENDA.
POTATO-HEAD.
I THOUGHT WE WERE GOING TO EAT THAT WHILE WE WATCHED A LATE MOVIE TOGETHER.
NOT IN THE MOOD.
I CAN CHANGE THAT.
I DOUBT IT.
SO WHAT DO YOU WANT TO DO?
WORK.
YOU'RE KIDDING.
DO I LOOK LIKE I'M KIDDING?
I DON'T KNOW, I'VE NEVER SEEN YOUR FACE WHEN YOU WERE KIDDING TO HAVE SOMETHING TO COMPARE IT TO.

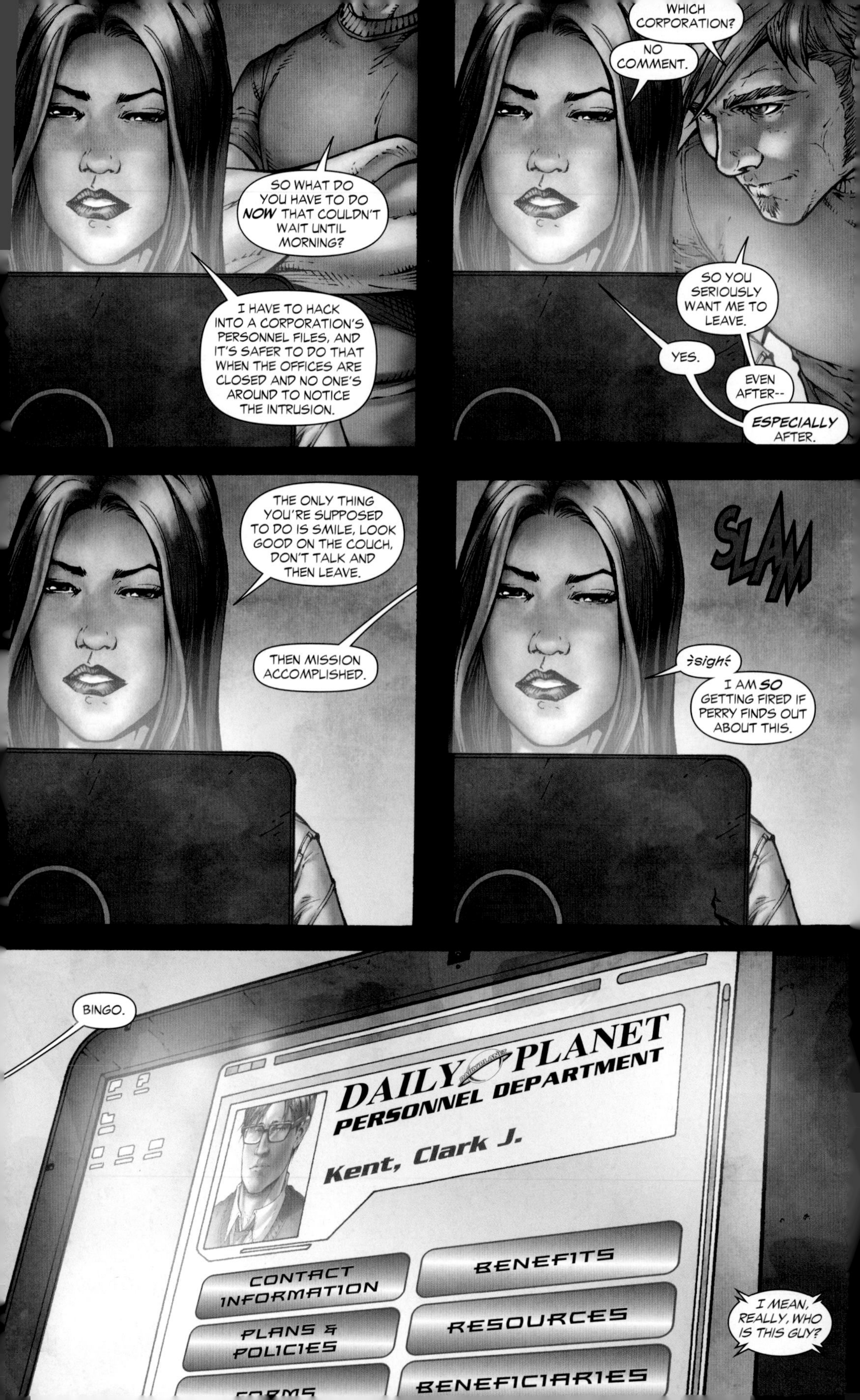

SO WHAT DO YOU HAVE TO DO NOW THAT COULDN'T WAIT UNTIL MORNING?
I HAVE TO HACK INTO A CORPORATION'S PERSONNEL FILES, AND IT'S SAFER TO DO THAT WHEN THE OFFICES ARE CLOSED AND NO ONE'S AROUND TO NOTICE THE INTRUSION.
WHICH CORPORATION?
NO COMMENT.
SO YOU SERIOUSLY WANT ME TO LEAVE.
YES.
EVEN AFTER--
ESPECIALLY AFTER.
THE ONLY THING YOU'RE SUPPOSED TO DO IS SMILE, LOOK GOOD ON THE COUCH, DON'T TALK AND THEN LEAVE.
THEN MISSION ACCOMPLISHED.
SLAM
sigh
I AM SO GETTING FIRED IF PERRY FINDS OUT ABOUT THIS.
BINGO.
DAILY PLANET
PERSONNEL DEPARTMENT
Kent, Clark J.
CONTACT INFORMATION
BENEFITS
PLANS & POLICIES
RESOURCES
BENEFICIARIES
I MEAN, REALLY, WHO IS THIS GUY?

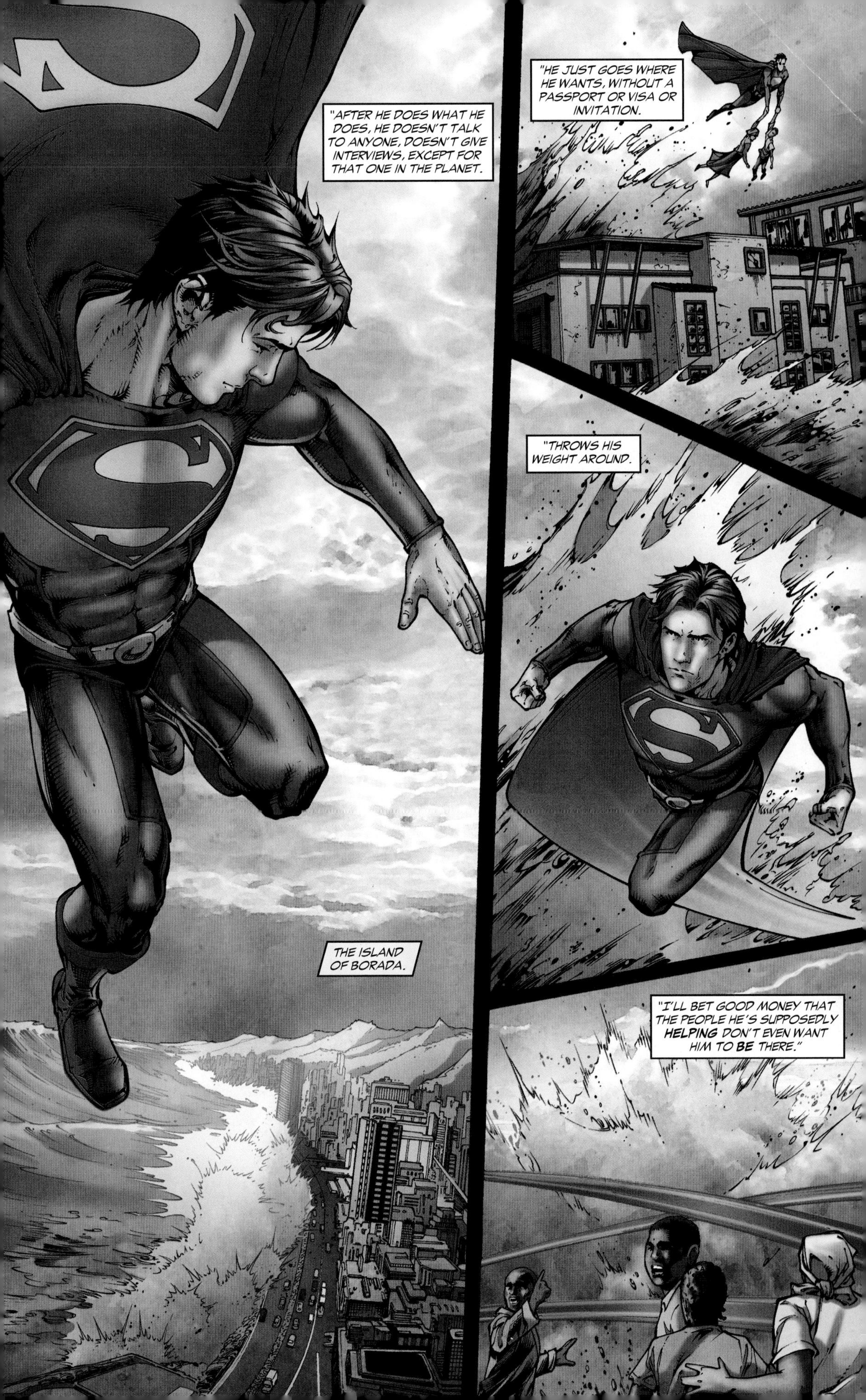
"AFTER HE DOES WHAT HE DOES, HE DOESN'T TALK TO ANYONE, DOESN'T GIVE INTERVIEWS, EXCEPT FOR THAT ONE IN THE PLANET.
THE ISLAND OF BORADA.
"HE JUST GOES WHERE HE WANTS, WITHOUT A PASSPORT OR VISA OR INVITATION.
"THROWS HIS WEIGHT AROUND.
"I'LL BET GOOD MONEY THAT THE PEOPLE HE'S SUPPOSEDLY HELPING DON'T EVEN WANT HIM TO BE THERE."

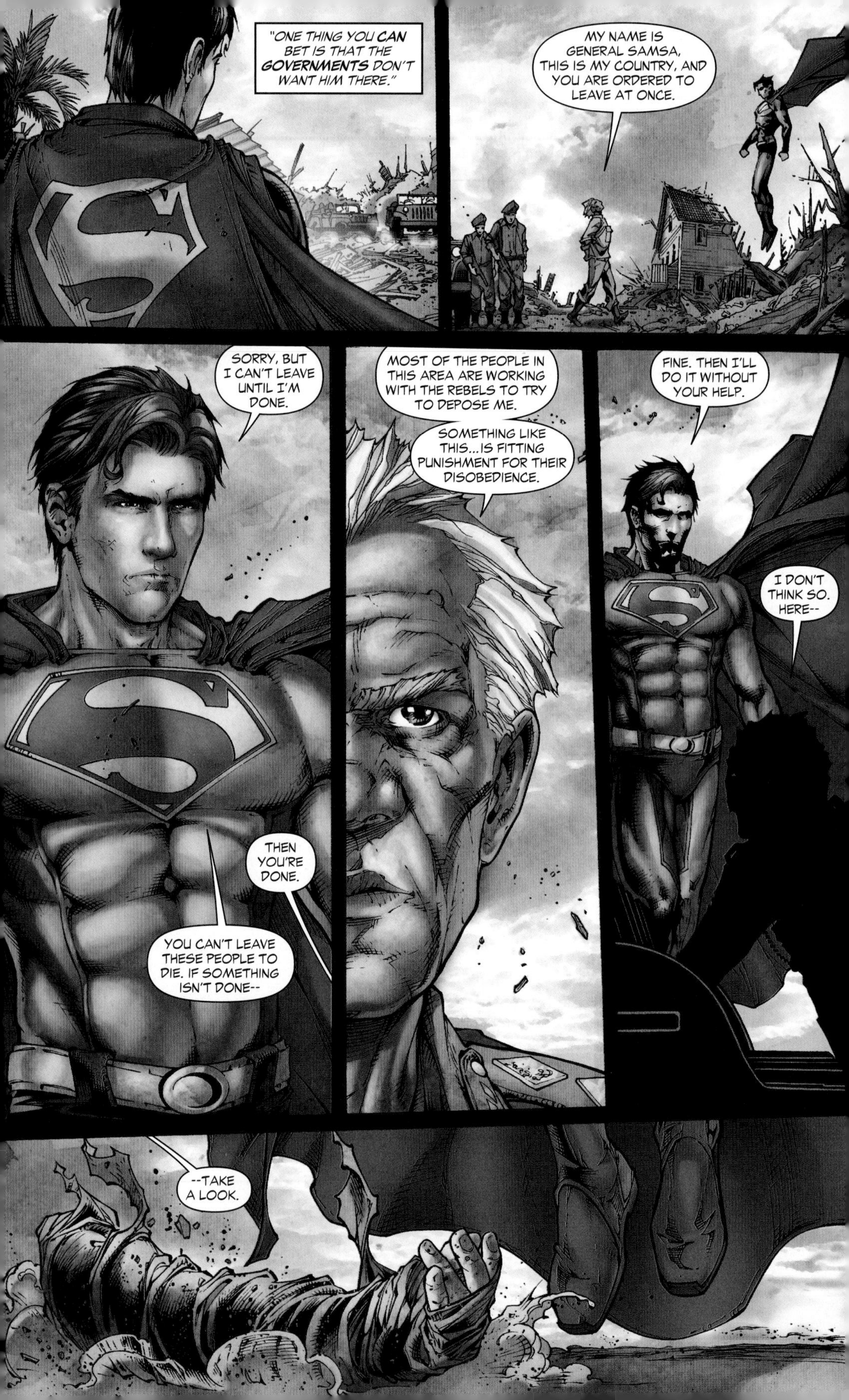
"ONE THING YOU CAN BET IS THAT THE GOVERNMENTS DON'T WANT HIM THERE."
MY NAME IS GENERAL SAMSA, THIS IS MY COUNTRY, AND YOU ARE ORDERED TO LEAVE AT ONCE.
SORRY, BUT I CAN'T LEAVE UNTIL I'M DONE.
THEN YOU'RE DONE.
YOU CAN'T LEAVE THESE PEOPLE TO DIE. IF SOMETHING ISN'T DONE--
MOST OF THE PEOPLE IN THIS AREA ARE WORKING WITH THE REBELS TO TRY TO DEPOSE ME.
SOMETHING LIKE THIS...IS FITTING PUNISHMENT FOR THEIR DISOBEDIENCE.
FINE. THEN I'LL DO IT WITHOUT YOUR HELP.
I DON'T THINK SO. HERE--
--TAKE A LOOK.

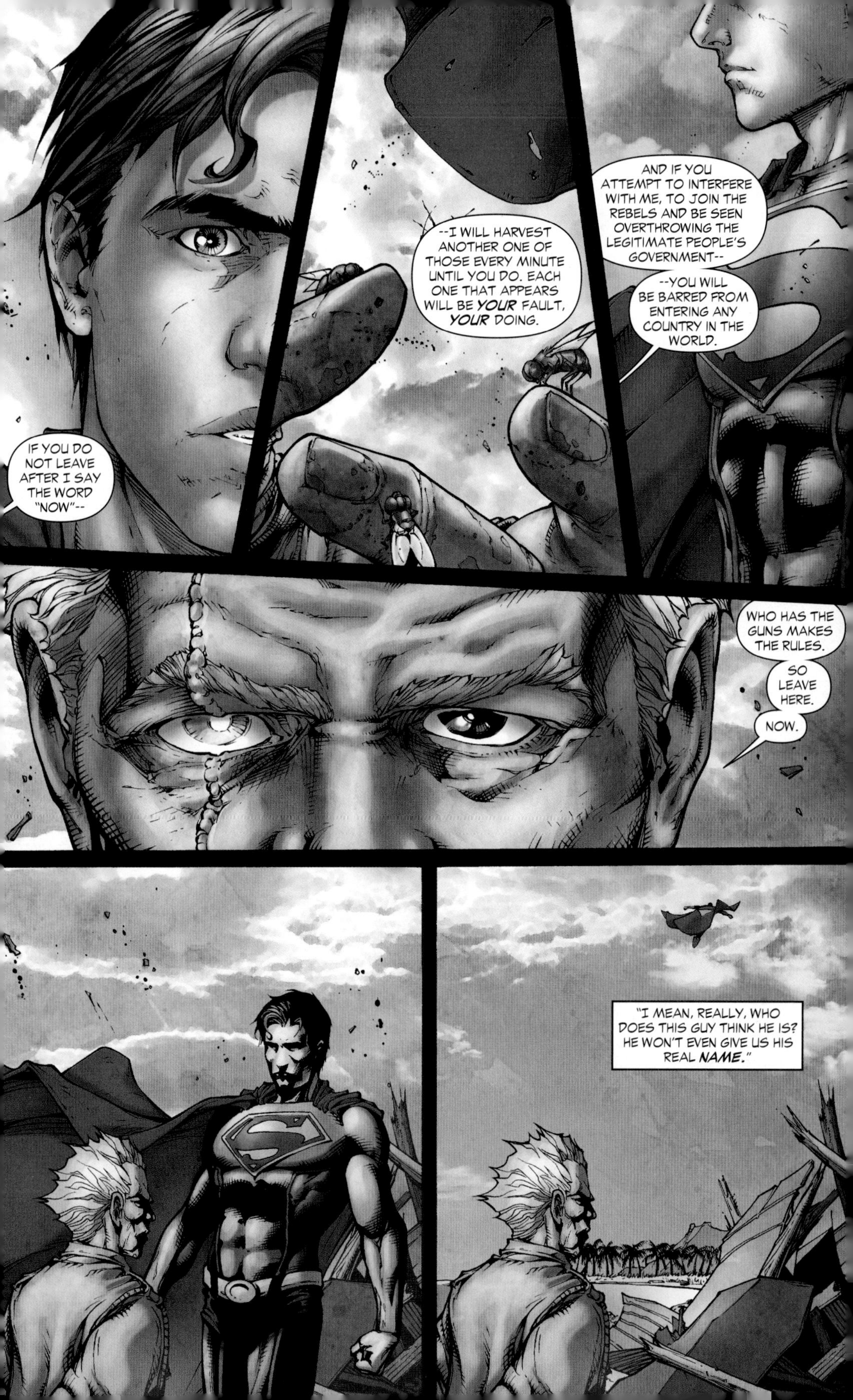
IF YOU DO NOT LEAVE AFTER I SAY THE WORD "NOW"--
--I WILL HARVEST ANOTHER ONE OF THOSE EVERY MINUTE UNTIL YOU DO. EACH ONE THAT APPEARS WILL BE YOUR FAULT, YOUR DOING.
AND IF YOU ATTEMPT TO INTERFERE WITH ME, TO JOIN THE REBELS AND BE SEEN OVERTHROWING THE LEGITIMATE PEOPLE'S GOVERNMENT--
--YOU WILL BE BARRED FROM ENTERING ANY COUNTRY IN THE WORLD.
WHO HAS THE GUNS MAKES THE RULES.
SO LEAVE HERE.
NOW.
"I MEAN, REALLY, WHO DOES THIS GUY THINK HE IS? HE WON'T EVEN GIVE US HIS REAL NAME."

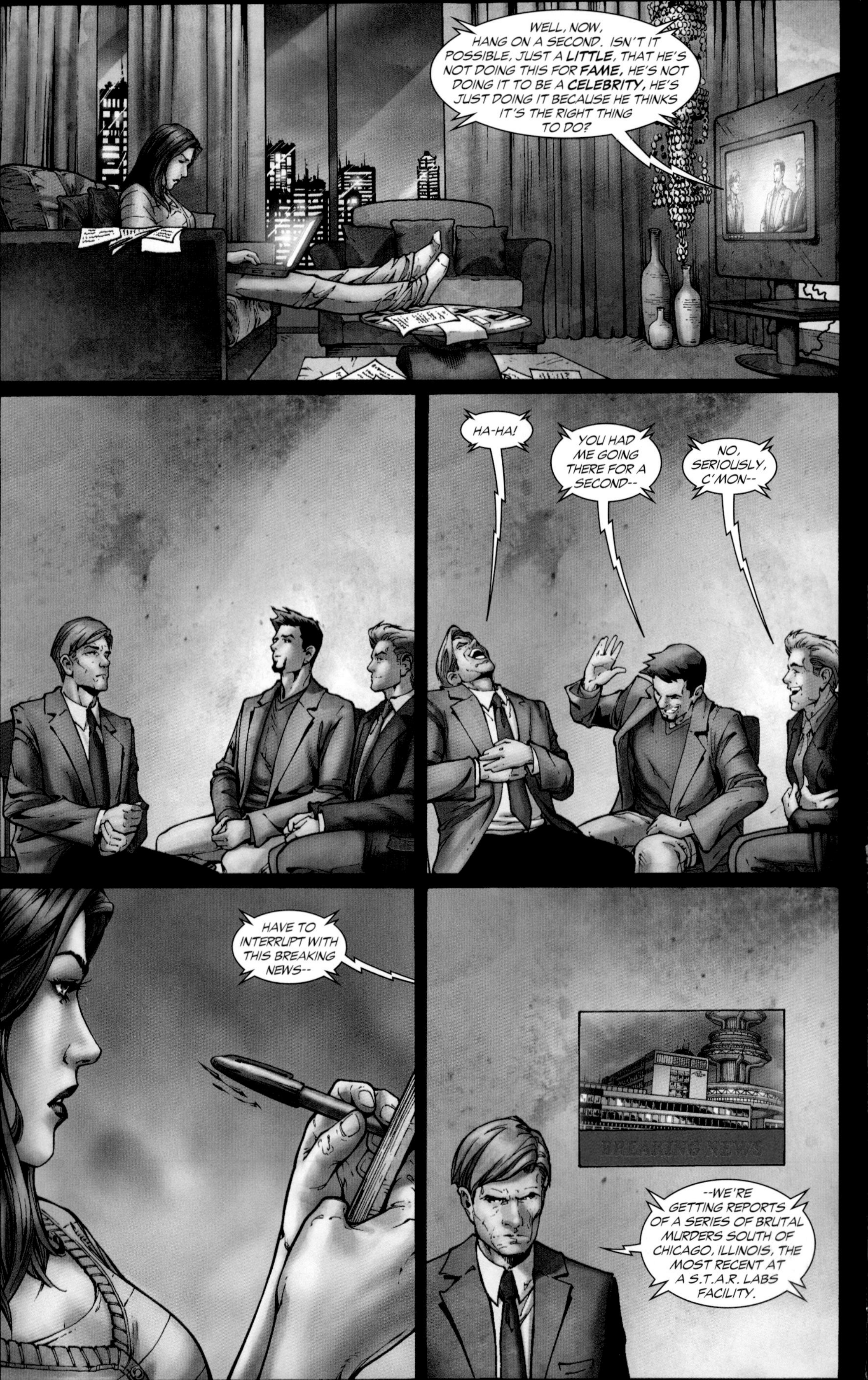
WELL, NOW, HANG ON A SECOND. ISN'T IT POSSIBLE, JUST A **LITTLE**, THAT HE'S NOT DOING THIS FOR **FAME**, HE'S NOT DOING IT TO BE A **CELEBRITY**, HE'S JUST DOING IT BECAUSE HE THINKS IT'S THE RIGHT THING TO DO?
HA-HA!
YOU HAD ME GOING THERE FOR A SECOND--
NO, SERIOUSLY, C'MON--
HAVE TO INTERRUPT WITH THIS BREAKING NEWS--
--WE'RE GETTING REPORTS OF A SERIES OF BRUTAL MURDERS SOUTH OF CHICAGO, ILLINOIS, THE MOST RECENT AT A S.T.A.R. LABS FACILITY.

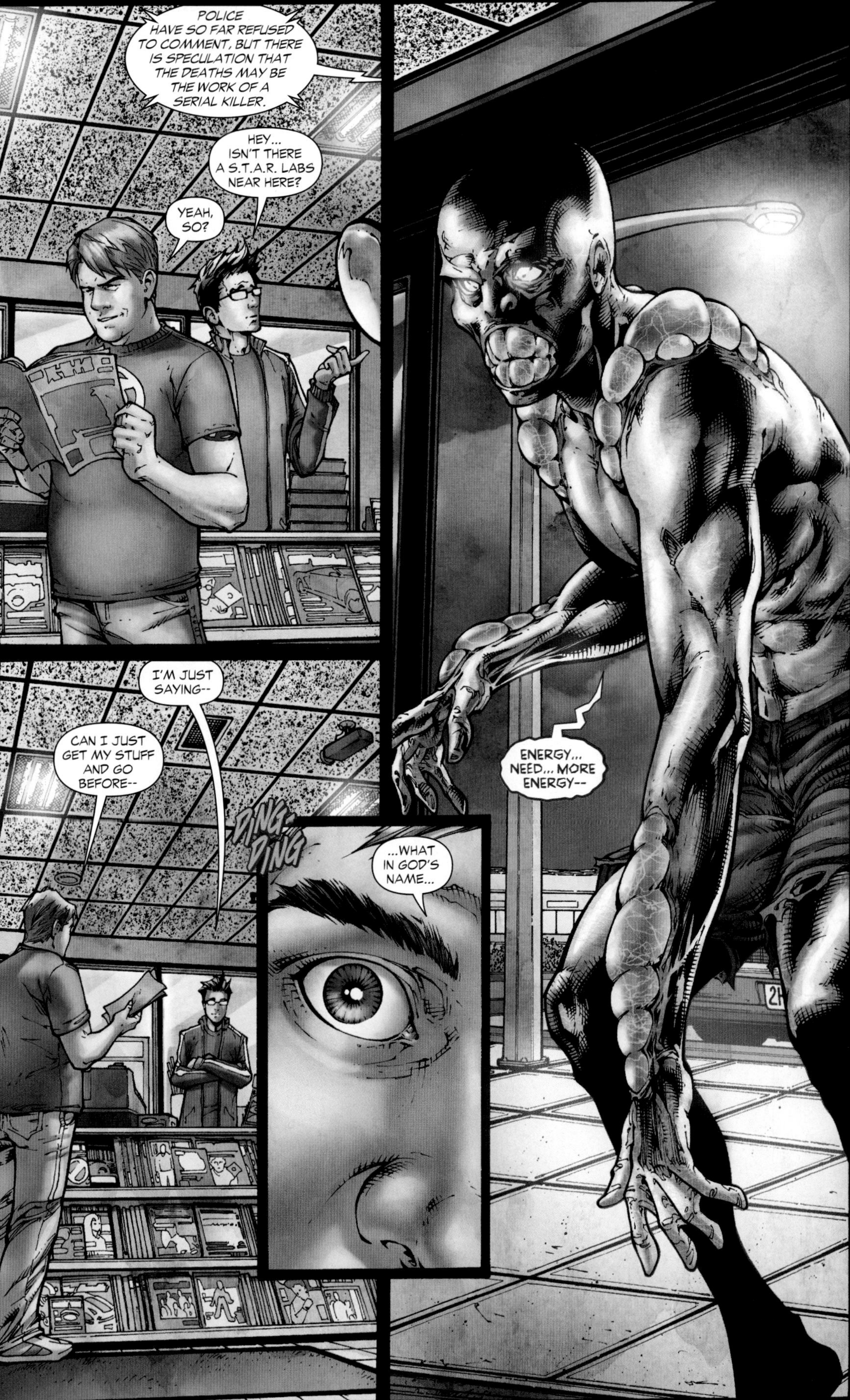
POLICE HAVE SO FAR REFUSED TO COMMENT, BUT THERE IS SPECULATION THAT THE DEATHS MAY BE THE WORK OF A SERIAL KILLER.
HEY... ISN'T THERE A S.T.A.R. LABS NEAR HERE?
YEAH, SO?
ENERGY... NEED... MORE ENERGY--
I'M JUST SAYING--
CAN I JUST GET MY STUFF AND GO BEFORE--
DING-DING
...WHAT IN GOD'S NAME...

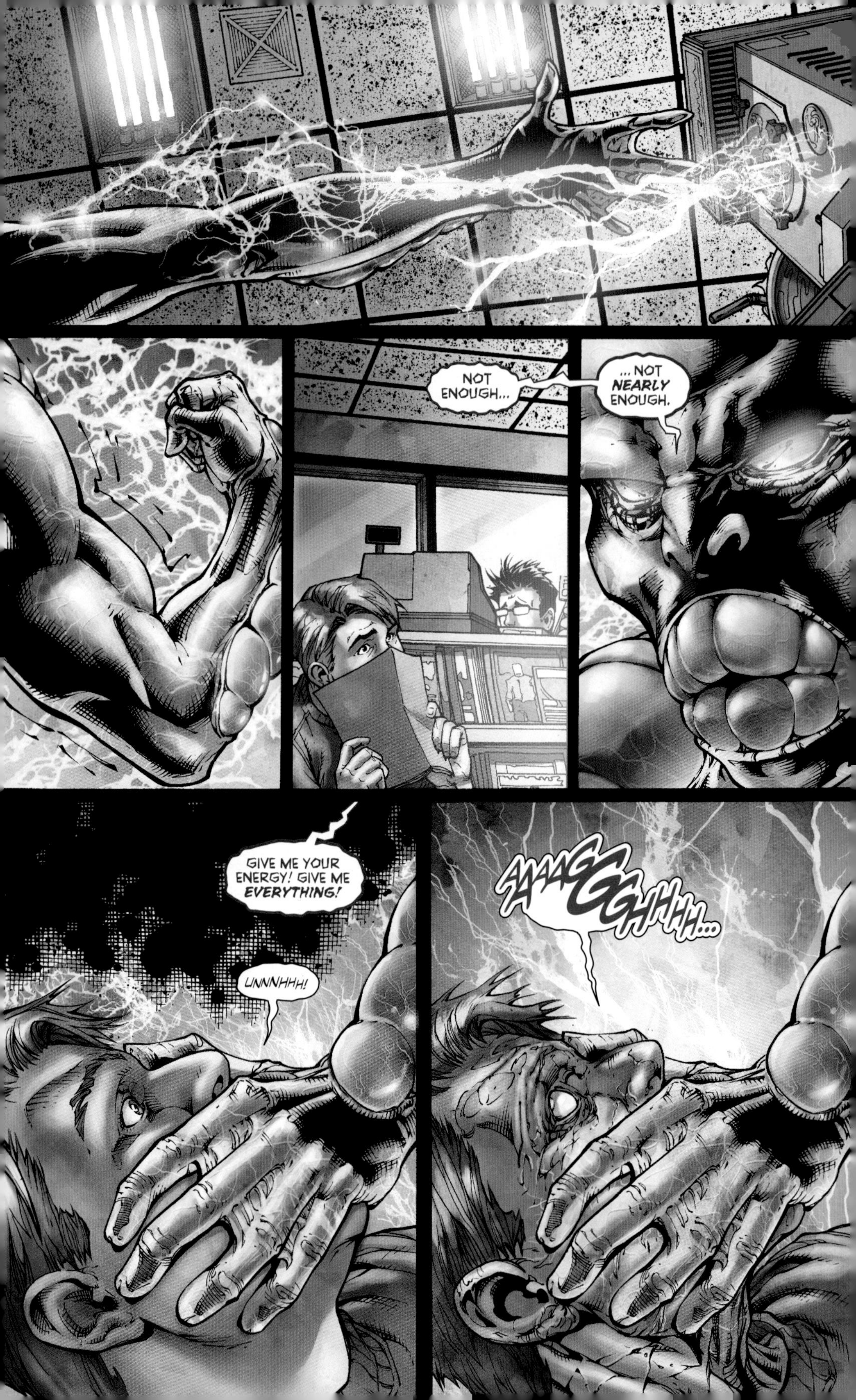
NOT ENOUGH...
...NOT NEARLY ENOUGH.
GIVE ME YOUR ENERGY! GIVE ME EVERYTHING!
UNNHHH!
AAAAGGGHHHH...

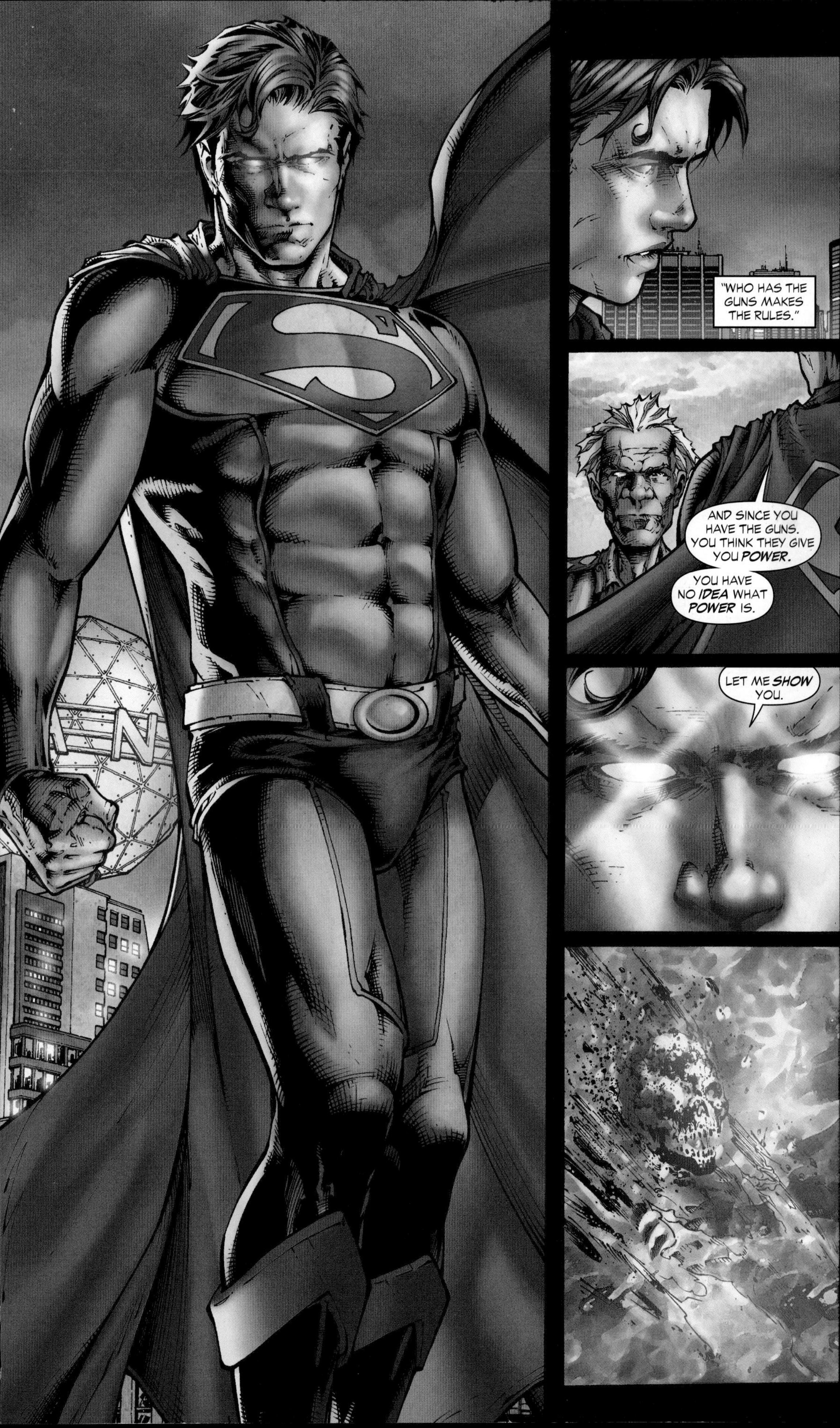
"WHO HAS THE GUNS MAKES THE RULES."
AND SINCE YOU HAVE THE GUNS. YOU THINK THEY GIVE YOU **POWER**.
YOU HAVE NO **IDEA** WHAT **POWER** IS.
LET ME **SHOW** YOU.

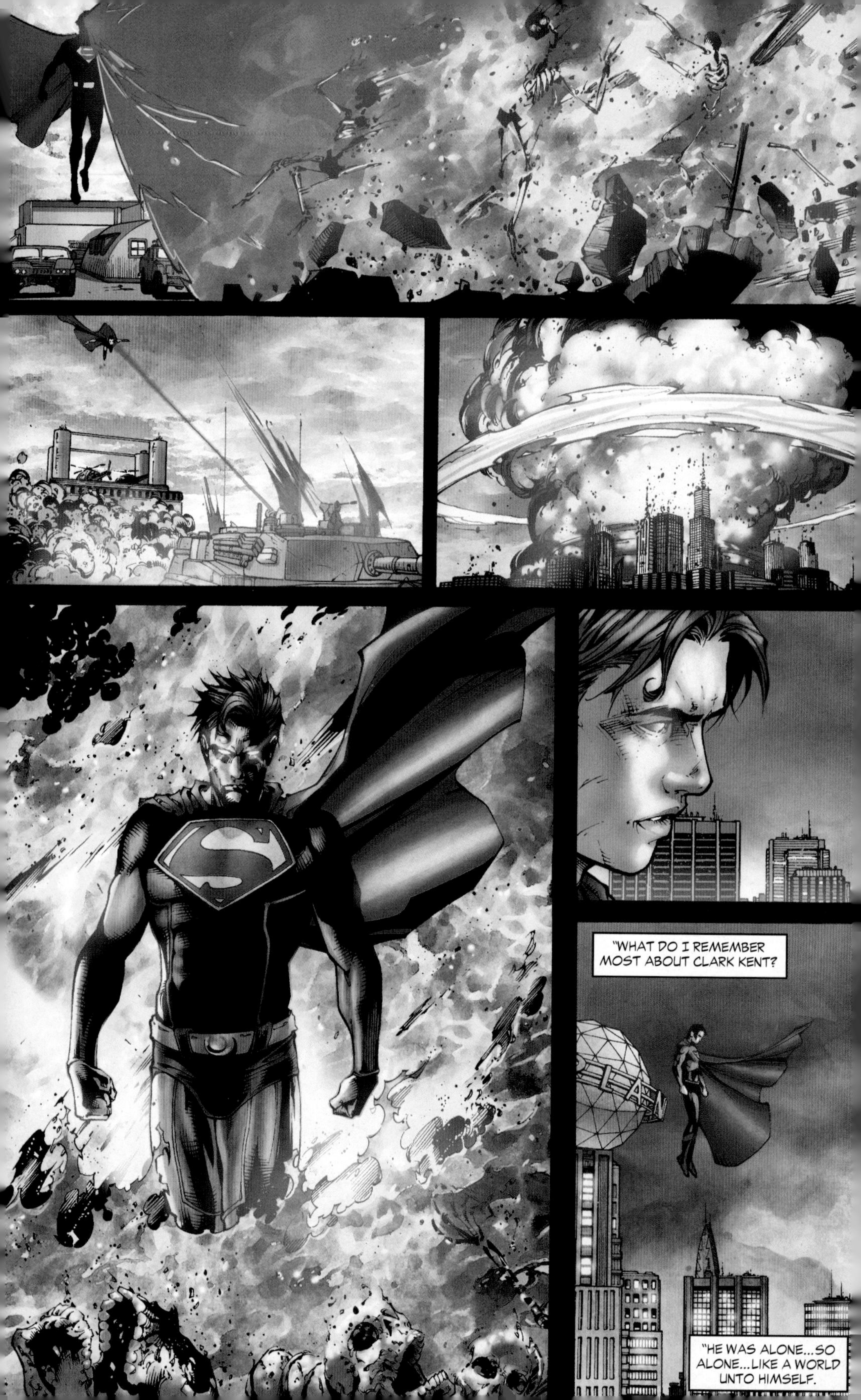
"WHAT DO I REMEMBER MOST ABOUT CLARK KENT?
"HE WAS ALONE...SO ALONE...LIKE A WORLD UNTO HIMSELF.

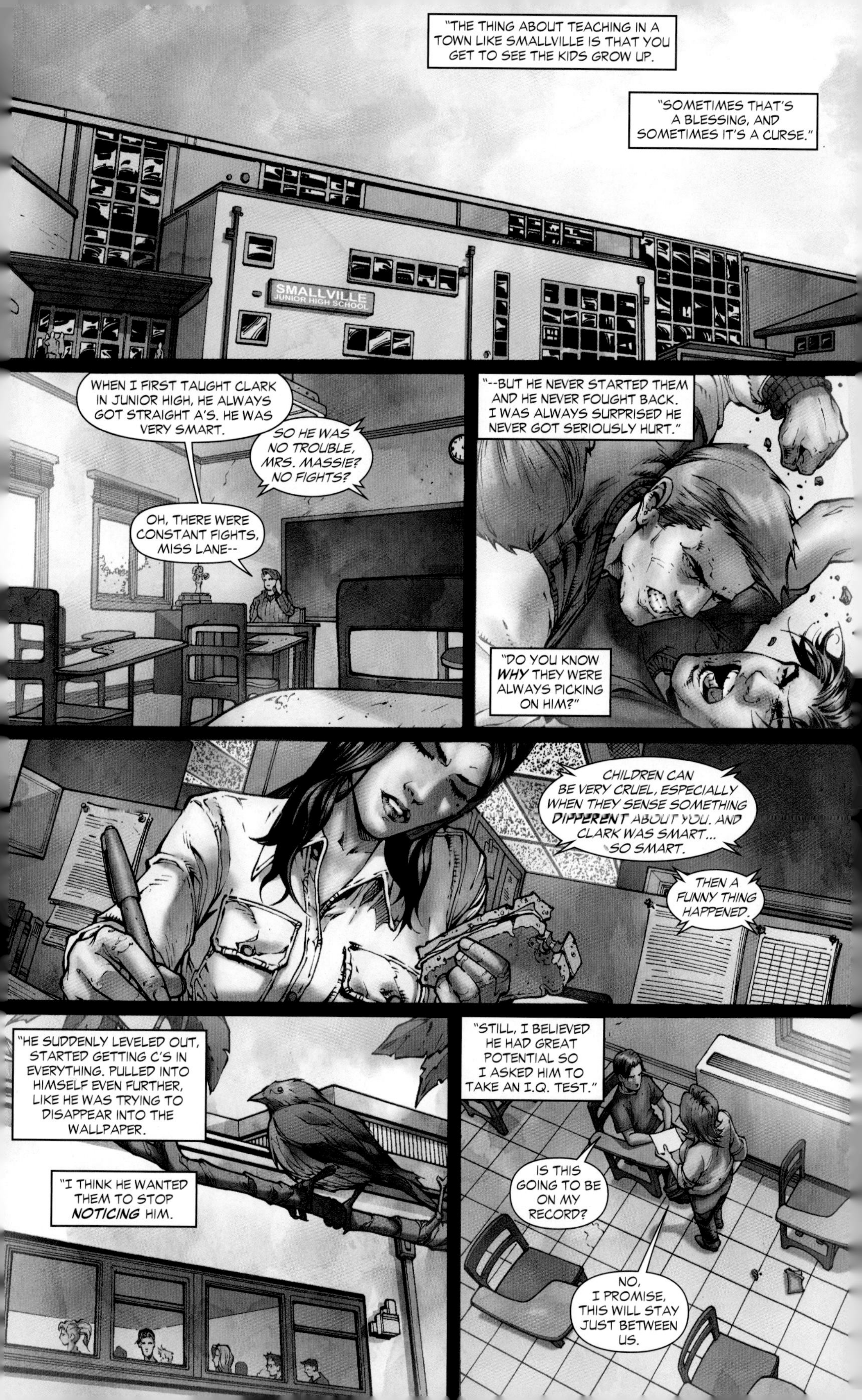
"THE THING ABOUT TEACHING IN A TOWN LIKE SMALLVILLE IS THAT YOU GET TO SEE THE KIDS GROW UP.
"SOMETIMES THAT'S A BLESSING, AND SOMETIMES IT'S A CURSE."
SMALLVILLE JUNIOR HIGH SCHOOL
WHEN I FIRST TAUGHT CLARK IN JUNIOR HIGH, HE ALWAYS GOT STRAIGHT A'S. HE WAS VERY SMART.
SO HE WAS NO TROUBLE, MRS. MASSIE? NO FIGHTS?
OH, THERE WERE CONSTANT FIGHTS, MISS LANE--
"--BUT HE NEVER STARTED THEM AND HE NEVER FOUGHT BACK. I WAS ALWAYS SURPRISED HE NEVER GOT SERIOUSLY HURT."
"DO YOU KNOW WHY THEY WERE ALWAYS PICKING ON HIM?"
CHILDREN CAN BE VERY CRUEL, ESPECIALLY WHEN THEY SENSE SOMETHING DIFFERENT ABOUT YOU. AND CLARK WAS SMART... SO SMART.
THEN A FUNNY THING HAPPENED.
"HE SUDDENLY LEVELED OUT, STARTED GETTING C'S IN EVERYTHING. PULLED INTO HIMSELF EVEN FURTHER, LIKE HE WAS TRYING TO DISAPPEAR INTO THE WALLPAPER.
"I THINK HE WANTED THEM TO STOP NOTICING HIM.
"STILL, I BELIEVED HE HAD GREAT POTENTIAL SO I ASKED HIM TO TAKE AN I.Q. TEST."
IS THIS GOING TO BE ON MY RECORD?
NO, I PROMISE, THIS WILL STAY JUST BETWEEN US.

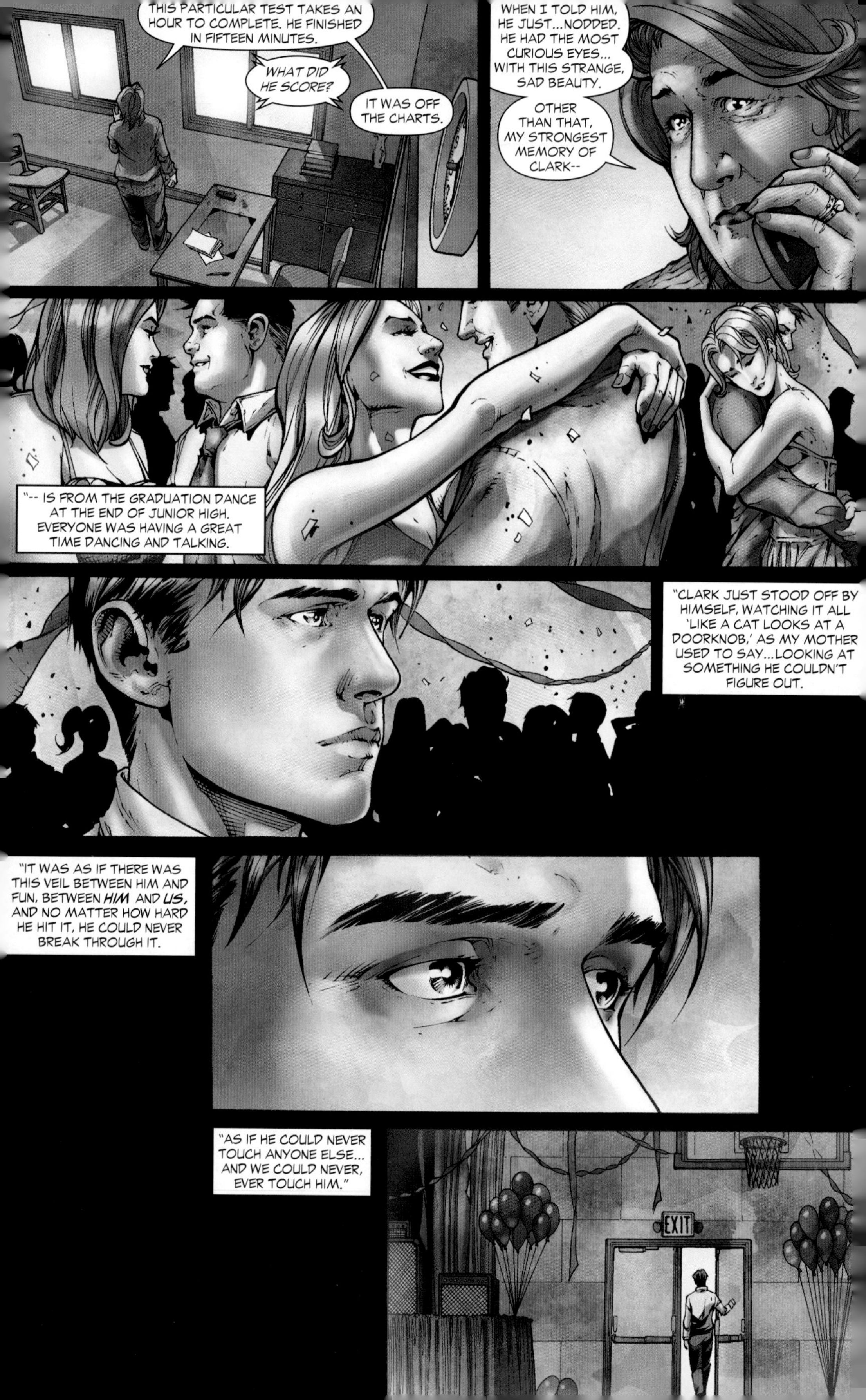
THIS PARTICULAR TEST TAKES AN HOUR TO COMPLETE. HE FINISHED IN FIFTEEN MINUTES.
WHAT DID HE SCORE?
IT WAS OFF THE CHARTS.
WHEN I TOLD HIM, HE JUST...NODDED. HE HAD THE MOST CURIOUS EYES... WITH THIS STRANGE, SAD BEAUTY.
OTHER THAN THAT, MY STRONGEST MEMORY OF CLARK--
"-- IS FROM THE GRADUATION DANCE AT THE END OF JUNIOR HIGH. EVERYONE WAS HAVING A GREAT TIME DANCING AND TALKING.
"CLARK JUST STOOD OFF BY HIMSELF, WATCHING IT ALL 'LIKE A CAT LOOKS AT A DOORKNOB,' AS MY MOTHER USED TO SAY...LOOKING AT SOMETHING HE COULDN'T FIGURE OUT.
"IT WAS AS IF THERE WAS THIS VEIL BETWEEN HIM AND FUN, BETWEEN *HIM* AND *US*, AND NO MATTER HOW HARD HE HIT IT, HE COULD NEVER BREAK THROUGH IT.
"AS IF HE COULD NEVER TOUCH ANYONE ELSE... AND WE COULD NEVER, EVER TOUCH HIM."
EXIT

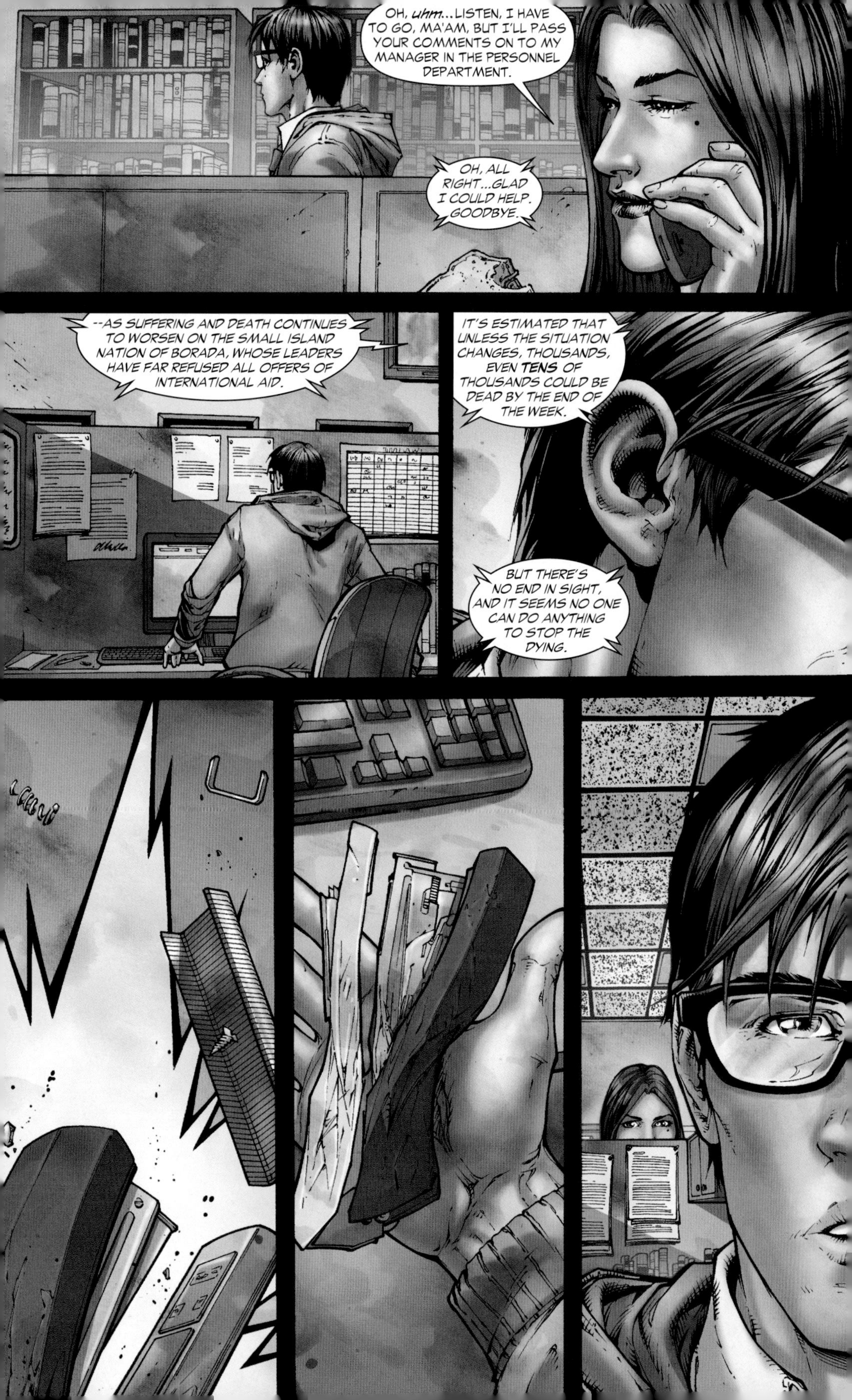
OH, uhm...LISTEN, I HAVE TO GO, MA'AM, BUT I'LL PASS YOUR COMMENTS ON TO MY MANAGER IN THE PERSONNEL DEPARTMENT.
OH, ALL RIGHT...GLAD I COULD HELP. GOODBYE.
--AS SUFFERING AND DEATH CONTINUES TO WORSEN ON THE SMALL ISLAND NATION OF BORADA, WHOSE LEADERS HAVE FAR REFUSED ALL OFFERS OF INTERNATIONAL AID.
IT'S ESTIMATED THAT UNLESS THE SITUATION CHANGES, THOUSANDS, EVEN TENS OF THOUSANDS COULD BE DEAD BY THE END OF THE WEEK.
BUT THERE'S NO END IN SIGHT, AND IT SEEMS NO ONE CAN DO ANYTHING TO STOP THE DYING.

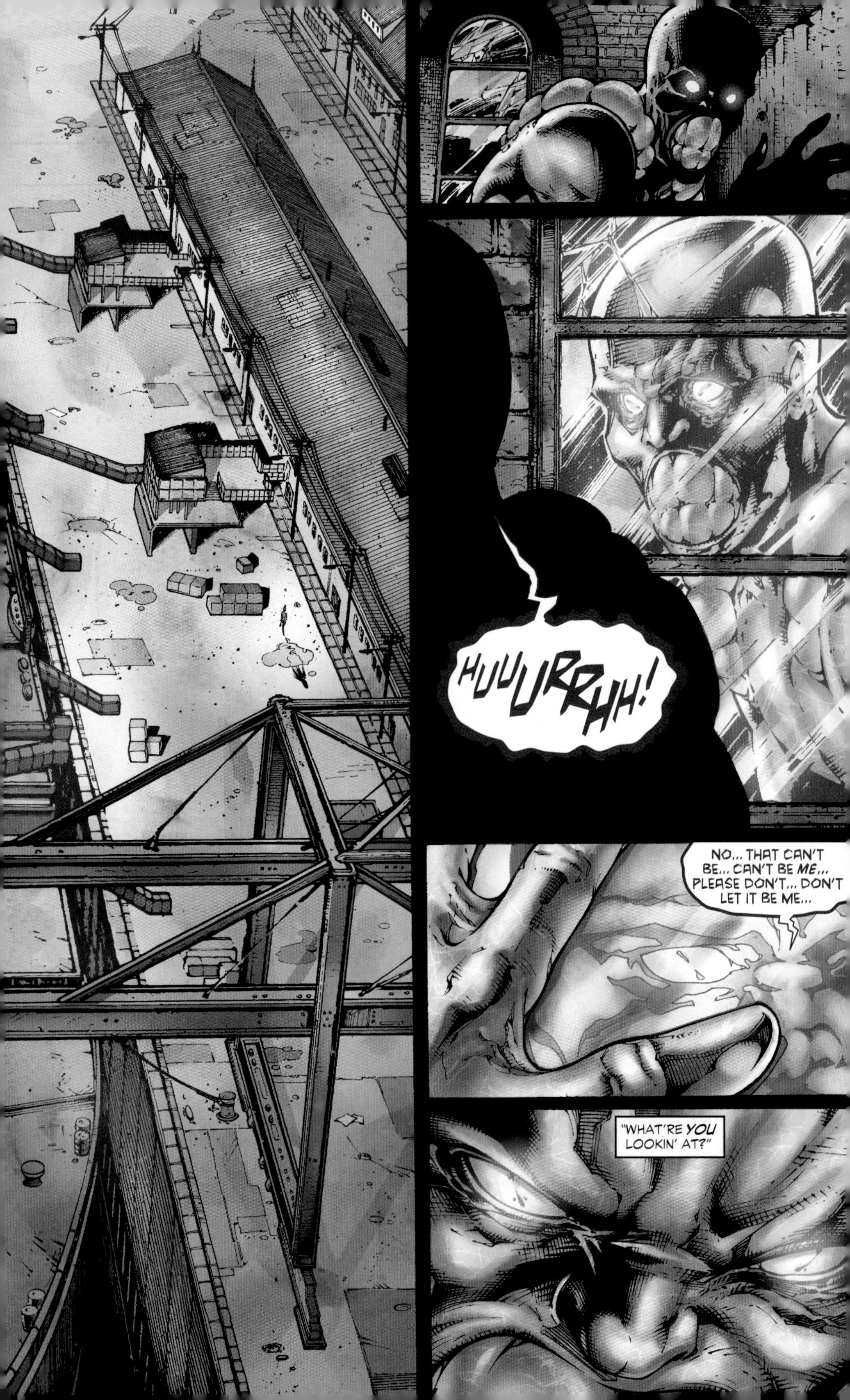
HUUURRHH!
NO... THAT CAN'T BE... CAN'T BE *ME*... PLEASE DON'T... DON'T LET IT BE ME...
"WHAT'RE *YOU* LOOKIN' AT?"

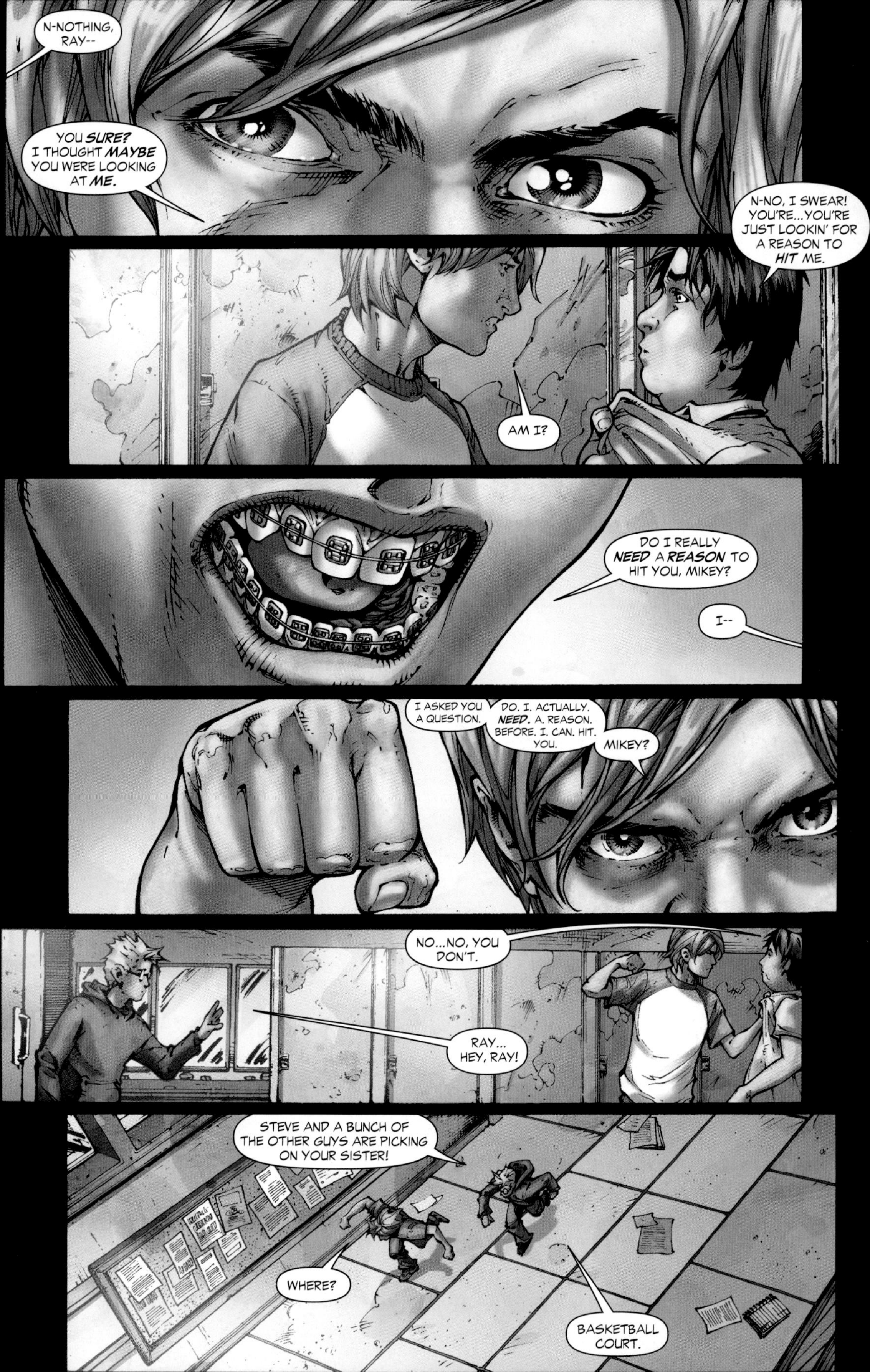
N-NOTHING, RAY--
YOU SURE? I THOUGHT MAYBE YOU WERE LOOKING AT ME.
N-NO, I SWEAR! YOU'RE...YOU'RE JUST LOOKIN' FOR A REASON TO HIT ME.
AM I?
DO I REALLY NEED A REASON TO HIT YOU, MIKEY?
I--
I ASKED YOU A QUESTION.
DO. I. ACTUALLY. NEED. A. REASON. BEFORE. I. CAN. HIT. YOU.
MIKEY?
NO...NO, YOU DON'T.
RAY... HEY, RAY!
STEVE AND A BUNCH OF THE OTHER GUYS ARE PICKING ON YOUR SISTER!
WHERE?
BASKETBALL COURT.

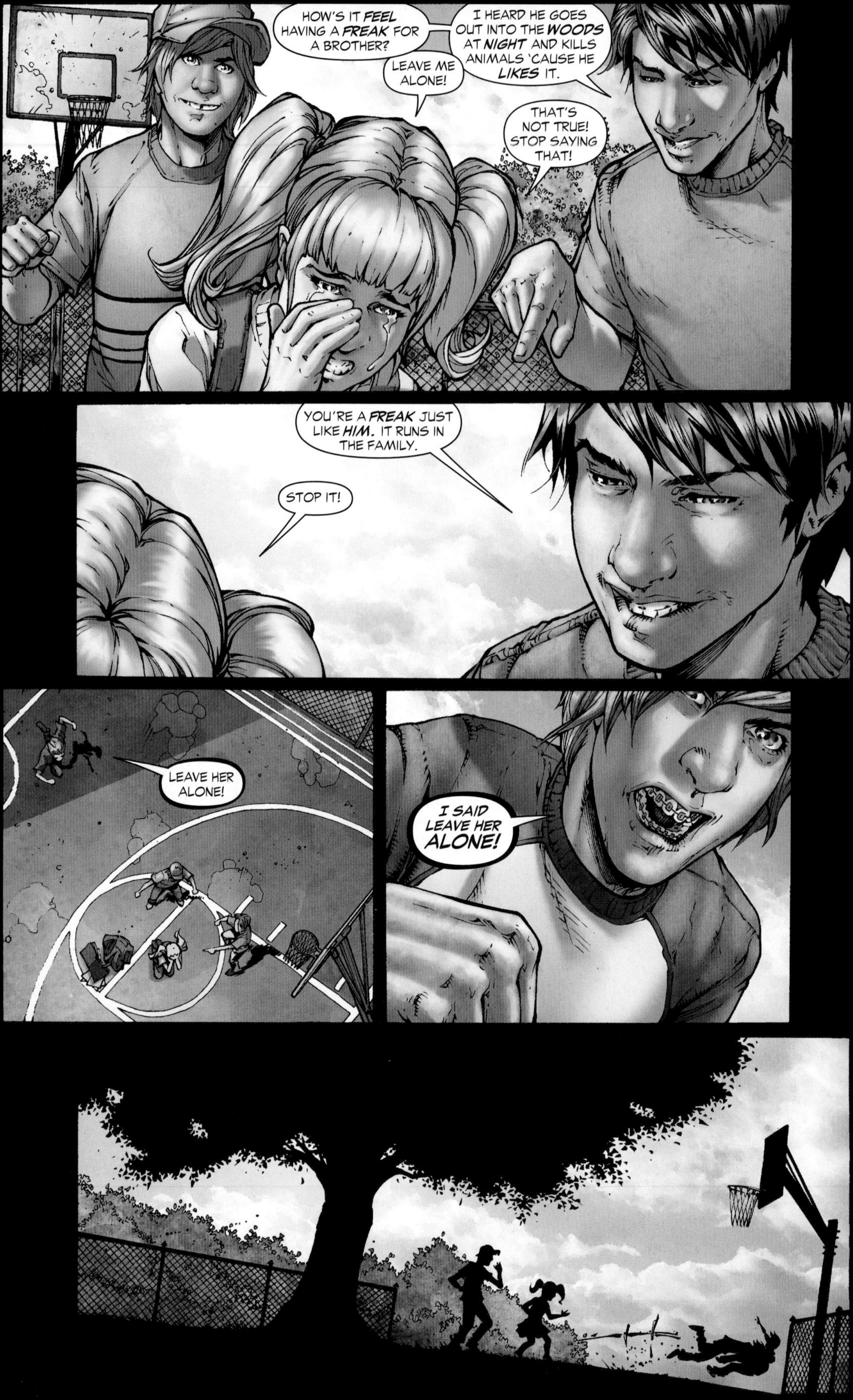
HOW'S IT FEEL HAVING A FREAK FOR A BROTHER?
I HEARD HE GOES OUT INTO THE WOODS AT NIGHT AND KILLS ANIMALS 'CAUSE HE LIKES IT.
LEAVE ME ALONE!
THAT'S NOT TRUE! STOP SAYING THAT!
YOU'RE A FREAK JUST LIKE HIM. IT RUNS IN THE FAMILY.
STOP IT!
LEAVE HER ALONE!
I SAID LEAVE HER ALONE!

GET 'IM!

NO!

ARE YOU CRAZY?

LEGGO!

GET HIM OFF ME! GET HIM OFF ME! **GET HIM OFF ME!**

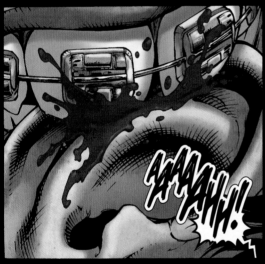

GYAAAAHH!!

HE BIT MY EAR OFF! HE BIT MY EAR OFF!

HE BIT MY FREAKING EAR OFF!--

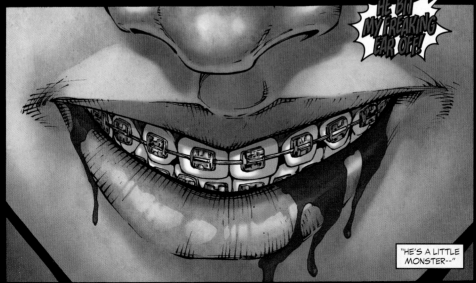

"HE'S A LITTLE MONSTER--"

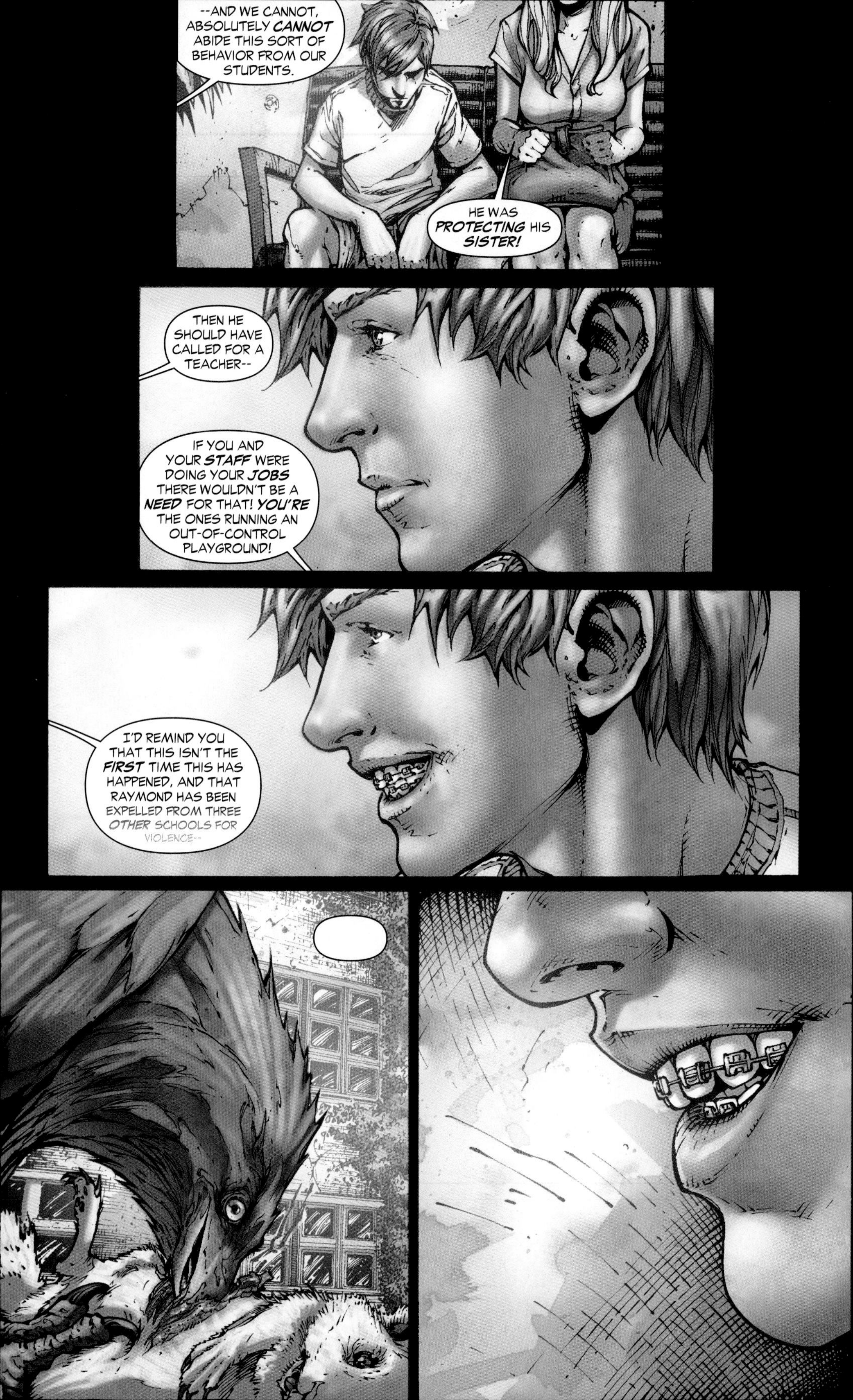
--AND WE CANNOT, ABSOLUTELY CANNOT ABIDE THIS SORT OF BEHAVIOR FROM OUR STUDENTS.
HE WAS PROTECTING HIS SISTER!
THEN HE SHOULD HAVE CALLED FOR A TEACHER--
IF YOU AND YOUR STAFF WERE DOING YOUR JOBS THERE WOULDN'T BE A NEED FOR THAT! YOU'RE THE ONES RUNNING AN OUT-OF-CONTROL PLAYGROUND!
I'D REMIND YOU THAT THIS ISN'T THE FIRST TIME THIS HAS HAPPENED, AND THAT RAYMOND HAS BEEN EXPELLED FROM THREE OTHER SCHOOLS FOR VIOLENCE--

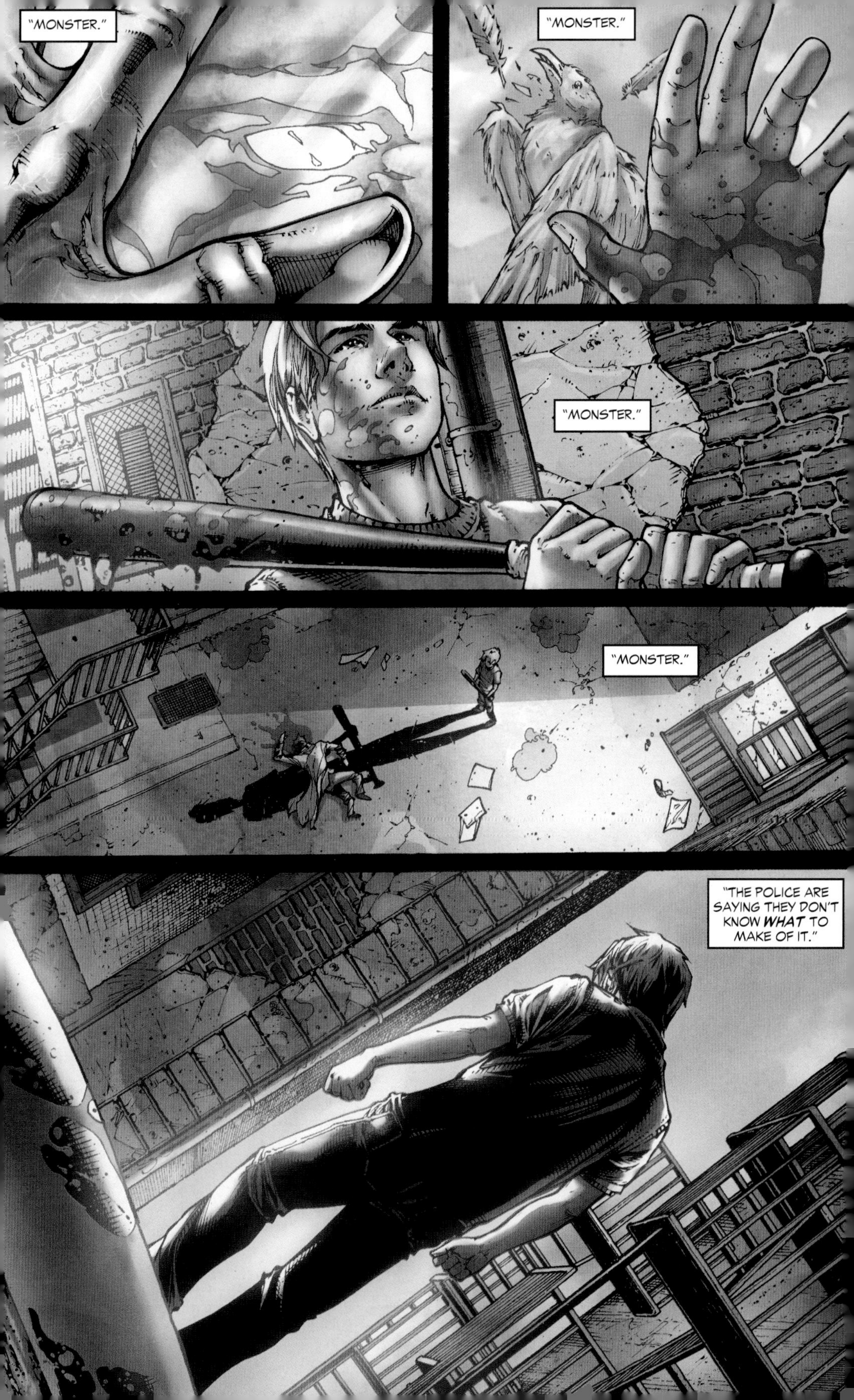
"MONSTER."
"MONSTER."
"MONSTER."
"MONSTER."
"THE POLICE ARE SAYING THEY DON'T KNOW *WHAT* TO MAKE OF IT."

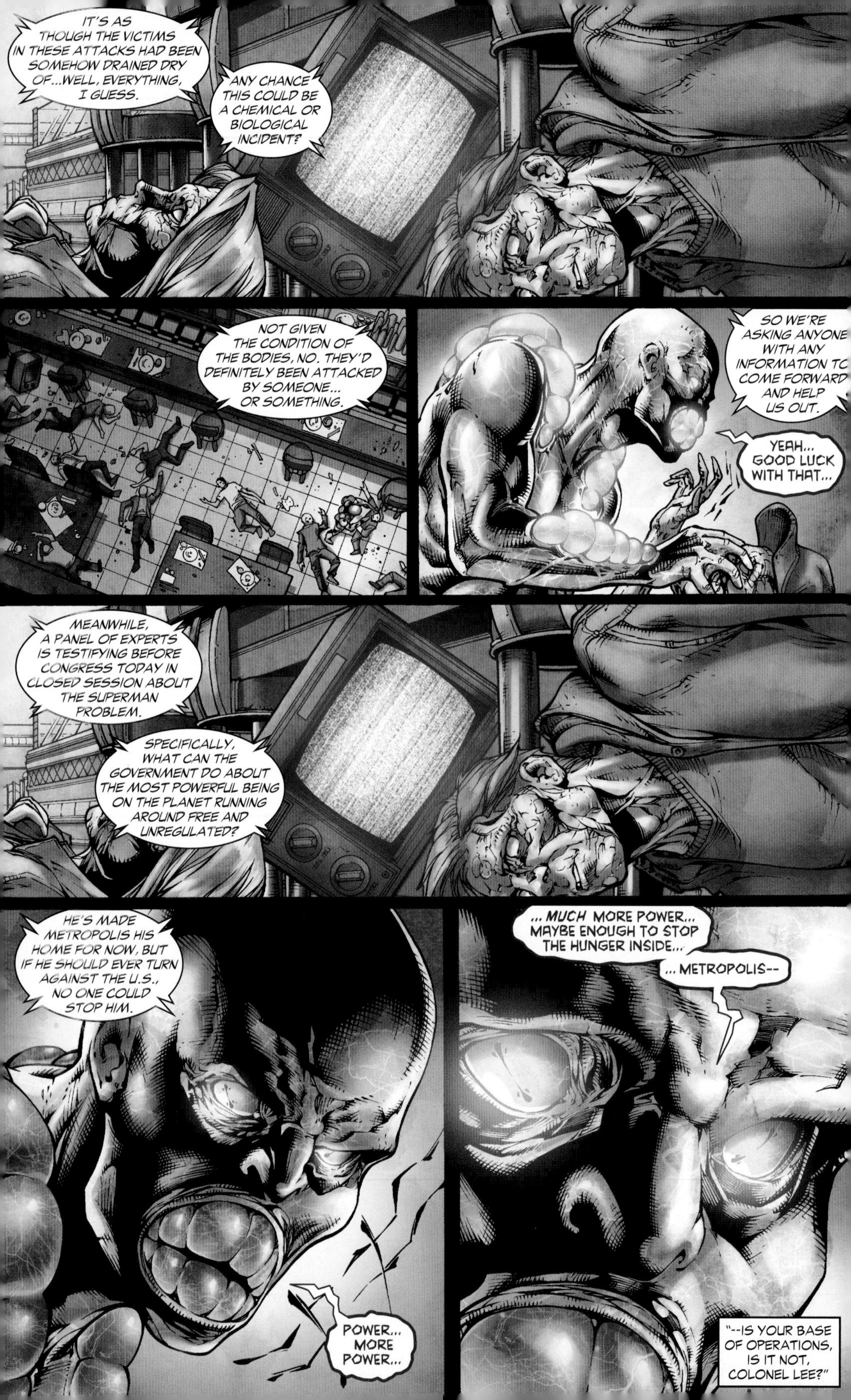
IT'S AS THOUGH THE VICTIMS IN THESE ATTACKS HAD BEEN SOMEHOW DRAINED DRY OF...WELL, EVERYTHING, I GUESS.
ANY CHANCE THIS COULD BE A CHEMICAL OR BIOLOGICAL INCIDENT?
NOT GIVEN THE CONDITION OF THE BODIES, NO. THEY'D DEFINITELY BEEN ATTACKED BY SOMEONE... OR SOMETHING.
SO WE'RE ASKING ANYONE WITH ANY INFORMATION TO COME FORWARD AND HELP US OUT.
YEAH... GOOD LUCK WITH THAT...
MEANWHILE, A PANEL OF EXPERTS IS TESTIFYING BEFORE CONGRESS TODAY IN CLOSED SESSION ABOUT THE SUPERMAN PROBLEM.
SPECIFICALLY, WHAT CAN THE GOVERNMENT DO ABOUT THE MOST POWERFUL BEING ON THE PLANET RUNNING AROUND FREE AND UNREGULATED?
HE'S MADE METROPOLIS HIS HOME FOR NOW, BUT IF HE SHOULD EVER TURN AGAINST THE U.S., NO ONE COULD STOP HIM.
POWER... MORE POWER...
...MUCH MORE POWER... MAYBE ENOUGH TO STOP THE HUNGER INSIDE...
...METROPOLIS--
"--IS YOUR BASE OF OPERATIONS, IS IT NOT, COLONEL LEE?"

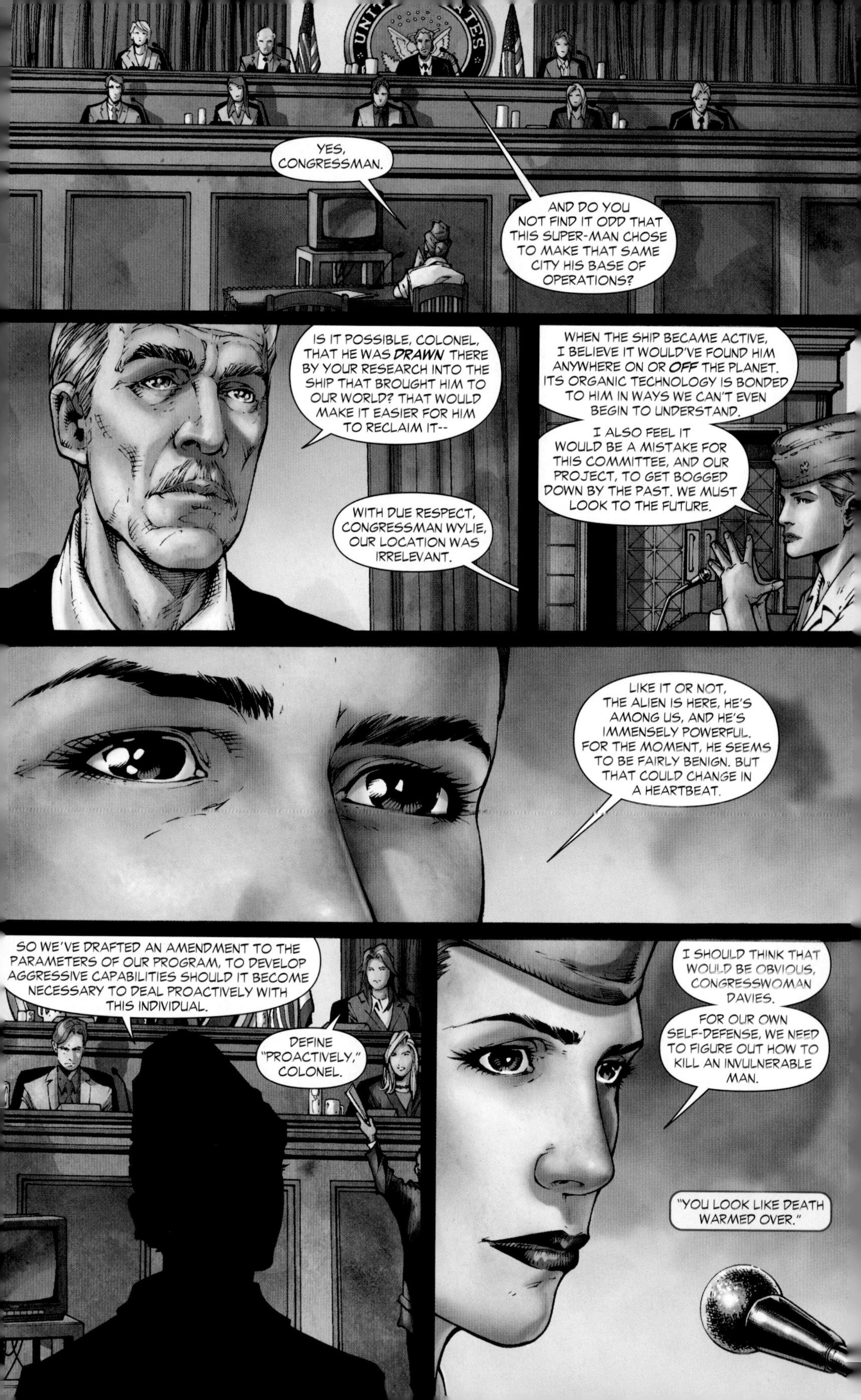

YES, CONGRESSMAN.
AND DO YOU NOT FIND IT ODD THAT THIS SUPER-MAN CHOSE TO MAKE THAT SAME CITY HIS BASE OF OPERATIONS?
IS IT POSSIBLE, COLONEL, THAT HE WAS DRAWN THERE BY YOUR RESEARCH INTO THE SHIP THAT BROUGHT HIM TO OUR WORLD? THAT WOULD MAKE IT EASIER FOR HIM TO RECLAIM IT--
WITH DUE RESPECT, CONGRESSMAN WYLIE, OUR LOCATION WAS IRRELEVANT.
WHEN THE SHIP BECAME ACTIVE, I BELIEVE IT WOULD'VE FOUND HIM ANYWHERE ON OR OFF THE PLANET. ITS ORGANIC TECHNOLOGY IS BONDED TO HIM IN WAYS WE CAN'T EVEN BEGIN TO UNDERSTAND.
I ALSO FEEL IT WOULD BE A MISTAKE FOR THIS COMMITTEE, AND OUR PROJECT, TO GET BOGGED DOWN BY THE PAST. WE MUST LOOK TO THE FUTURE.
LIKE IT OR NOT, THE ALIEN IS HERE, HE'S AMONG US, AND HE'S IMMENSELY POWERFUL. FOR THE MOMENT, HE SEEMS TO BE FAIRLY BENIGN. BUT THAT COULD CHANGE IN A HEARTBEAT.
SO WE'VE DRAFTED AN AMENDMENT TO THE PARAMETERS OF OUR PROGRAM, TO DEVELOP AGGRESSIVE CAPABILITIES SHOULD IT BECOME NECESSARY TO DEAL PROACTIVELY WITH THIS INDIVIDUAL.
DEFINE "PROACTIVELY," COLONEL.
I SHOULD THINK THAT WOULD BE OBVIOUS, CONGRESSWOMAN DAVIES.
FOR OUR OWN SELF-DEFENSE, WE NEED TO FIGURE OUT HOW TO KILL AN INVULNERABLE MAN.
"YOU LOOK LIKE DEATH WARMED OVER."

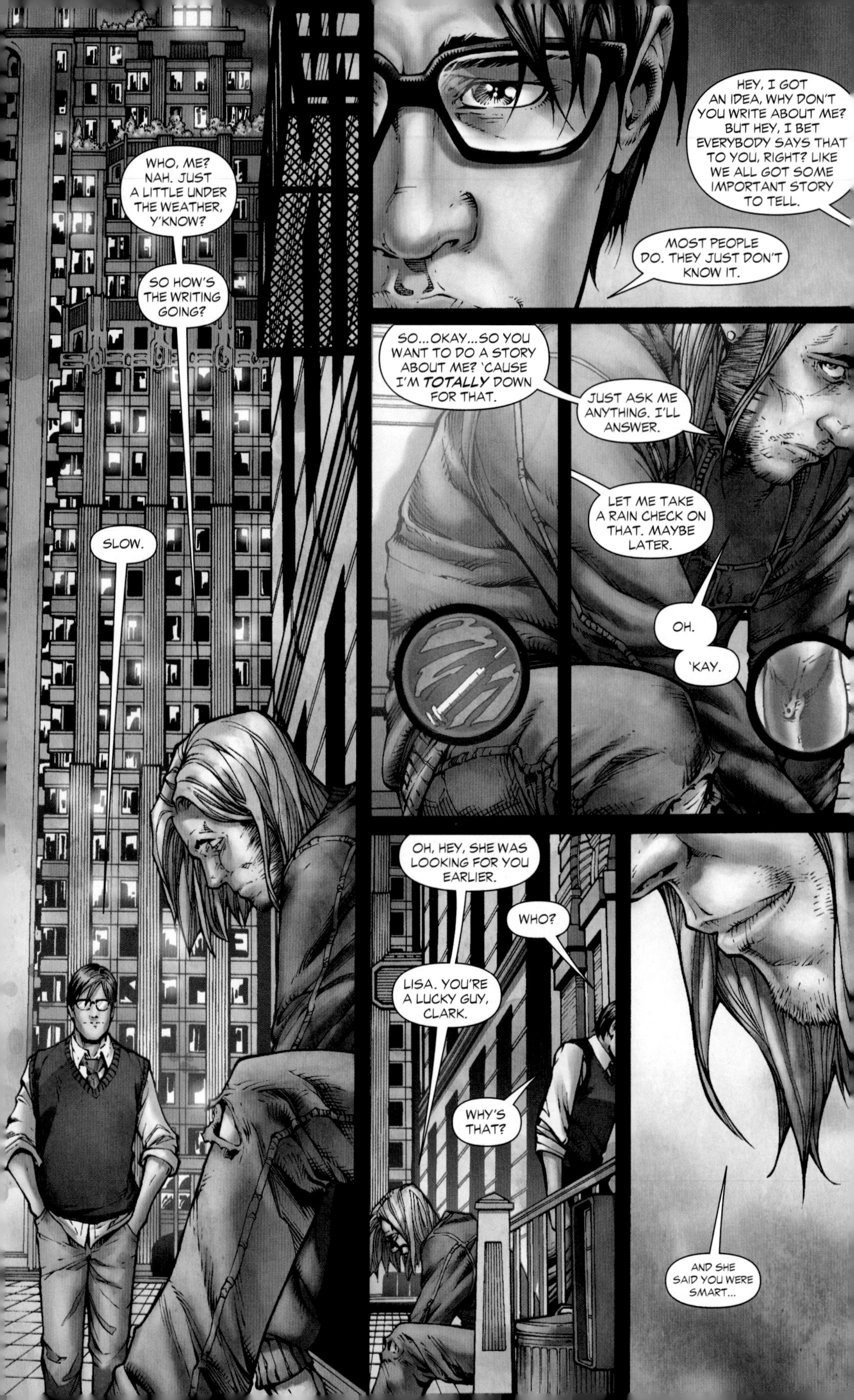
WHO, ME? NAH. JUST A LITTLE UNDER THE WEATHER, Y'KNOW?
SO HOW'S THE WRITING GOING?
SLOW.
HEY, I GOT AN IDEA, WHY DON'T YOU WRITE ABOUT ME? BUT HEY, I BET EVERYBODY SAYS THAT TO YOU, RIGHT? LIKE WE ALL GOT SOME IMPORTANT STORY TO TELL.
MOST PEOPLE DO. THEY JUST DON'T KNOW IT.
SO...OKAY...SO YOU WANT TO DO A STORY ABOUT ME? 'CAUSE I'M *TOTALLY* DOWN FOR THAT.
JUST ASK ME ANYTHING. I'LL ANSWER.
LET ME TAKE A RAIN CHECK ON THAT. MAYBE LATER.
OH.
'KAY.
OH, HEY, SHE WAS LOOKING FOR YOU EARLIER.
WHO?
LISA. YOU'RE A LUCKY GUY, CLARK.
WHY'S THAT?
AND SHE SAID YOU WERE SMART...

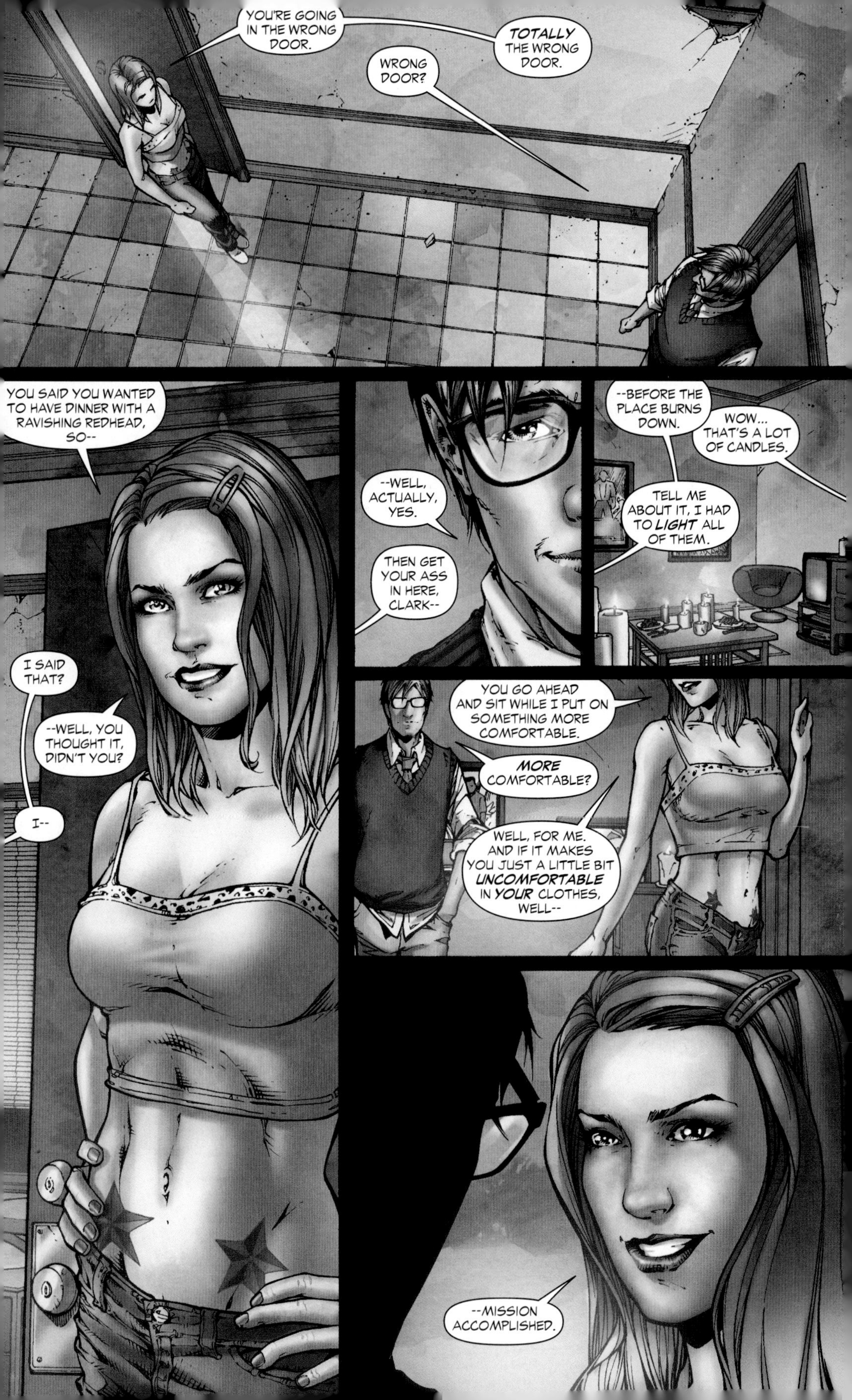
YOU'RE GOING IN THE WRONG DOOR.
TOTALLY THE WRONG DOOR.
WRONG DOOR?
YOU SAID YOU WANTED TO HAVE DINNER WITH A RAVISHING REDHEAD, SO--
I SAID THAT?
--WELL, YOU THOUGHT IT, DIDN'T YOU?
I--
--WELL, ACTUALLY, YES.
THEN GET YOUR ASS IN HERE, CLARK--
--BEFORE THE PLACE BURNS DOWN.
WOW... THAT'S A LOT OF CANDLES.
TELL ME ABOUT IT, I HAD TO LIGHT ALL OF THEM.
YOU GO AHEAD AND SIT WHILE I PUT ON SOMETHING MORE COMFORTABLE.
MORE COMFORTABLE?
WELL, FOR ME. AND IF IT MAKES YOU JUST A LITTLE BIT UNCOMFORTABLE IN YOUR CLOTHES, WELL--
--MISSION ACCOMPLISHED.

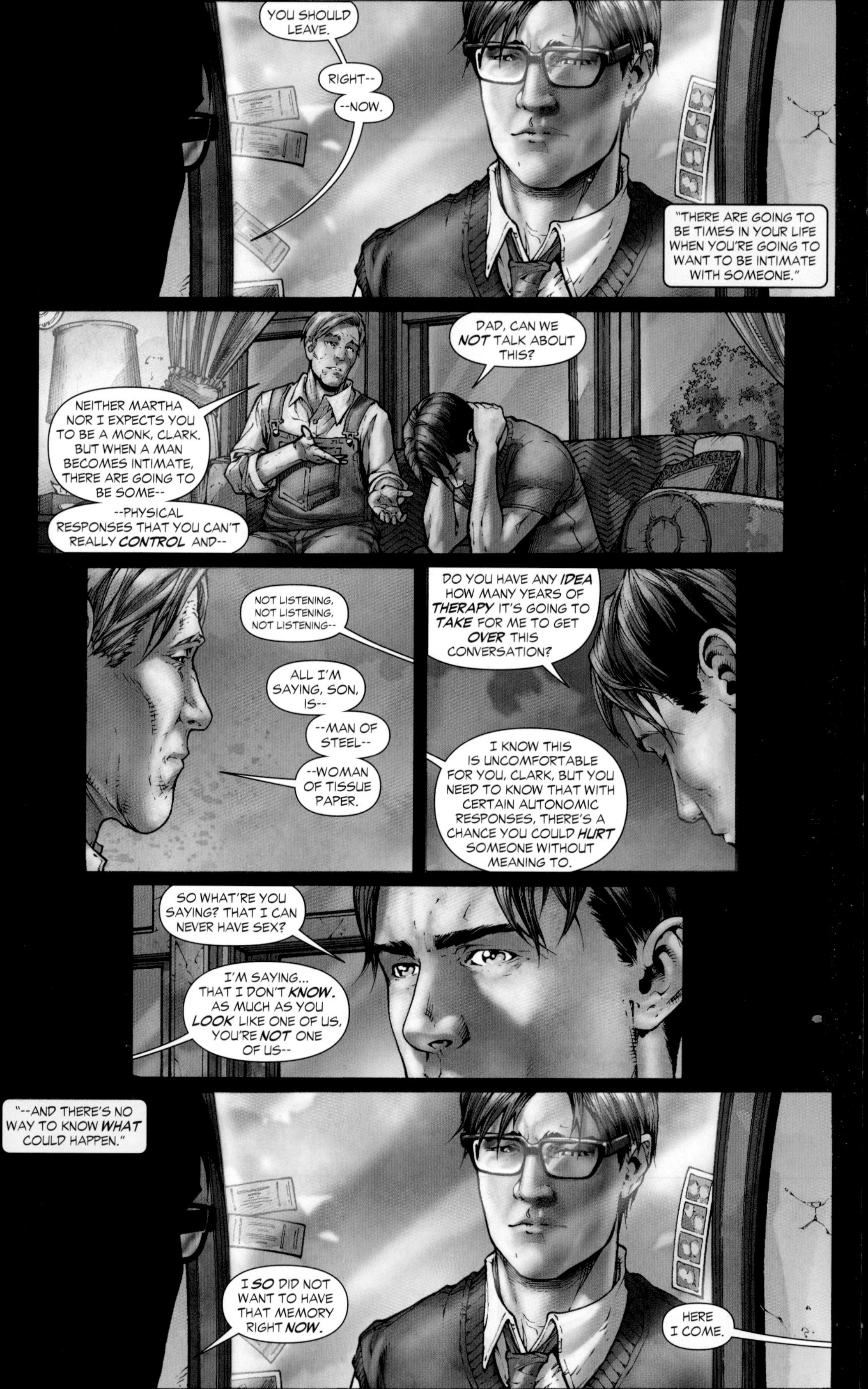
YOU SHOULD LEAVE.
RIGHT--
--NOW.
"THERE ARE GOING TO BE TIMES IN YOUR LIFE WHEN YOU'RE GOING TO WANT TO BE INTIMATE WITH SOMEONE."
NEITHER MARTHA NOR I EXPECTS YOU TO BE A MONK, CLARK. BUT WHEN A MAN BECOMES INTIMATE, THERE ARE GOING TO BE SOME--
--PHYSICAL RESPONSES THAT YOU CAN'T REALLY CONTROL AND--
DAD, CAN WE NOT TALK ABOUT THIS?
NOT LISTENING, NOT LISTENING, NOT LISTENING--
ALL I'M SAYING, SON, IS--
--MAN OF STEEL--
--WOMAN OF TISSUE PAPER.
DO YOU HAVE ANY IDEA HOW MANY YEARS OF THERAPY IT'S GOING TO TAKE FOR ME TO GET OVER THIS CONVERSATION?
I KNOW THIS IS UNCOMFORTABLE FOR YOU, CLARK, BUT YOU NEED TO KNOW THAT WITH CERTAIN AUTONOMIC RESPONSES, THERE'S A CHANCE YOU COULD HURT SOMEONE WITHOUT MEANING TO.
SO WHAT'RE YOU SAYING? THAT I CAN NEVER HAVE SEX?
I'M SAYING... THAT I DON'T KNOW. AS MUCH AS YOU LOOK LIKE ONE OF US, YOU'RE NOT ONE OF US--
"--AND THERE'S NO WAY TO KNOW WHAT COULD HAPPEN."
I SO DID NOT WANT TO HAVE THAT MEMORY RIGHT NOW.
HERE I COME.

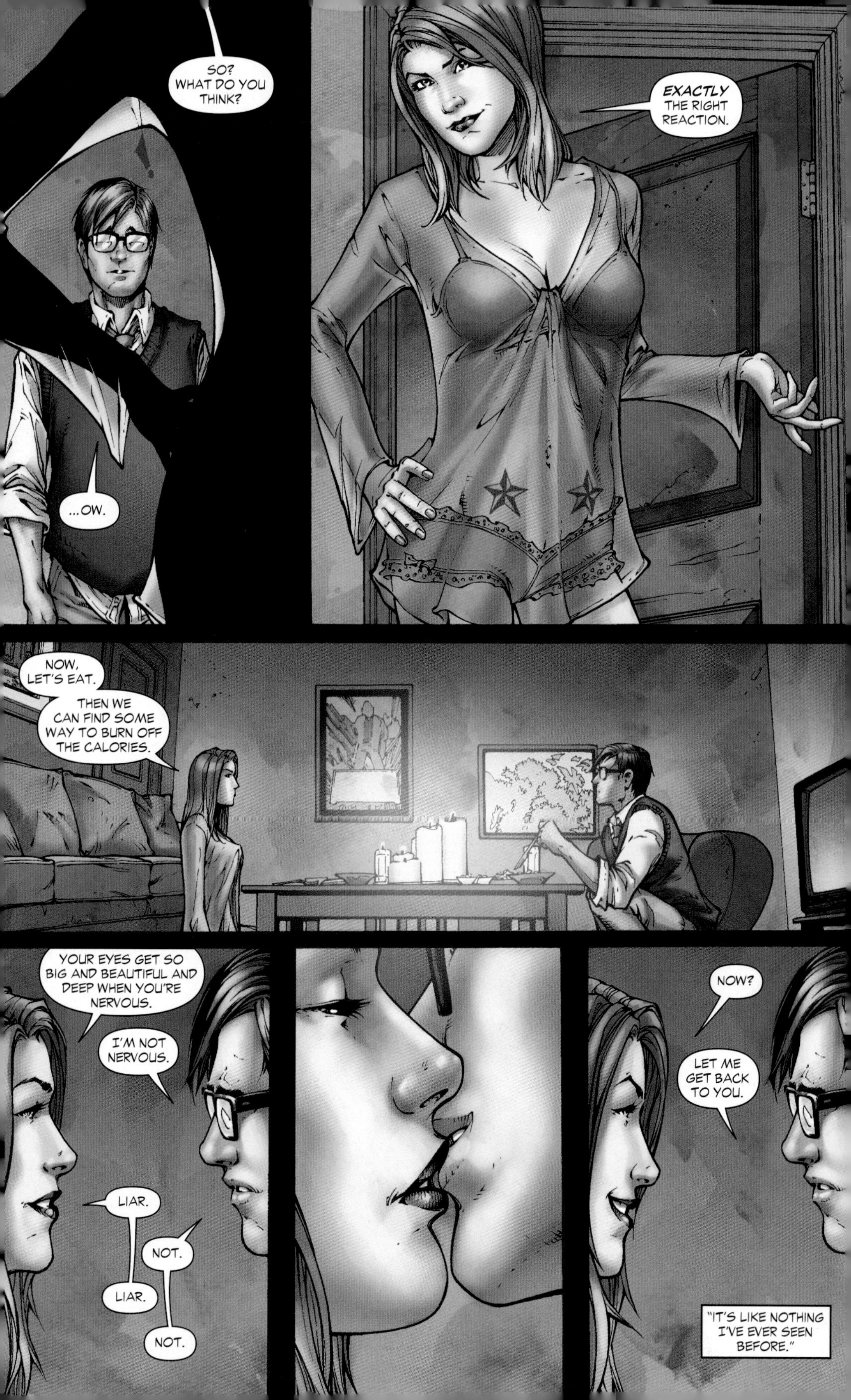
SO? WHAT DO YOU THINK?
...OW.
EXACTLY THE RIGHT REACTION.
NOW, LET'S EAT.
THEN WE CAN FIND SOME WAY TO BURN OFF THE CALORIES.
YOUR EYES GET SO BIG AND BEAUTIFUL AND DEEP WHEN YOU'RE NERVOUS.
I'M NOT NERVOUS.
LIAR.
NOT.
LIAR.
NOT.
NOW?
LET ME GET BACK TO YOU.
"IT'S LIKE NOTHING I'VE EVER SEEN BEFORE."

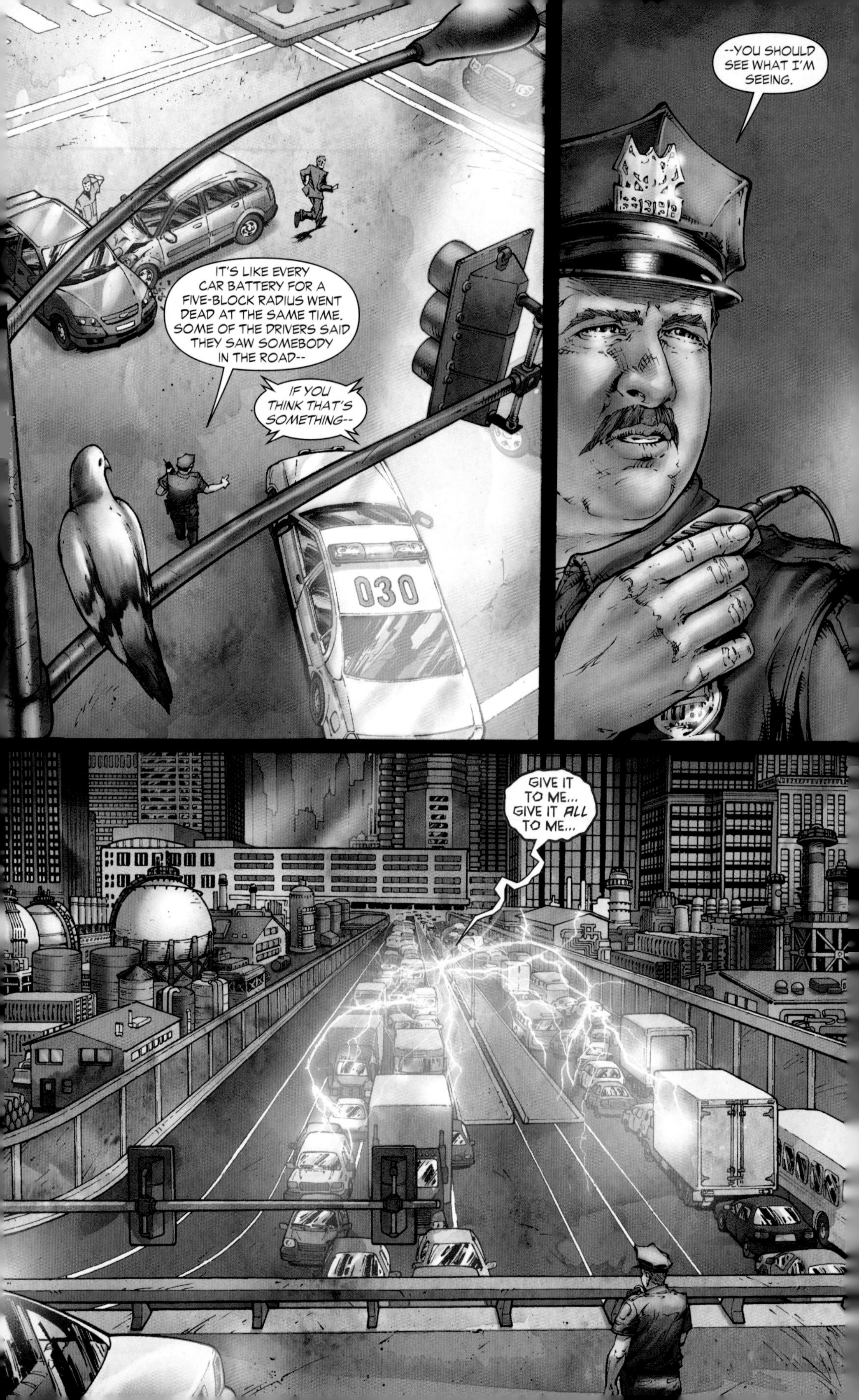
IT'S LIKE EVERY CAR BATTERY FOR A FIVE-BLOCK RADIUS WENT DEAD AT THE SAME TIME. SOME OF THE DRIVERS SAID THEY SAW SOMEBODY IN THE ROAD--
IF YOU THINK THAT'S SOMETHING--
030
--YOU SHOULD SEE WHAT I'M SEEING.
GIVE IT TO ME... GIVE IT ALL TO ME...

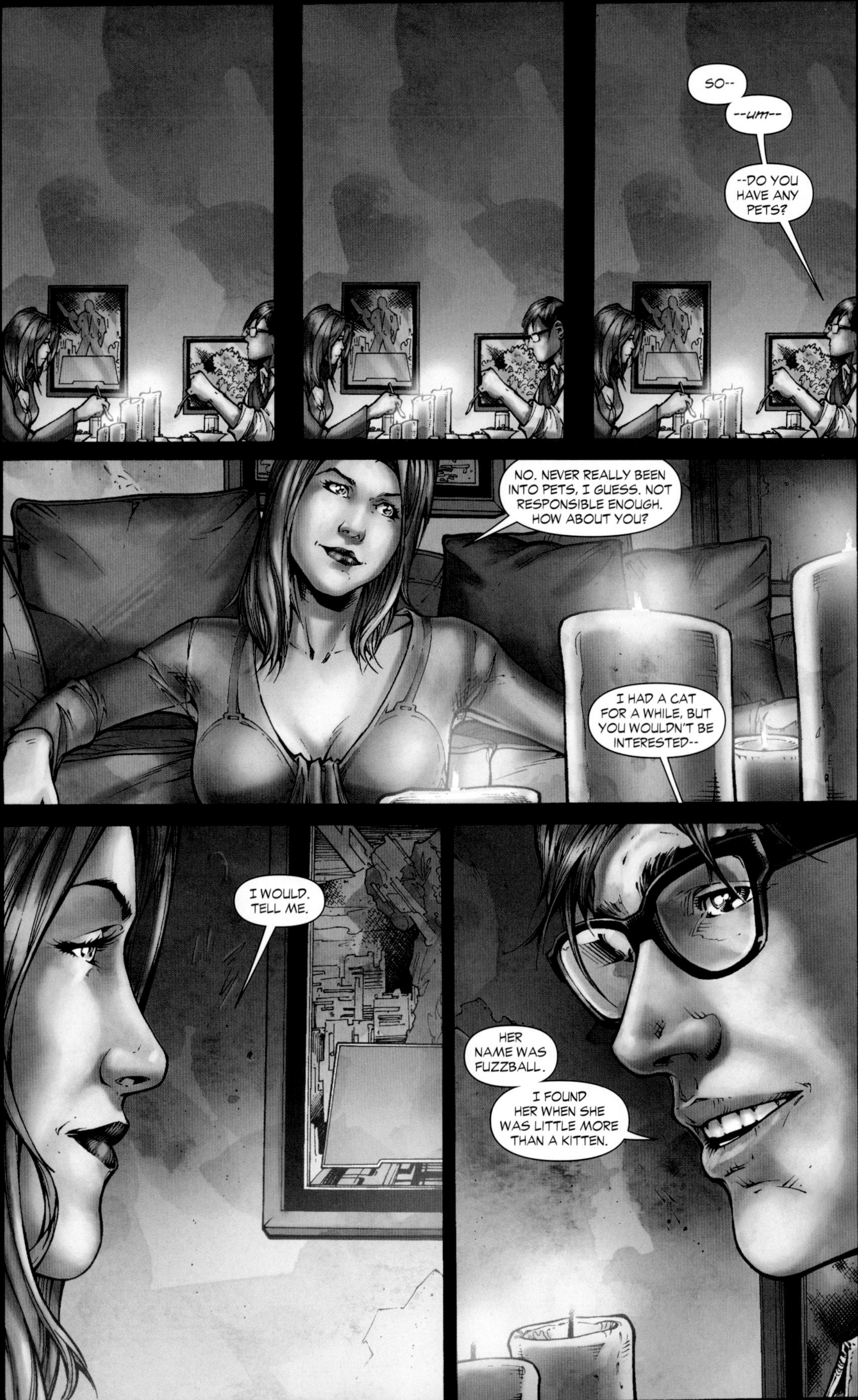
SO--
--UM--
--DO YOU HAVE ANY PETS?
NO. NEVER REALLY BEEN INTO PETS, I GUESS. NOT RESPONSIBLE ENOUGH. HOW ABOUT YOU?
I HAD A CAT FOR A WHILE, BUT YOU WOULDN'T BE INTERESTED--
I WOULD. TELL ME.
HER NAME WAS FUZZBALL.
I FOUND HER WHEN SHE WAS LITTLE MORE THAN A KITTEN.

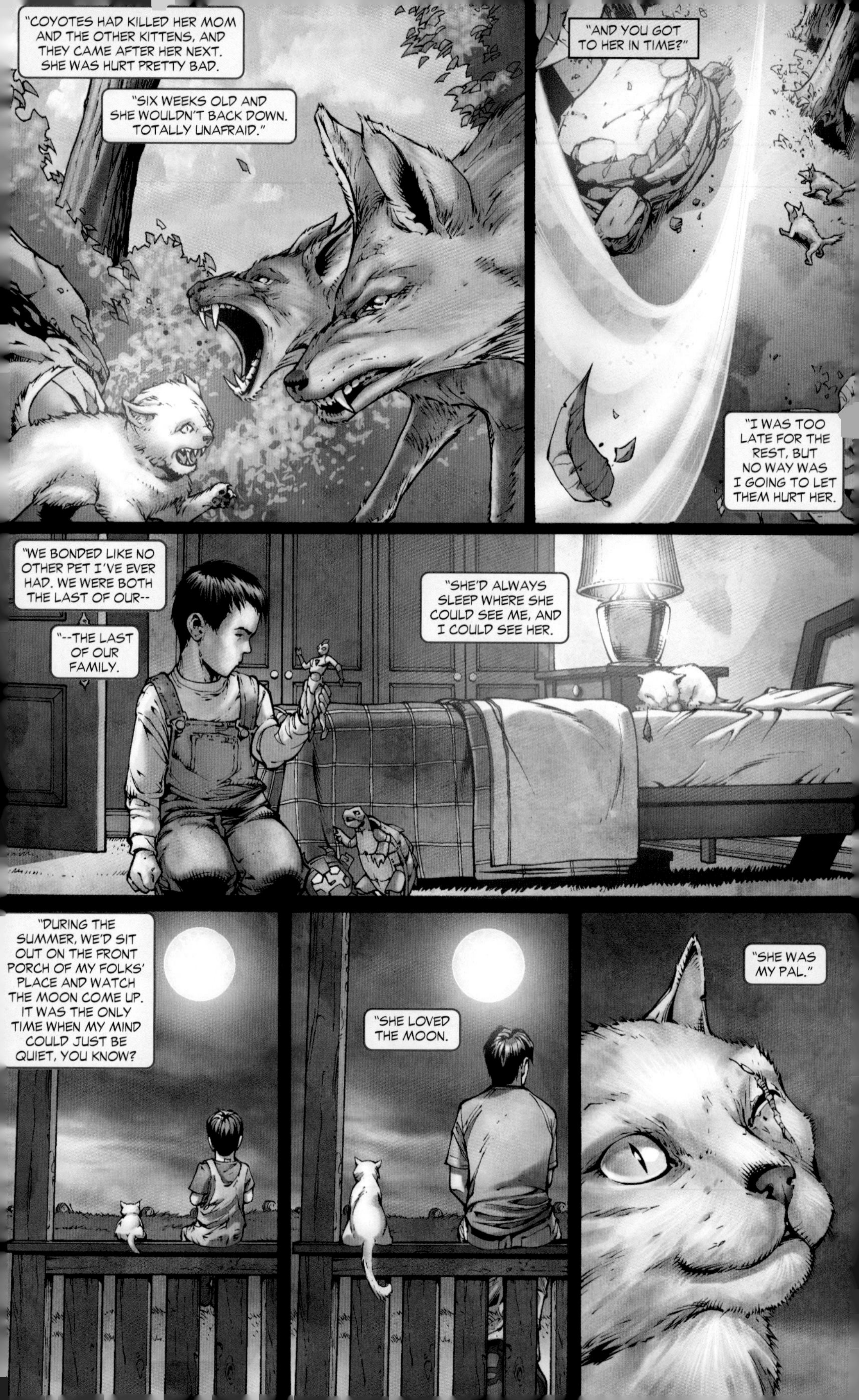
"COYOTES HAD KILLED HER MOM AND THE OTHER KITTENS, AND THEY CAME AFTER HER NEXT. SHE WAS HURT PRETTY BAD.
"SIX WEEKS OLD AND SHE WOULDN'T BACK DOWN. TOTALLY UNAFRAID."
"AND YOU GOT TO HER IN TIME?"
"I WAS TOO LATE FOR THE REST, BUT NO WAY WAS I GOING TO LET THEM HURT HER.
"WE BONDED LIKE NO OTHER PET I'VE EVER HAD. WE WERE BOTH THE LAST OF OUR--
"--THE LAST OF OUR FAMILY.
"SHE'D ALWAYS SLEEP WHERE SHE COULD SEE ME, AND I COULD SEE HER.
"DURING THE SUMMER, WE'D SIT OUT ON THE FRONT PORCH OF MY FOLKS' PLACE AND WATCH THE MOON COME UP. IT WAS THE ONLY TIME WHEN MY MIND COULD JUST BE QUIET, YOU KNOW?
"SHE LOVED THE MOON.
"SHE WAS MY PAL."

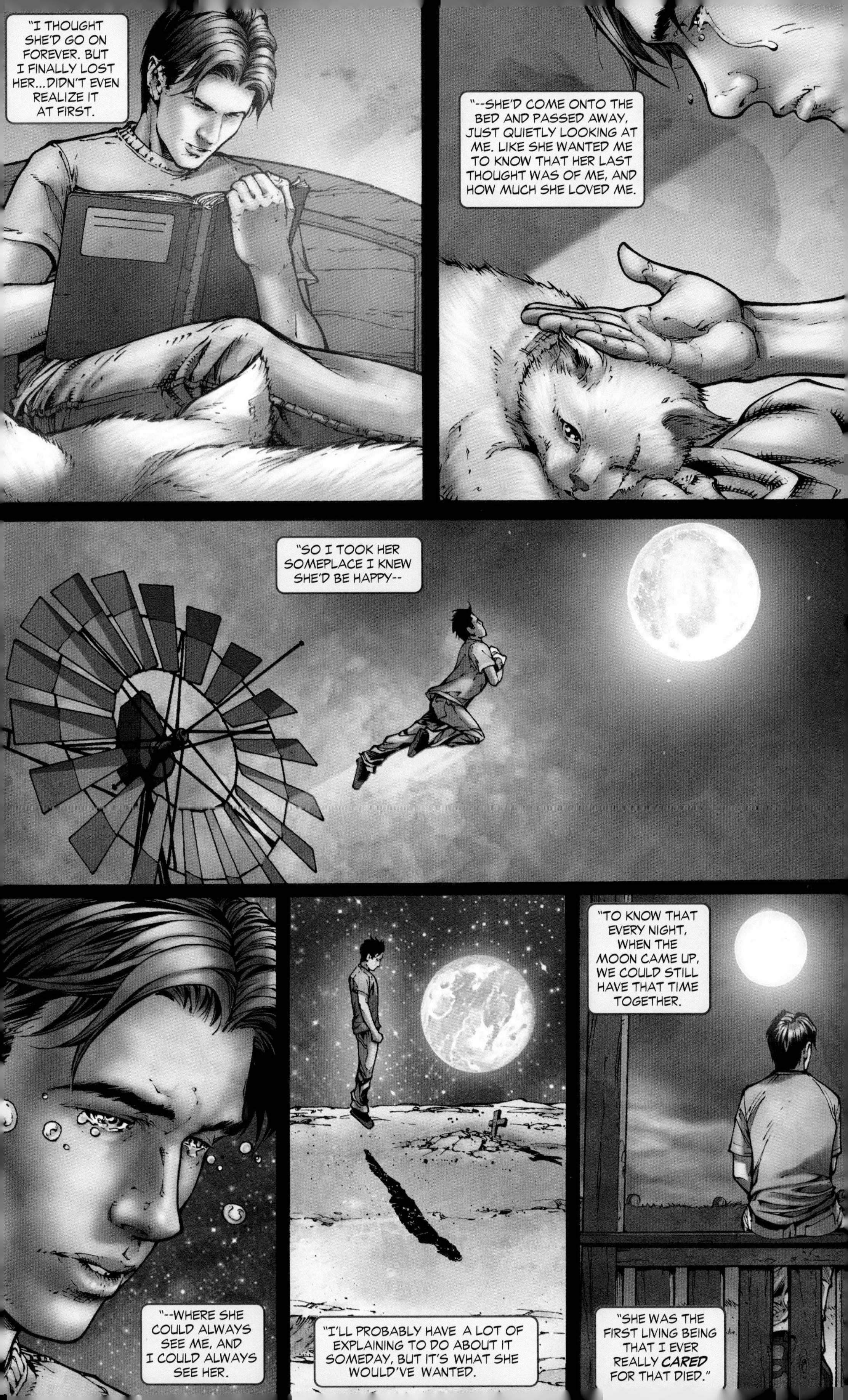
"I THOUGHT SHE'D GO ON FOREVER. BUT I FINALLY LOST HER...DIDN'T EVEN REALIZE IT AT FIRST.
"--SHE'D COME ONTO THE BED AND PASSED AWAY, JUST QUIETLY LOOKING AT ME. LIKE SHE WANTED ME TO KNOW THAT HER LAST THOUGHT WAS OF ME, AND HOW MUCH SHE LOVED ME.
"SO I TOOK HER SOMEPLACE I KNEW SHE'D BE HAPPY--
"--WHERE SHE COULD ALWAYS SEE ME, AND I COULD ALWAYS SEE HER.
"I'LL PROBABLY HAVE A LOT OF EXPLAINING TO DO ABOUT IT SOMEDAY, BUT IT'S WHAT SHE WOULD'VE WANTED.
"TO KNOW THAT EVERY NIGHT, WHEN THE MOON CAME UP, WE COULD STILL HAVE THAT TIME TOGETHER.
"SHE WAS THE FIRST LIVING BEING THAT I EVER REALLY *CARED* FOR THAT DIED."

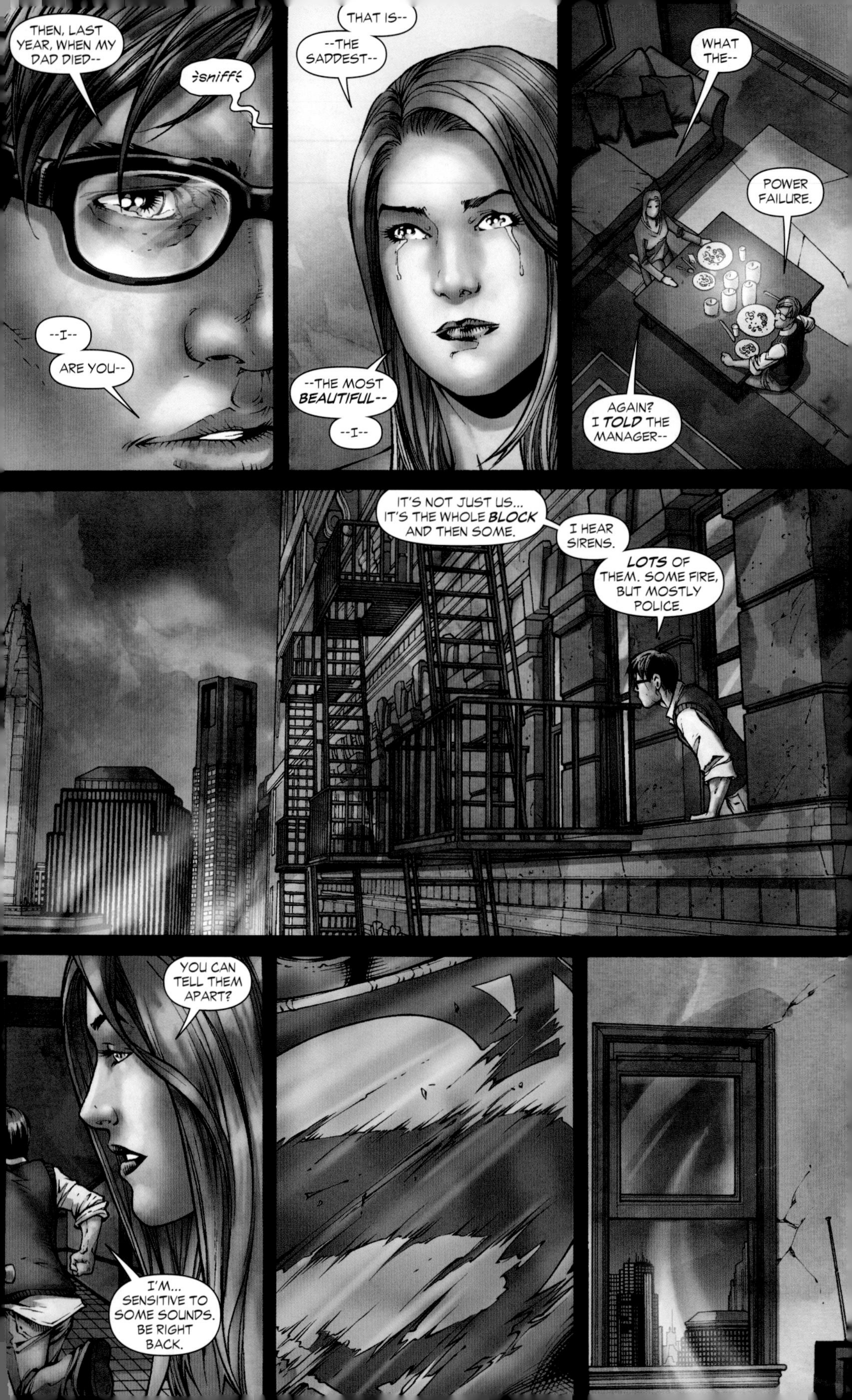
THEN, LAST YEAR, WHEN MY DAD DIED--
⩥sniff⩤
--I--
ARE YOU--
THAT IS--
--THE SADDEST--
--THE MOST *BEAUTIFUL*--
--I--
WHAT THE--
POWER FAILURE.
AGAIN? I *TOLD* THE MANAGER--
IT'S NOT JUST US... IT'S THE WHOLE *BLOCK* AND THEN SOME.
I HEAR SIRENS.
LOTS OF THEM. SOME FIRE, BUT MOSTLY POLICE.
YOU CAN TELL THEM APART?
I'M... SENSITIVE TO SOME SOUNDS. BE RIGHT BACK.

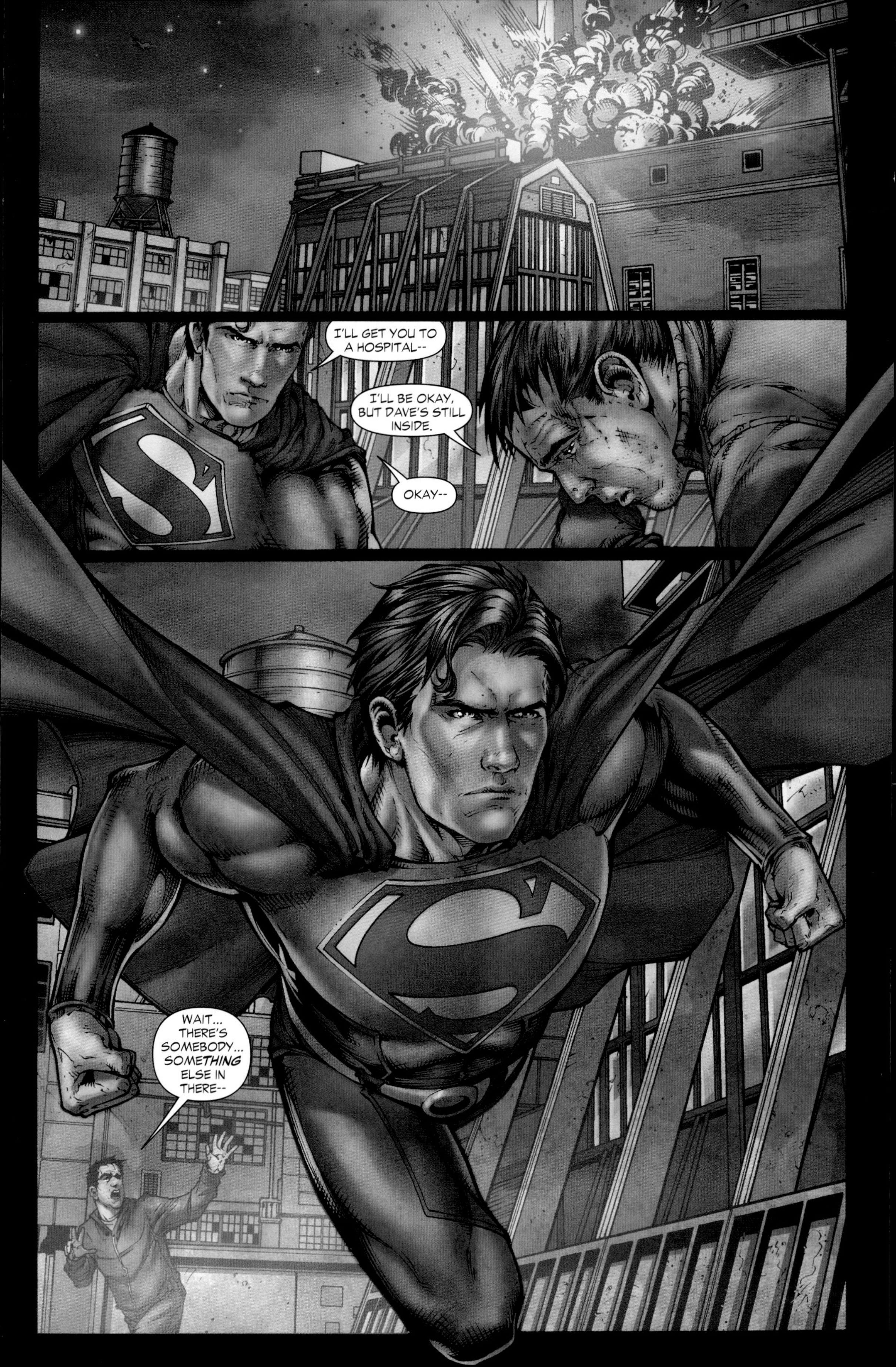
I'LL GET YOU TO A HOSPITAL--
I'LL BE OKAY, BUT DAVE'S STILL INSIDE.
OKAY--
WAIT... THERE'S SOMEBODY... SOME*THING* ELSE IN THERE--

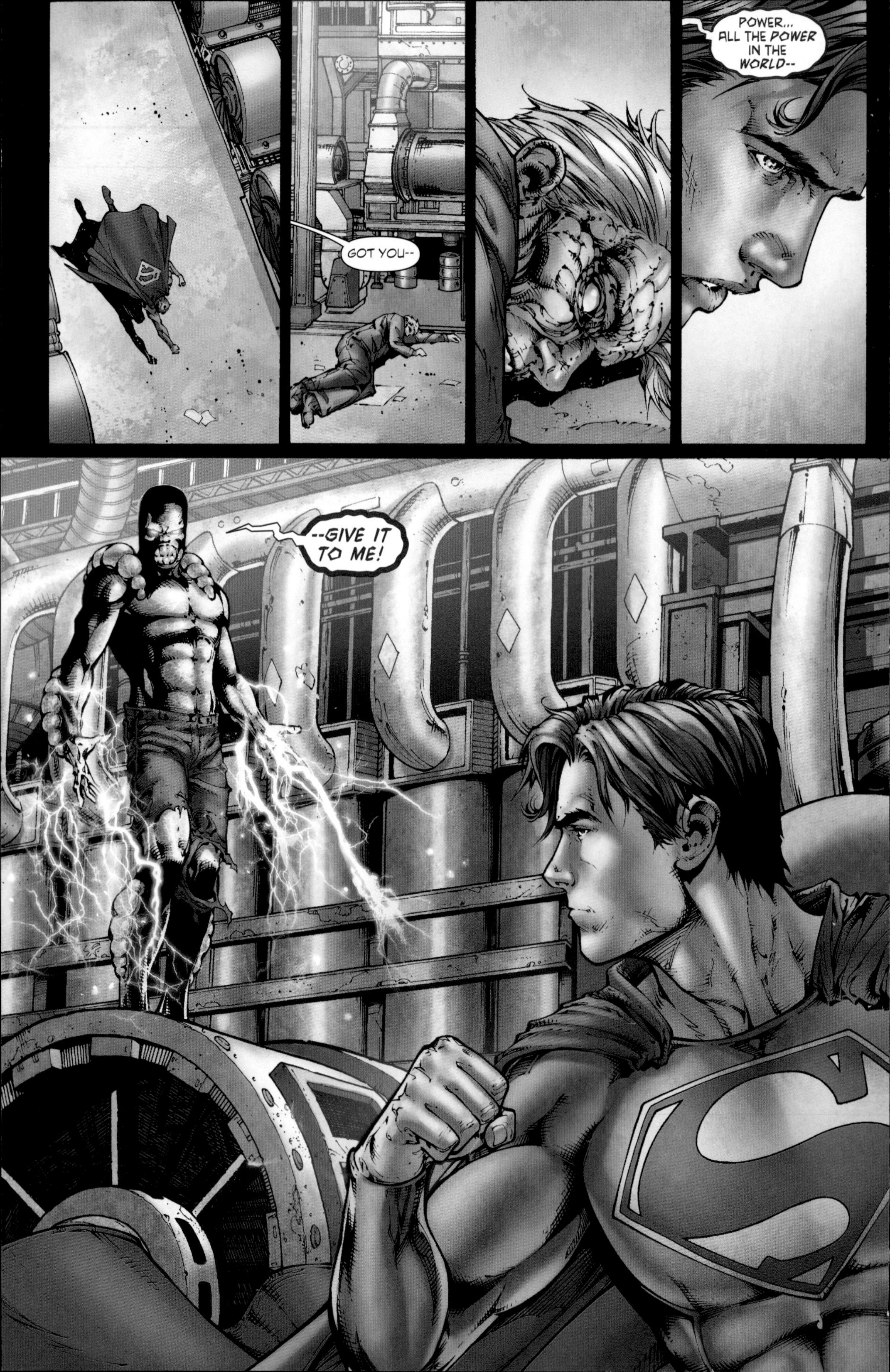
GOT YOU--
POWER... ALL THE POWER IN THE WORLD--
--GIVE IT TO ME!

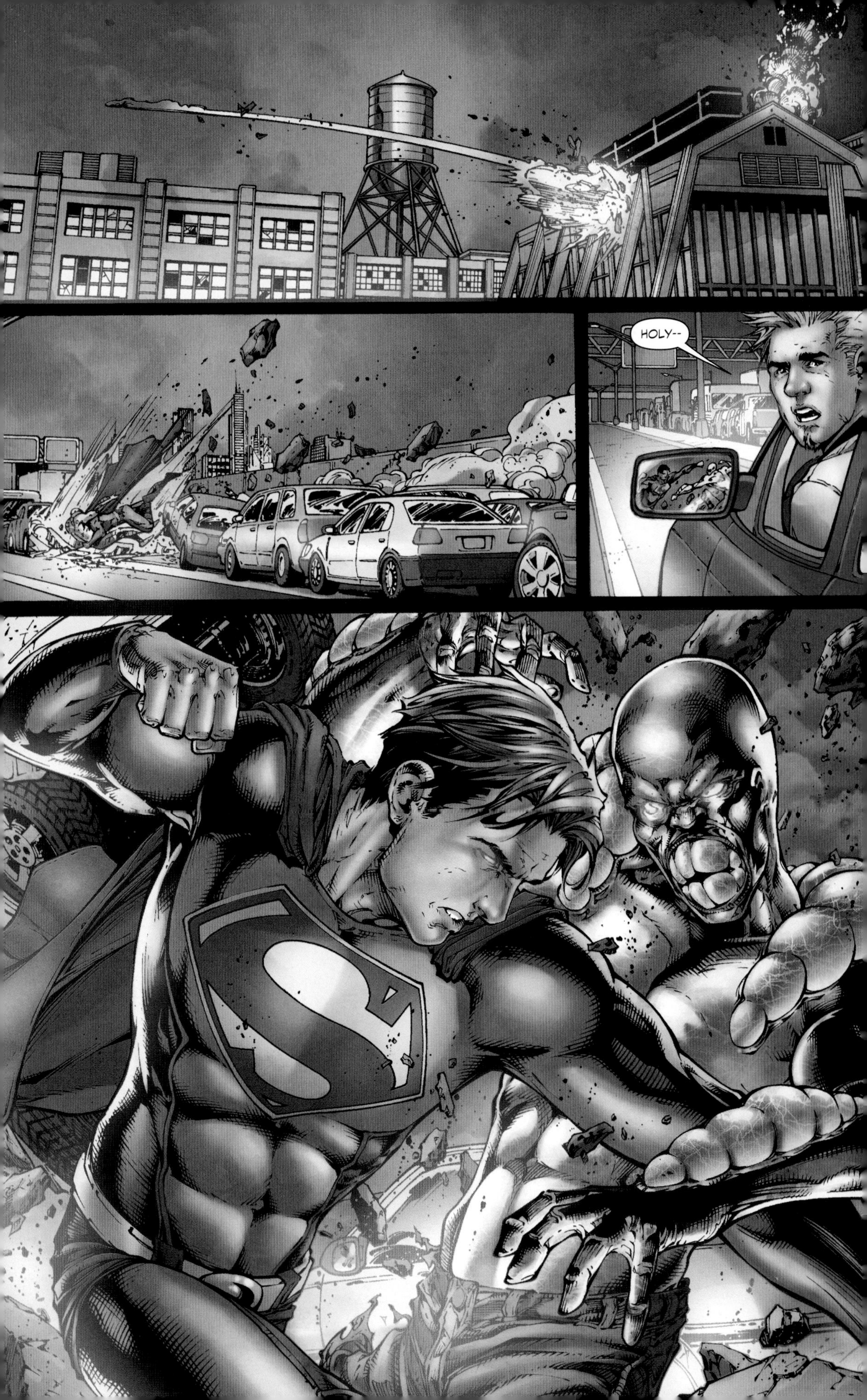
HOLY--

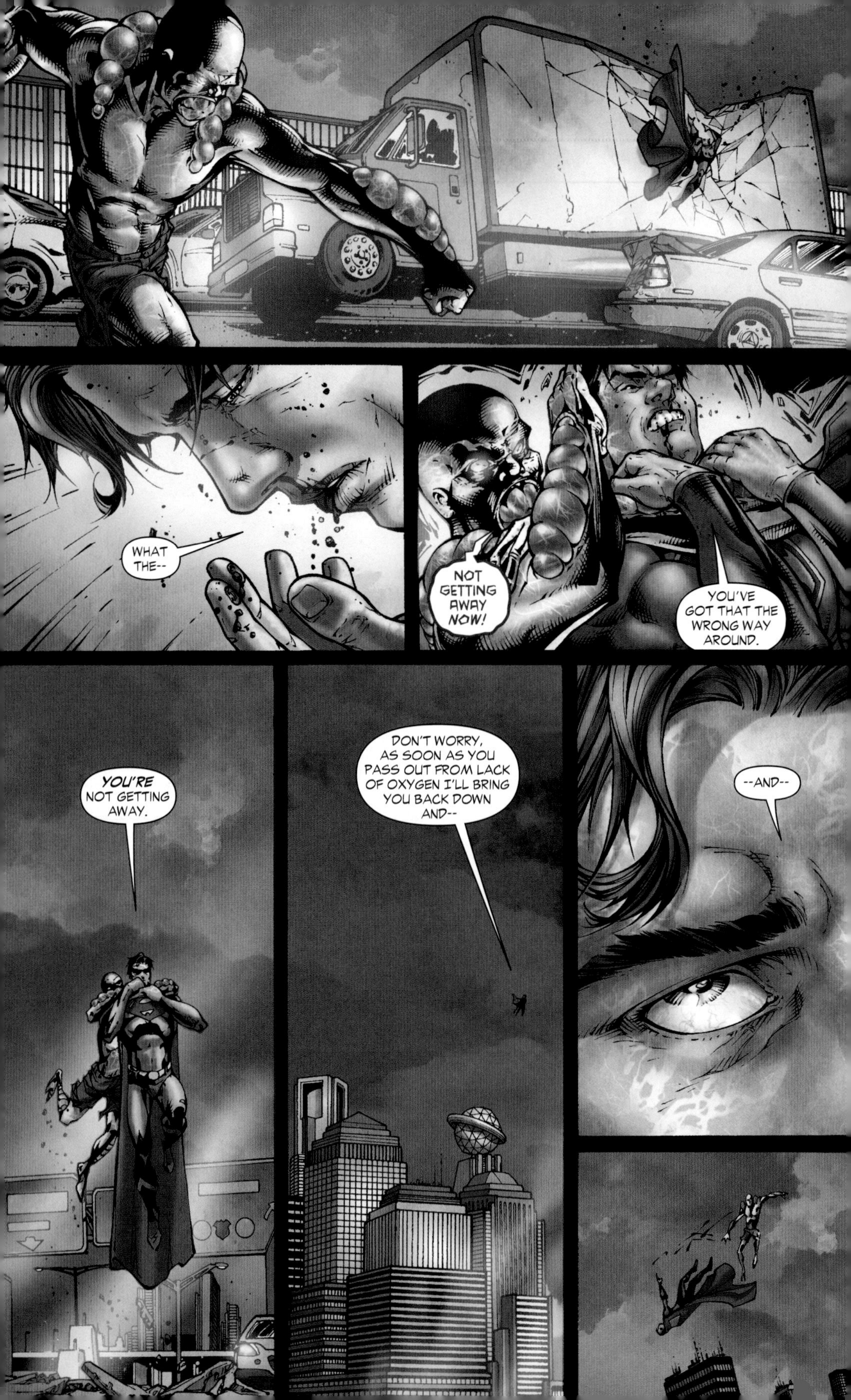
WHAT THE--
NOT GETTING AWAY NOW!
YOU'VE GOT THAT THE WRONG WAY AROUND.
YOU'RE NOT GETTING AWAY.
DON'T WORRY, AS SOON AS YOU PASS OUT FROM LACK OF OXYGEN I'LL BRING YOU BACK DOWN AND--
--AND--

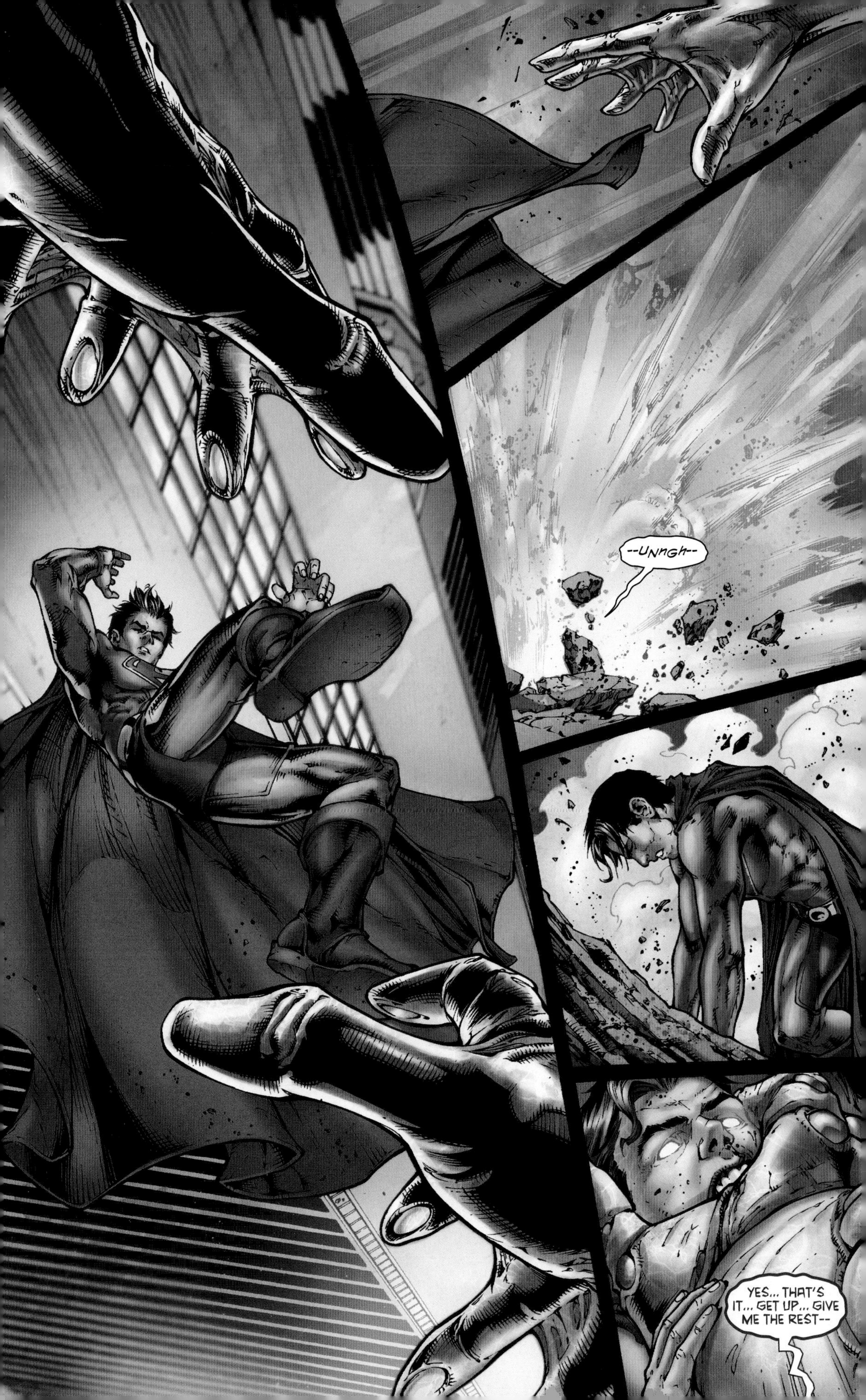
--Unngh--
YES... THAT'S IT... GET UP... GIVE ME THE REST--

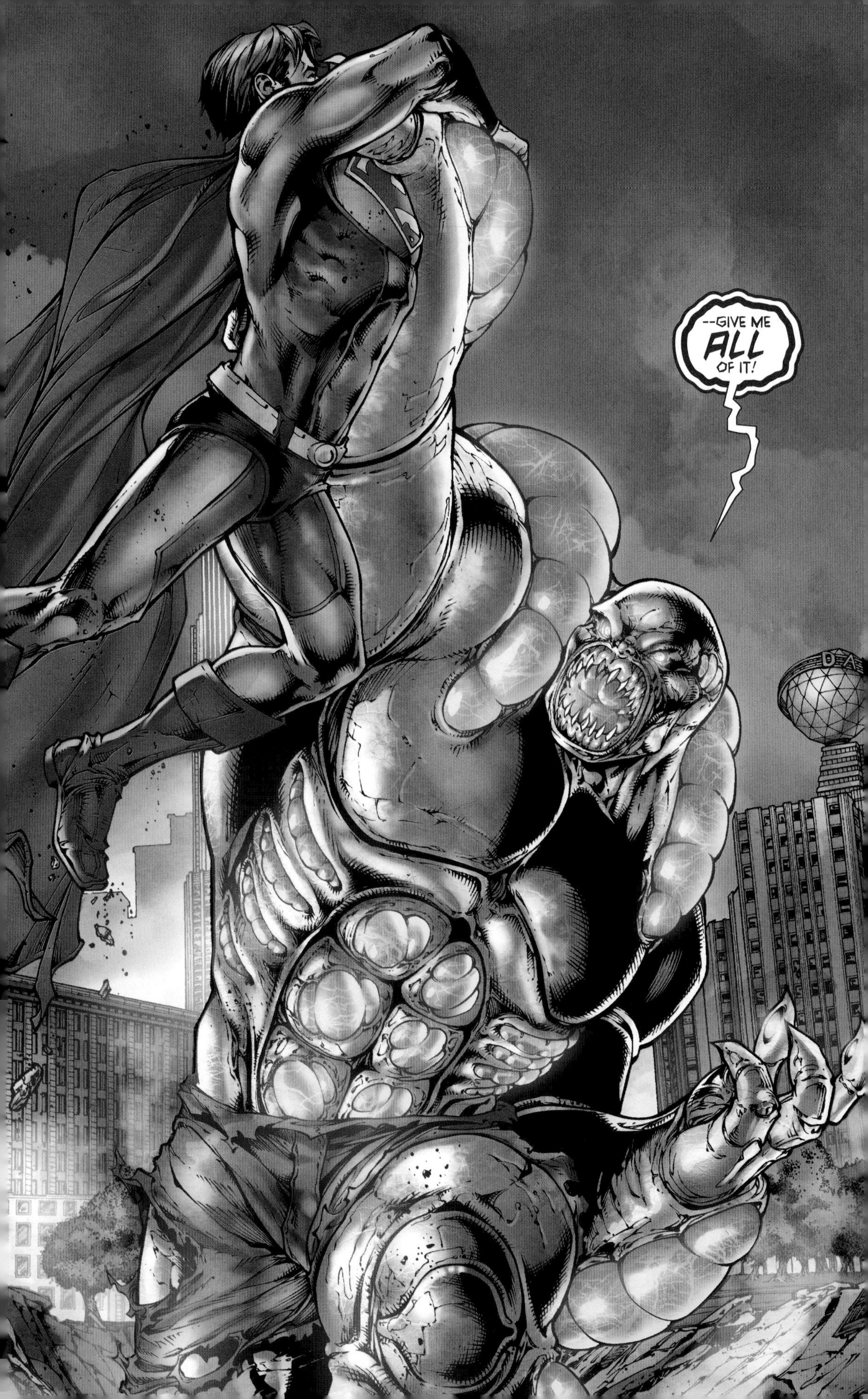
--GIVE ME ALL OF IT!

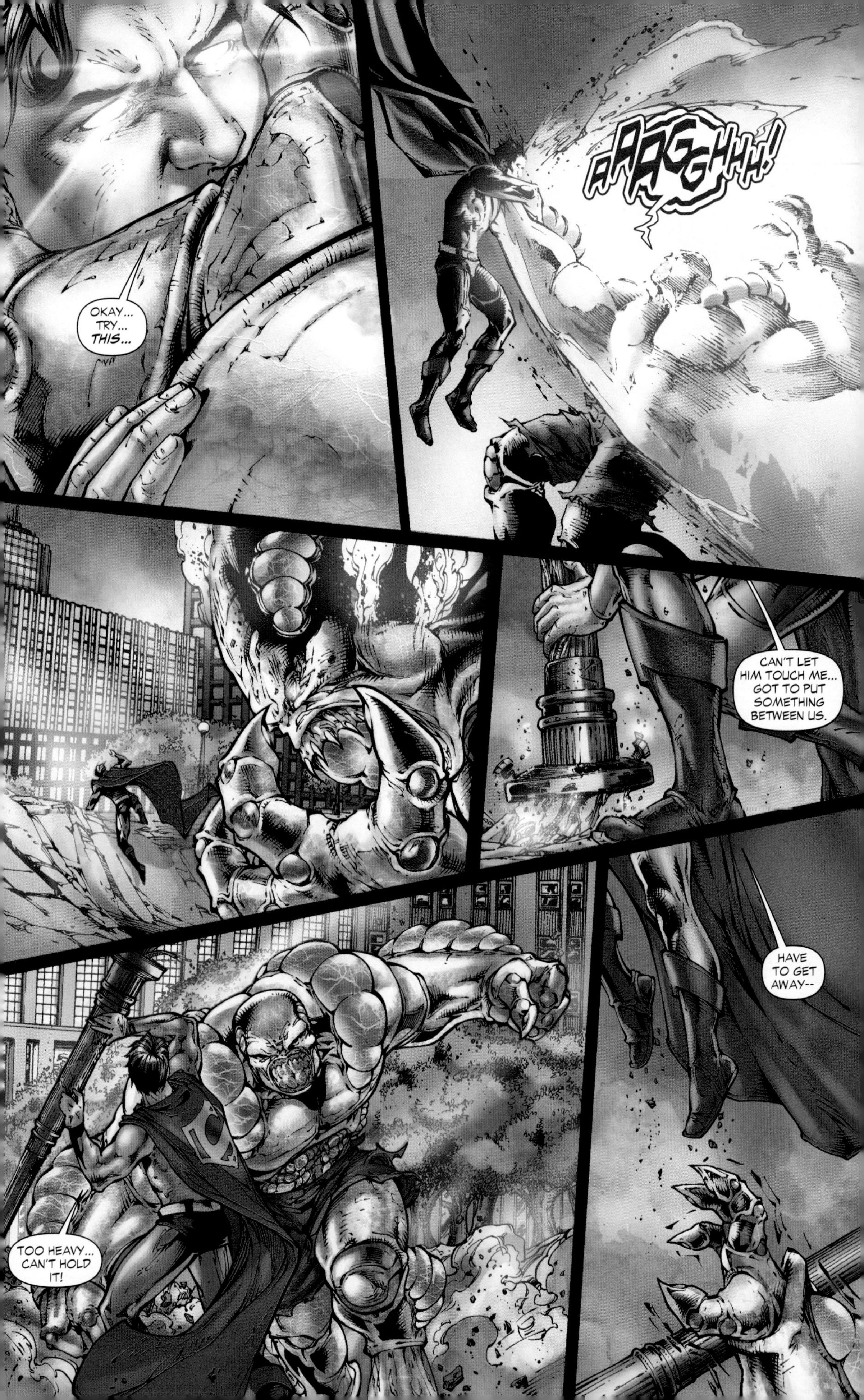
OKAY... TRY... THIS...
AAAGGHHH!
CAN'T LET HIM TOUCH ME... GOT TO PUT SOMETHING BETWEEN US.
HAVE TO GET AWAY--
TOO HEAVY... CAN'T HOLD IT!

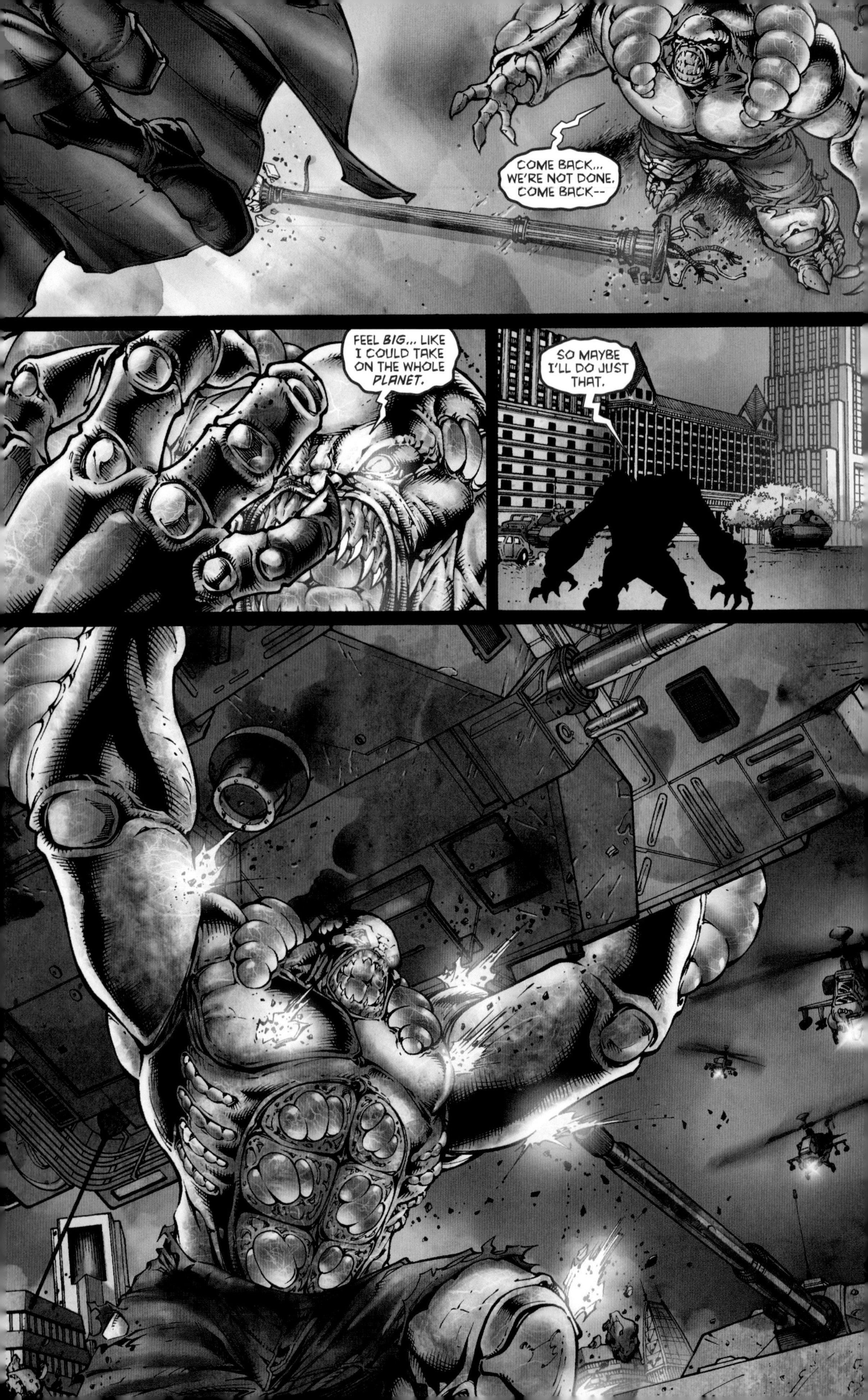
COME BACK... WE'RE NOT DONE. COME BACK--
FEEL *BIG*... LIKE I COULD TAKE ON THE WHOLE *PLANET*.
SO MAYBE I'LL DO JUST THAT.

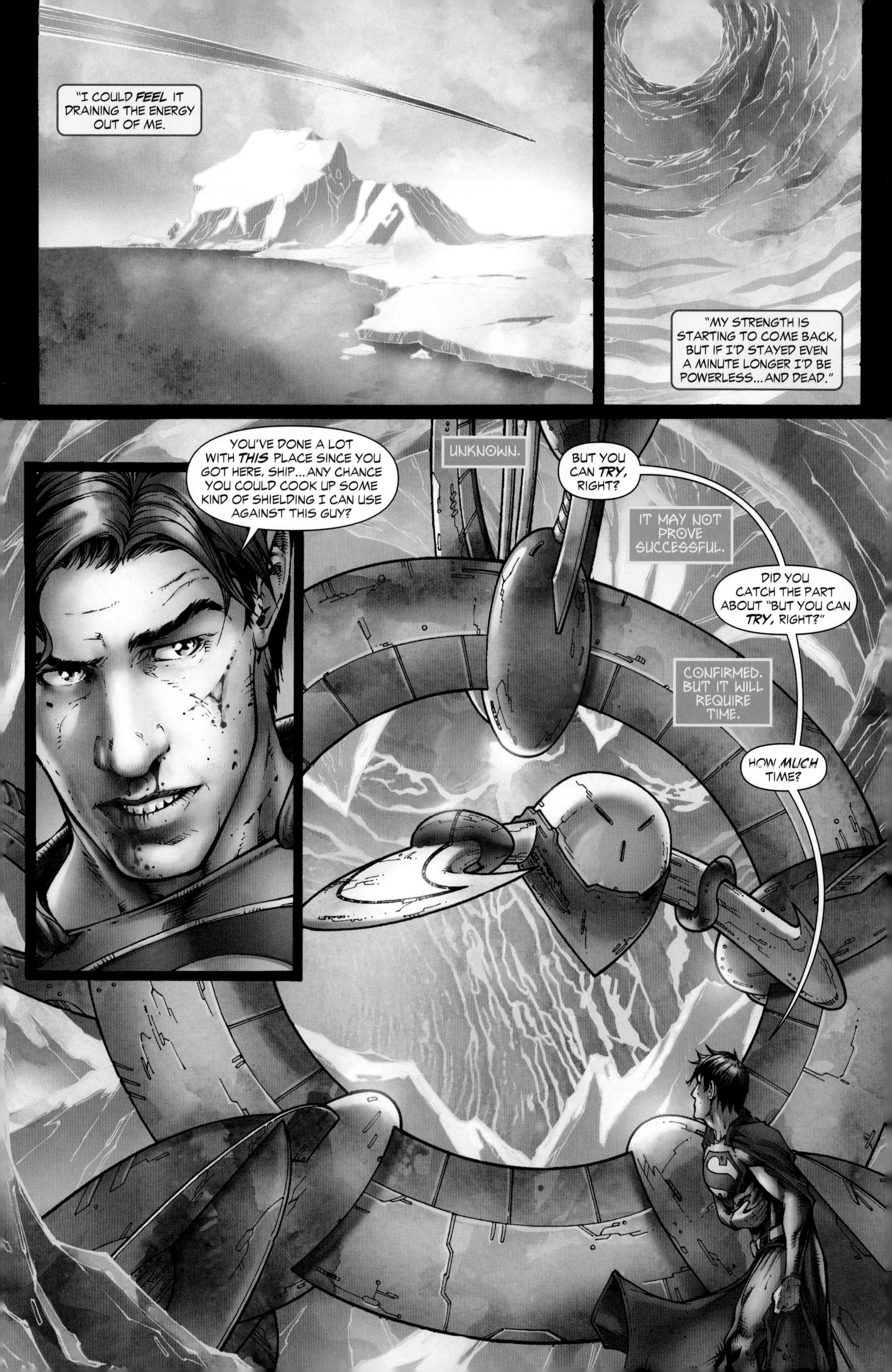
"I COULD FEEL IT DRAINING THE ENERGY OUT OF ME.
"MY STRENGTH IS STARTING TO COME BACK, BUT IF I'D STAYED EVEN A MINUTE LONGER I'D BE POWERLESS...AND DEAD."
YOU'VE DONE A LOT WITH THIS PLACE SINCE YOU GOT HERE, SHIP...ANY CHANCE YOU COULD COOK UP SOME KIND OF SHIELDING I CAN USE AGAINST THIS GUY?
UNKNOWN.
BUT YOU CAN TRY, RIGHT?
IT MAY NOT PROVE SUCCESSFUL.
DID YOU CATCH THE PART ABOUT "BUT YOU CAN TRY, RIGHT?"
CONFIRMED. BUT IT WILL REQUIRE TIME.
HOW MUCH TIME?

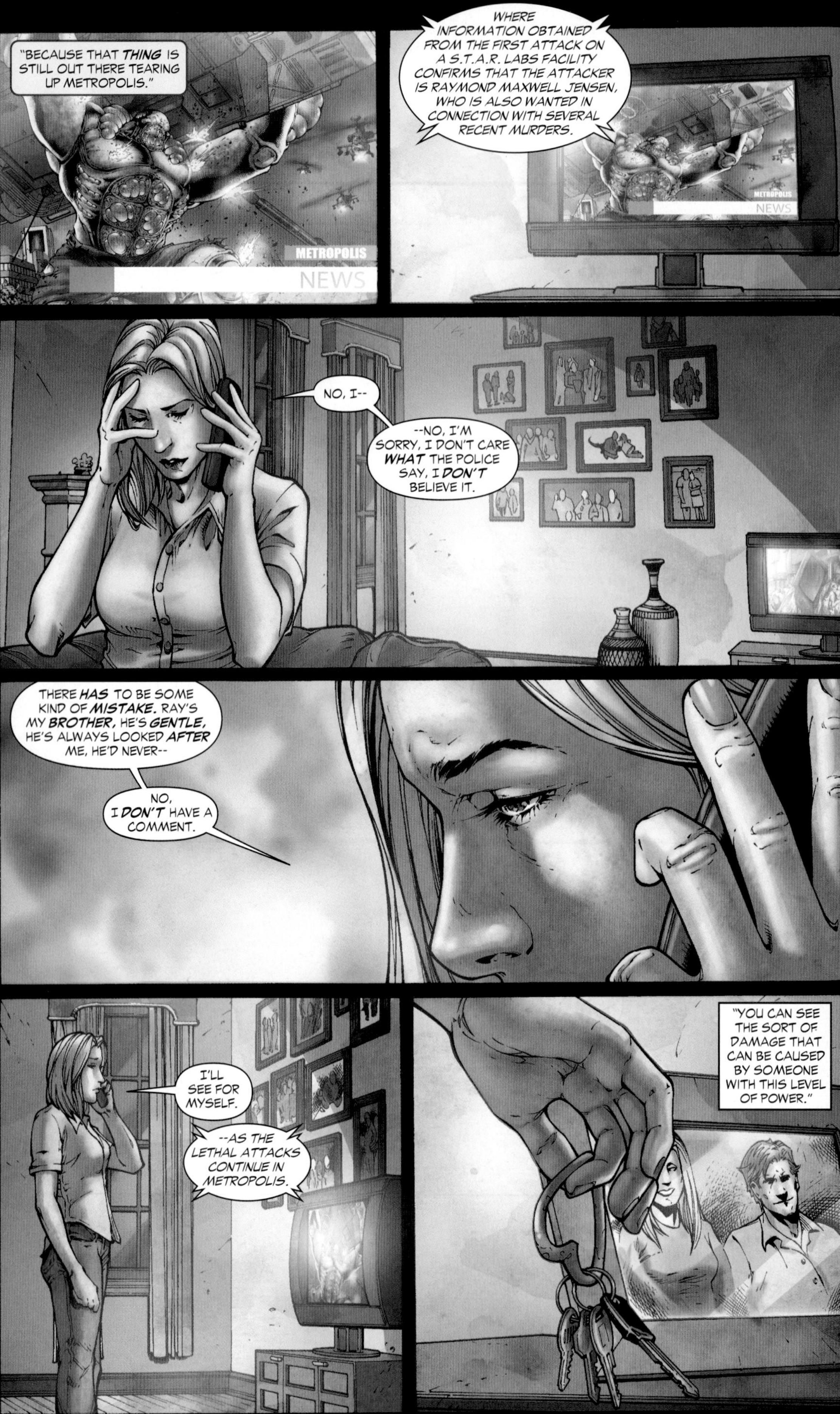
"BECAUSE THAT THING IS STILL OUT THERE TEARING UP METROPOLIS."
METROPOLIS
NEWS
WHERE INFORMATION OBTAINED FROM THE FIRST ATTACK ON A S.T.A.R. LABS FACILITY CONFIRMS THAT THE ATTACKER IS RAYMOND MAXWELL JENSEN, WHO IS ALSO WANTED IN CONNECTION WITH SEVERAL RECENT MURDERS.
METROPOLIS
NEWS
NO, I--
--NO, I'M SORRY, I DON'T CARE WHAT THE POLICE SAY, I DON'T BELIEVE IT.
THERE HAS TO BE SOME KIND OF MISTAKE. RAY'S MY BROTHER, HE'S GENTLE, HE'S ALWAYS LOOKED AFTER ME, HE'D NEVER--
NO, I DON'T HAVE A COMMENT.
I'LL SEE FOR MYSELF.
--AS THE LETHAL ATTACKS CONTINUE IN METROPOLIS.
"YOU CAN SEE THE SORT OF DAMAGE THAT CAN BE CAUSED BY SOMEONE WITH THIS LEVEL OF POWER."

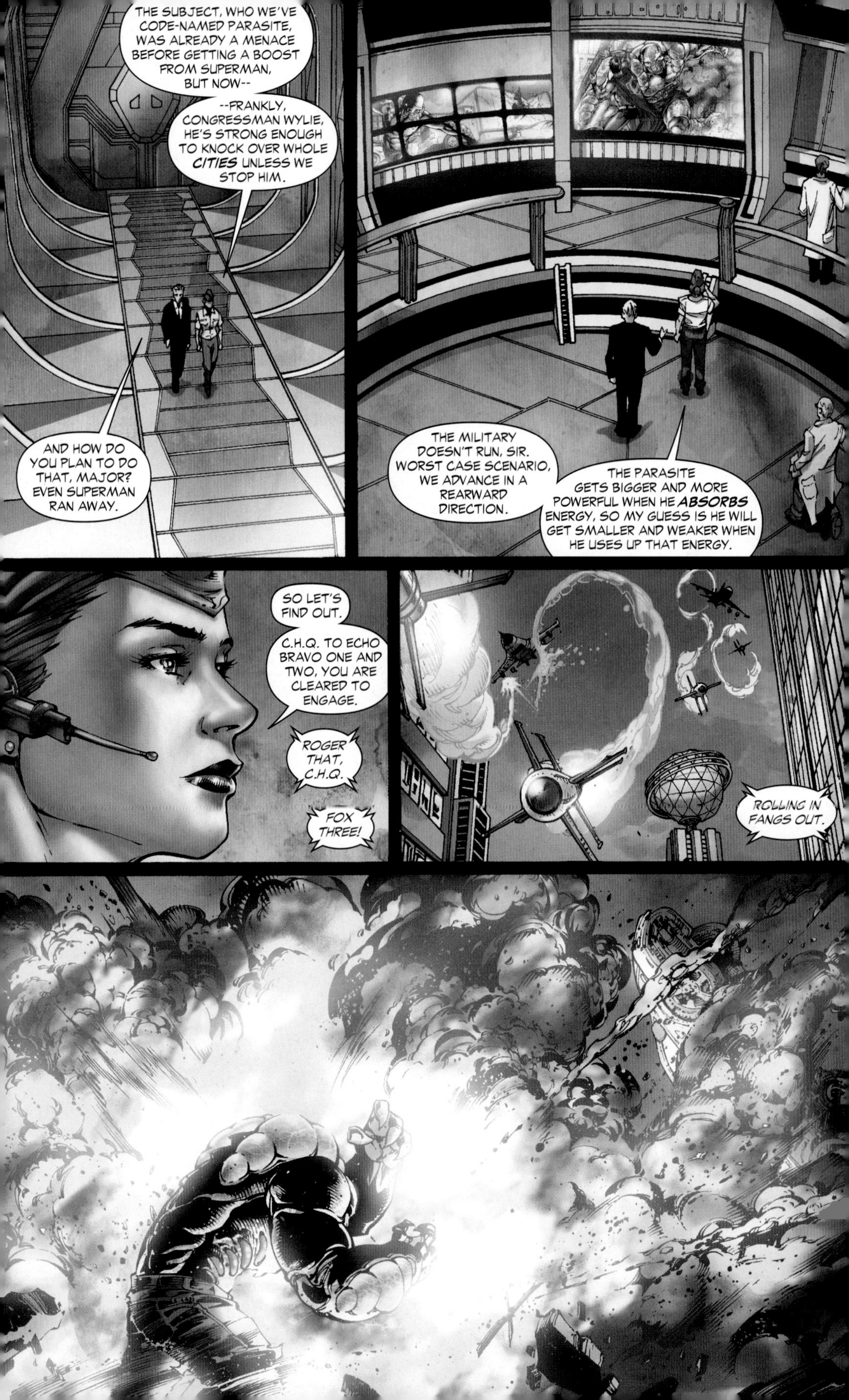
THE SUBJECT, WHO WE'VE CODE-NAMED PARASITE, WAS ALREADY A MENACE BEFORE GETTING A BOOST FROM SUPERMAN, BUT NOW--
--FRANKLY, CONGRESSMAN WYLIE, HE'S STRONG ENOUGH TO KNOCK OVER WHOLE CITIES UNLESS WE STOP HIM.
AND HOW DO YOU PLAN TO DO THAT, MAJOR? EVEN SUPERMAN RAN AWAY.
THE MILITARY DOESN'T RUN, SIR. WORST CASE SCENARIO, WE ADVANCE IN A REARWARD DIRECTION.
THE PARASITE GETS BIGGER AND MORE POWERFUL WHEN HE ABSORBS ENERGY, SO MY GUESS IS HE WILL GET SMALLER AND WEAKER WHEN HE USES UP THAT ENERGY.
SO LET'S FIND OUT.
C.H.Q. TO ECHO BRAVO ONE AND TWO, YOU ARE CLEARED TO ENGAGE.
ROGER THAT, C.H.Q.
FOX THREE!
ROLLING IN FANGS OUT.

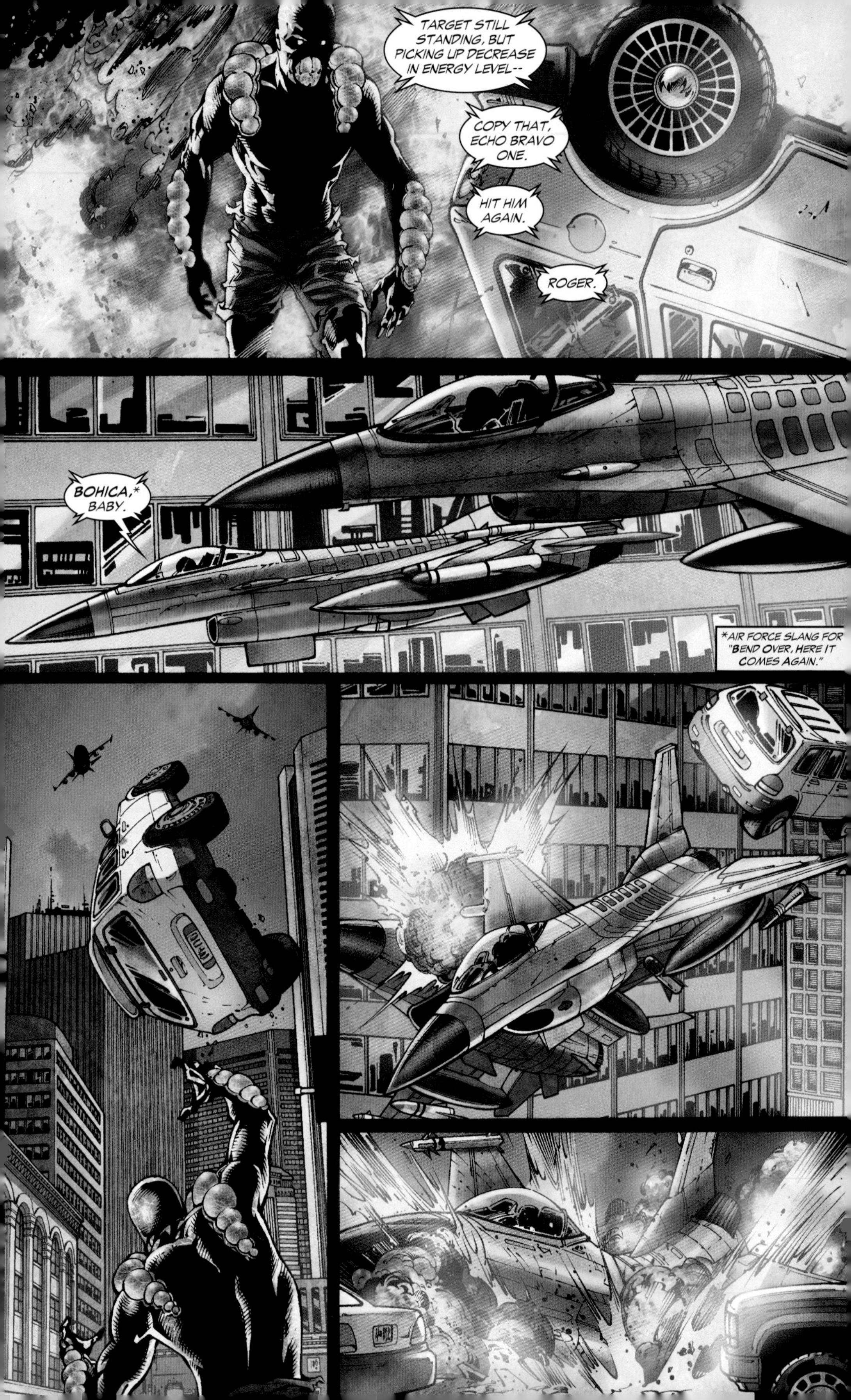
TARGET STILL STANDING, BUT PICKING UP DECREASE IN ENERGY LEVEL--
COPY THAT, ECHO BRAVO ONE.
HIT HIM AGAIN.
ROGER.
BOHICA,* BABY.
*AIR FORCE SLANG FOR "BEND OVER, HERE IT COMES AGAIN."

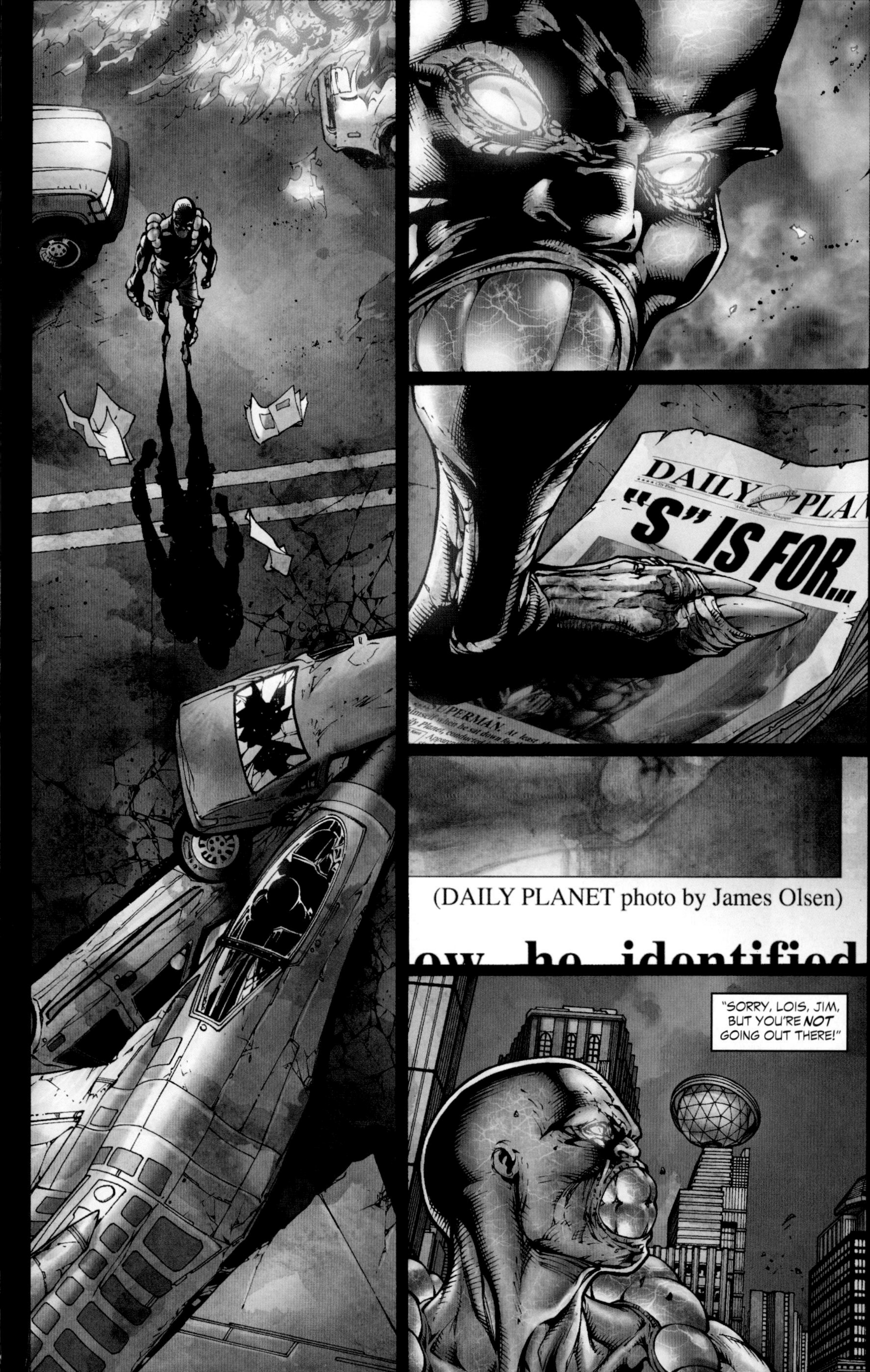
DAILY PLANET
"S" IS FOR...
(DAILY PLANET photo by James Olsen)
ow he identified
"SORRY, LOIS, JIM, BUT YOU'RE NOT GOING OUT THERE!"

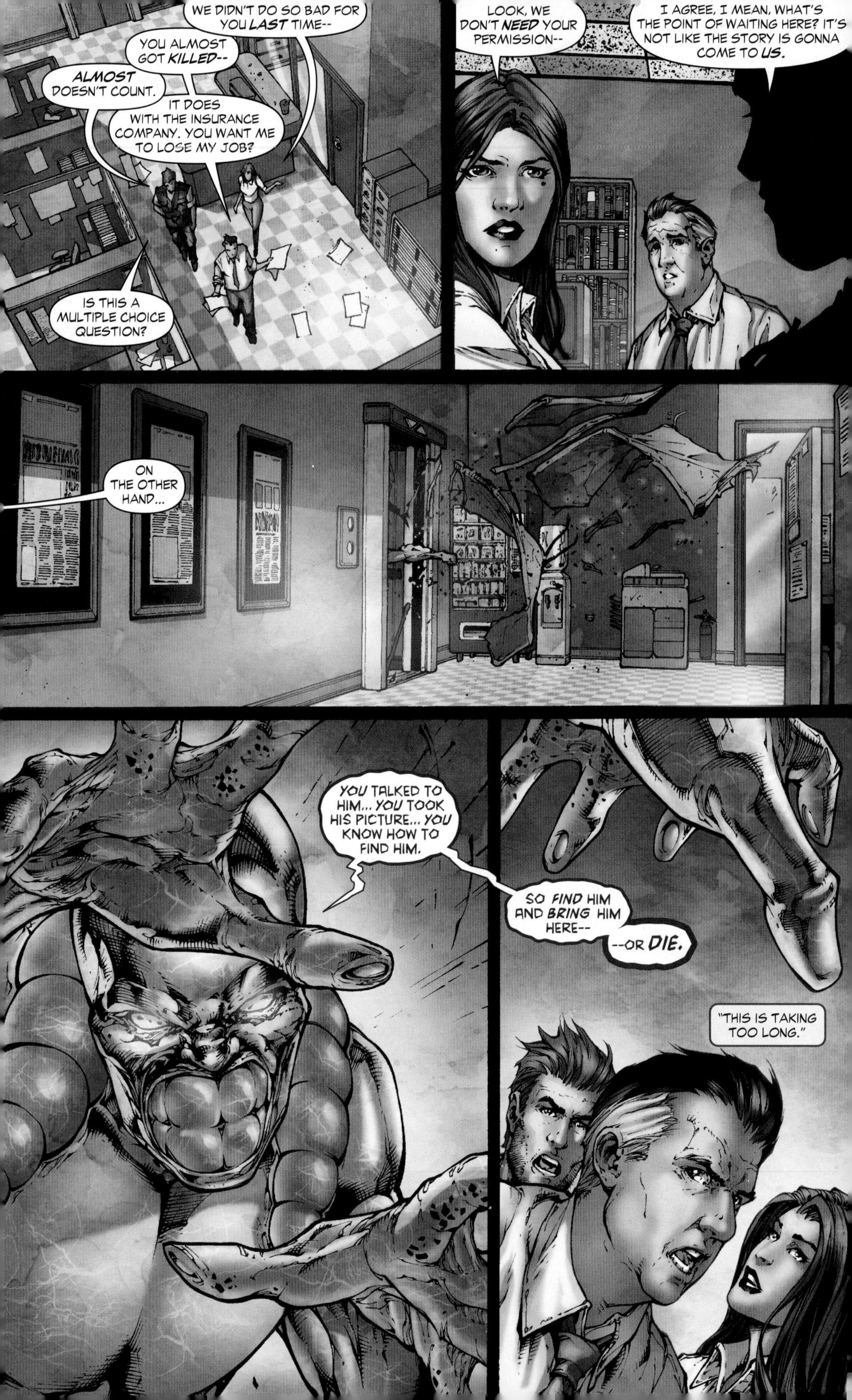
WE DIDN'T DO SO BAD FOR YOU LAST TIME--
YOU ALMOST GOT KILLED--
ALMOST DOESN'T COUNT.
IT DOES WITH THE INSURANCE COMPANY. YOU WANT ME TO LOSE MY JOB?
IS THIS A MULTIPLE CHOICE QUESTION?
LOOK, WE DON'T NEED YOUR PERMISSION--
I AGREE, I MEAN, WHAT'S THE POINT OF WAITING HERE? IT'S NOT LIKE THE STORY IS GONNA COME TO US.
ON THE OTHER HAND...
YOU TALKED TO HIM... YOU TOOK HIS PICTURE... YOU KNOW HOW TO FIND HIM.
SO FIND HIM AND BRING HIM HERE--
--OR DIE.
"THIS IS TAKING TOO LONG."

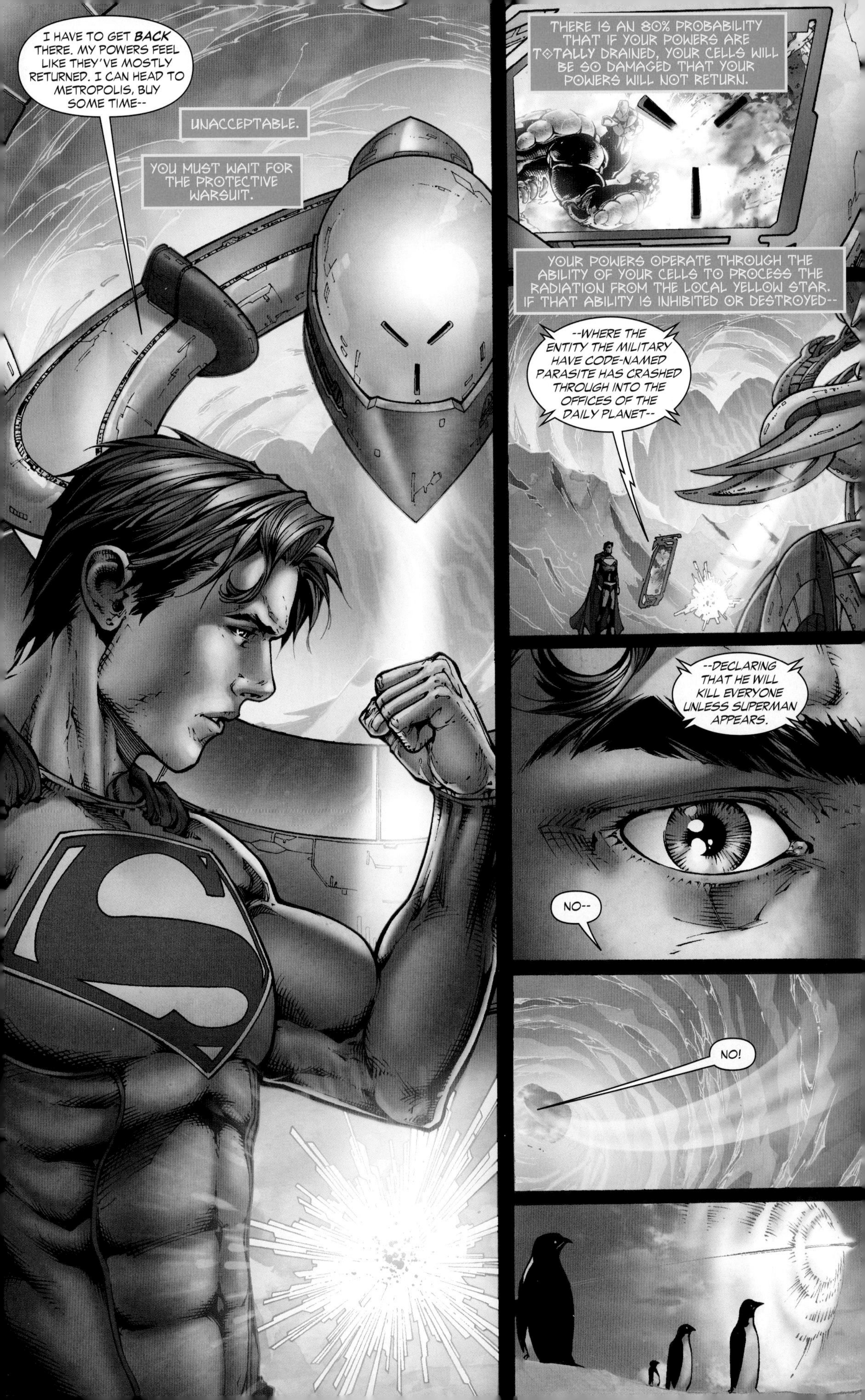
I HAVE TO GET BACK THERE. MY POWERS FEEL LIKE THEY'VE MOSTLY RETURNED. I CAN HEAD TO METROPOLIS, BUY SOME TIME--
UNACCEPTABLE.
YOU MUST WAIT FOR THE PROTECTIVE WARSUIT.
THERE IS AN 80% PROBABILITY THAT IF YOUR POWERS ARE TOTALLY DRAINED, YOUR CELLS WILL BE SO DAMAGED THAT YOUR POWERS WILL NOT RETURN.
YOUR POWERS OPERATE THROUGH THE ABILITY OF YOUR CELLS TO PROCESS THE RADIATION FROM THE LOCAL YELLOW STAR. IF THAT ABILITY IS INHIBITED OR DESTROYED--
--WHERE THE ENTITY THE MILITARY HAVE CODE-NAMED PARASITE HAS CRASHED THROUGH INTO THE OFFICES OF THE DAILY PLANET--
--DECLARING THAT HE WILL KILL EVERYONE UNLESS SUPERMAN APPEARS.
NO--
NO!

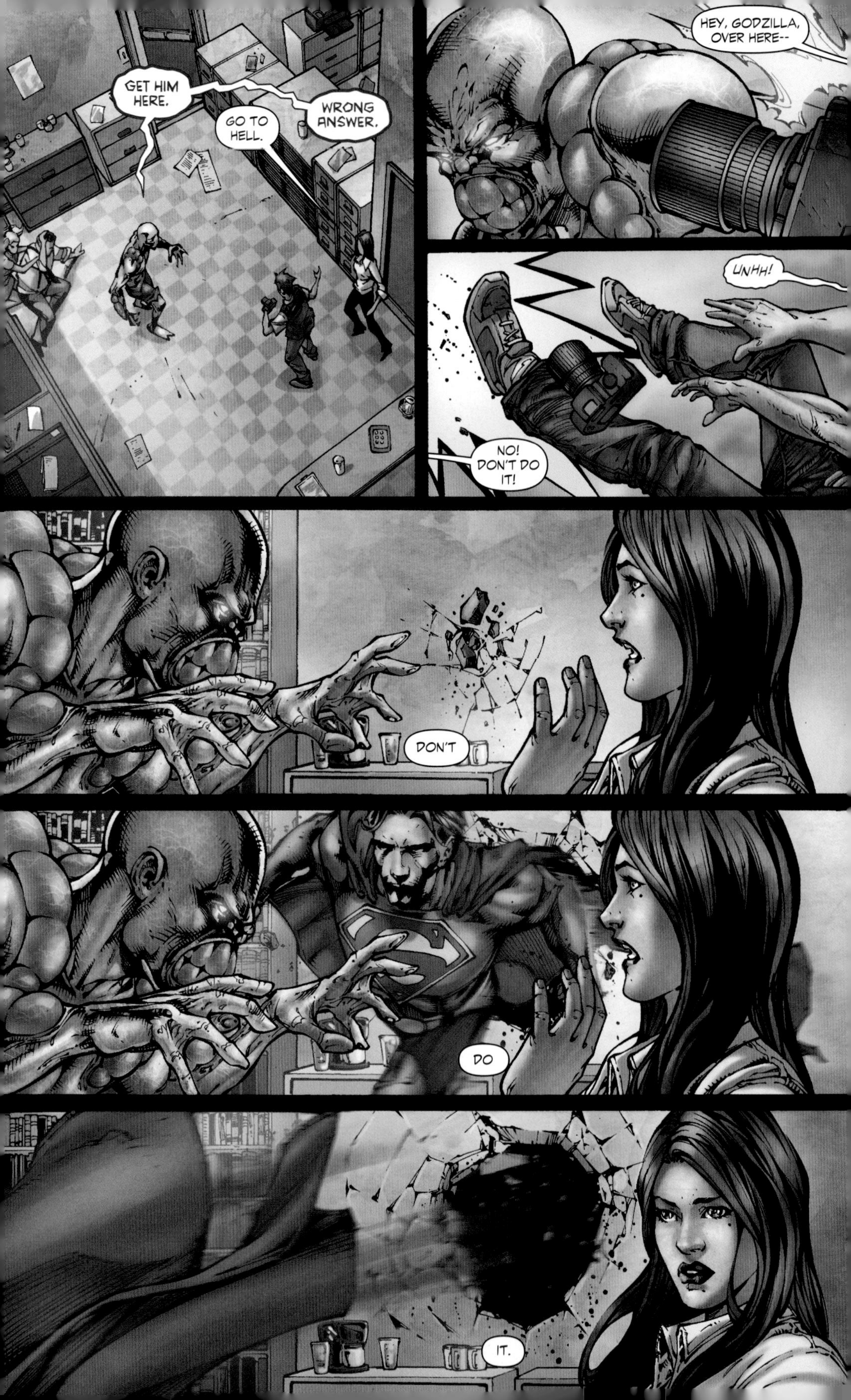
GET HIM HERE.
GO TO HELL.
WRONG ANSWER.
HEY, GODZILLA, OVER HERE--
UNHH!
NO! DON'T DO IT!
DON'T
DO
IT.

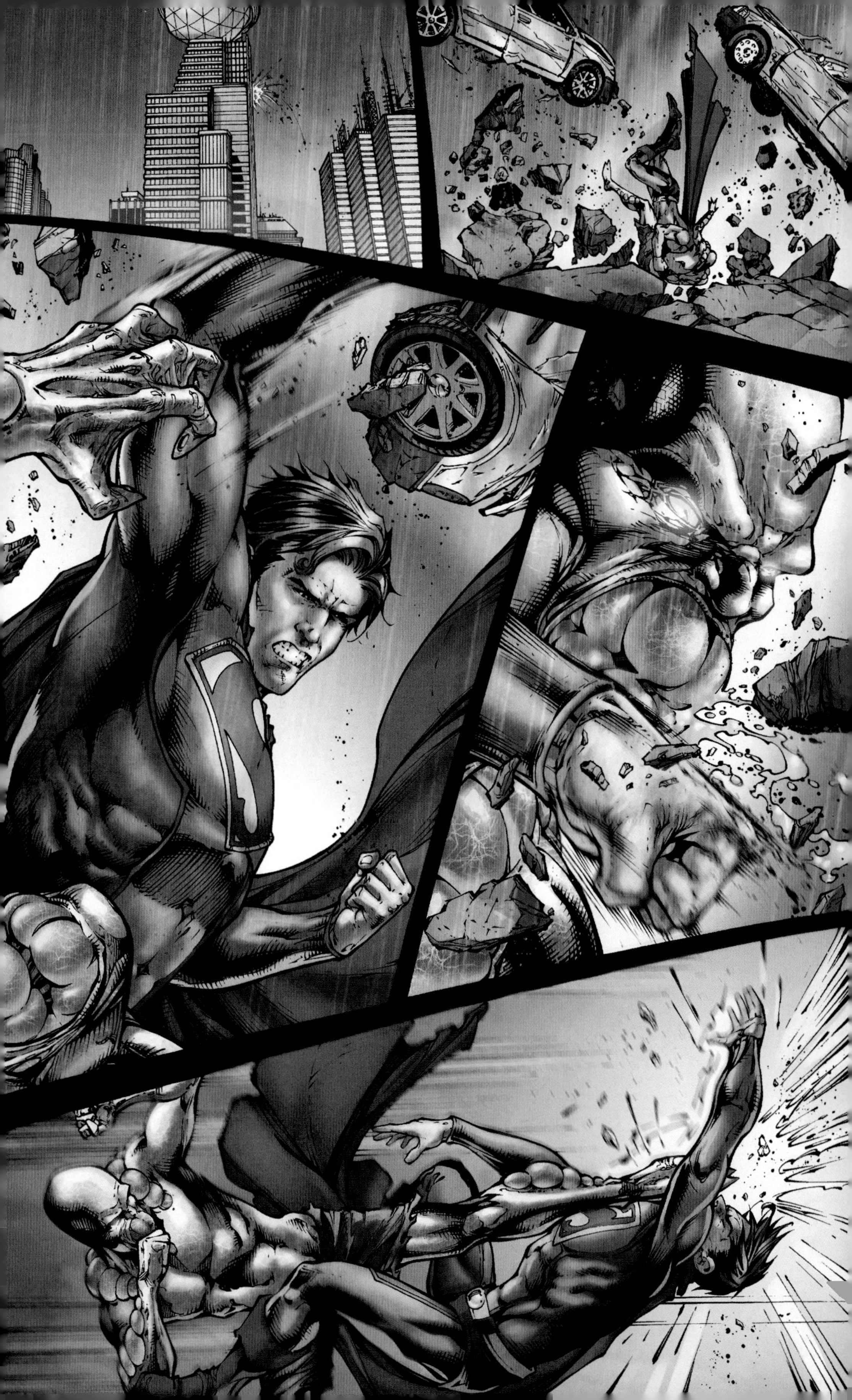

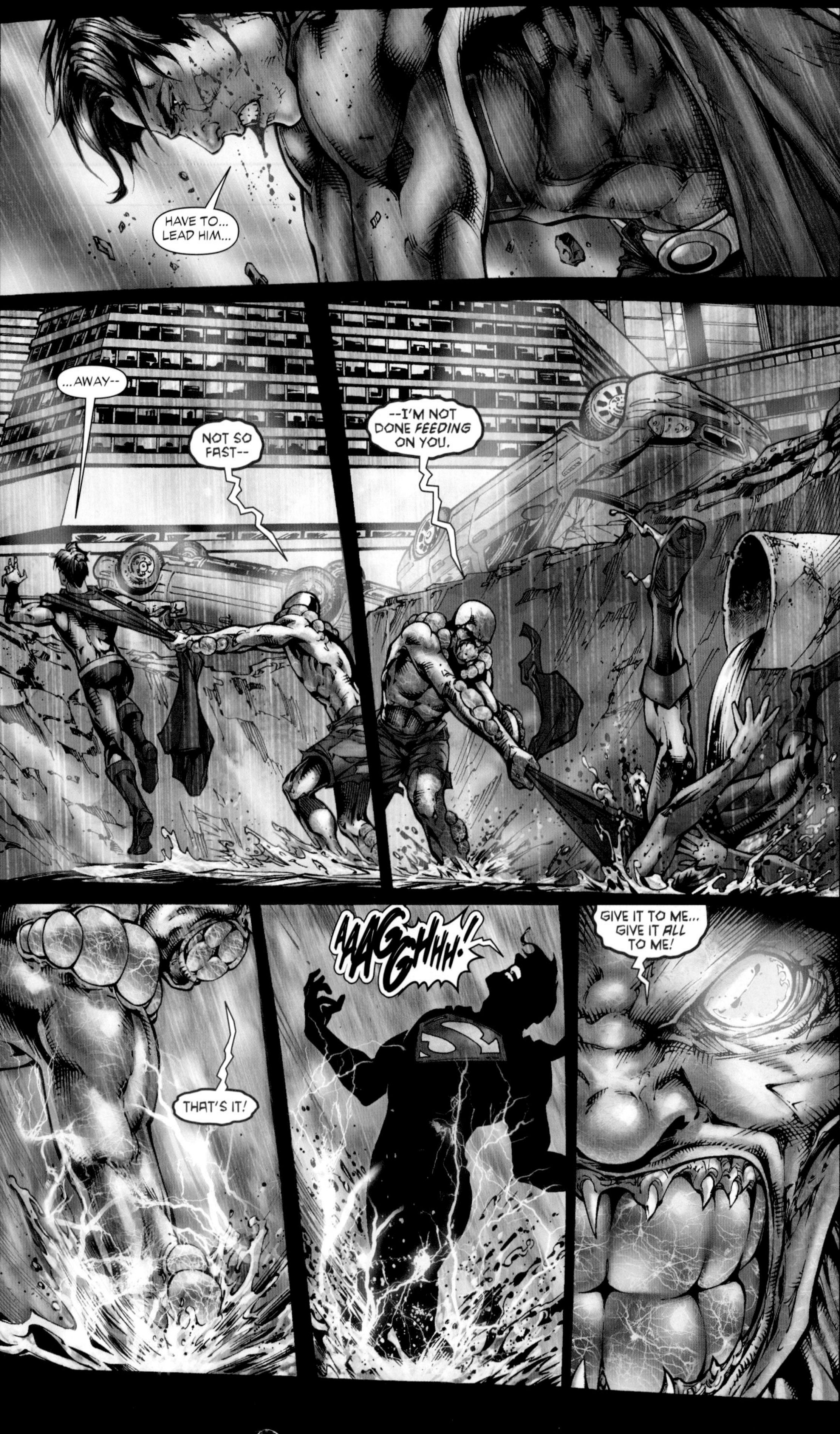
HAVE TO... LEAD HIM...
...AWAY--
NOT SO FAST--
--I'M NOT DONE FEEDING ON YOU.
THAT'S IT!
AAAGGHHH!
GIVE IT TO ME... GIVE IT ALL TO ME!

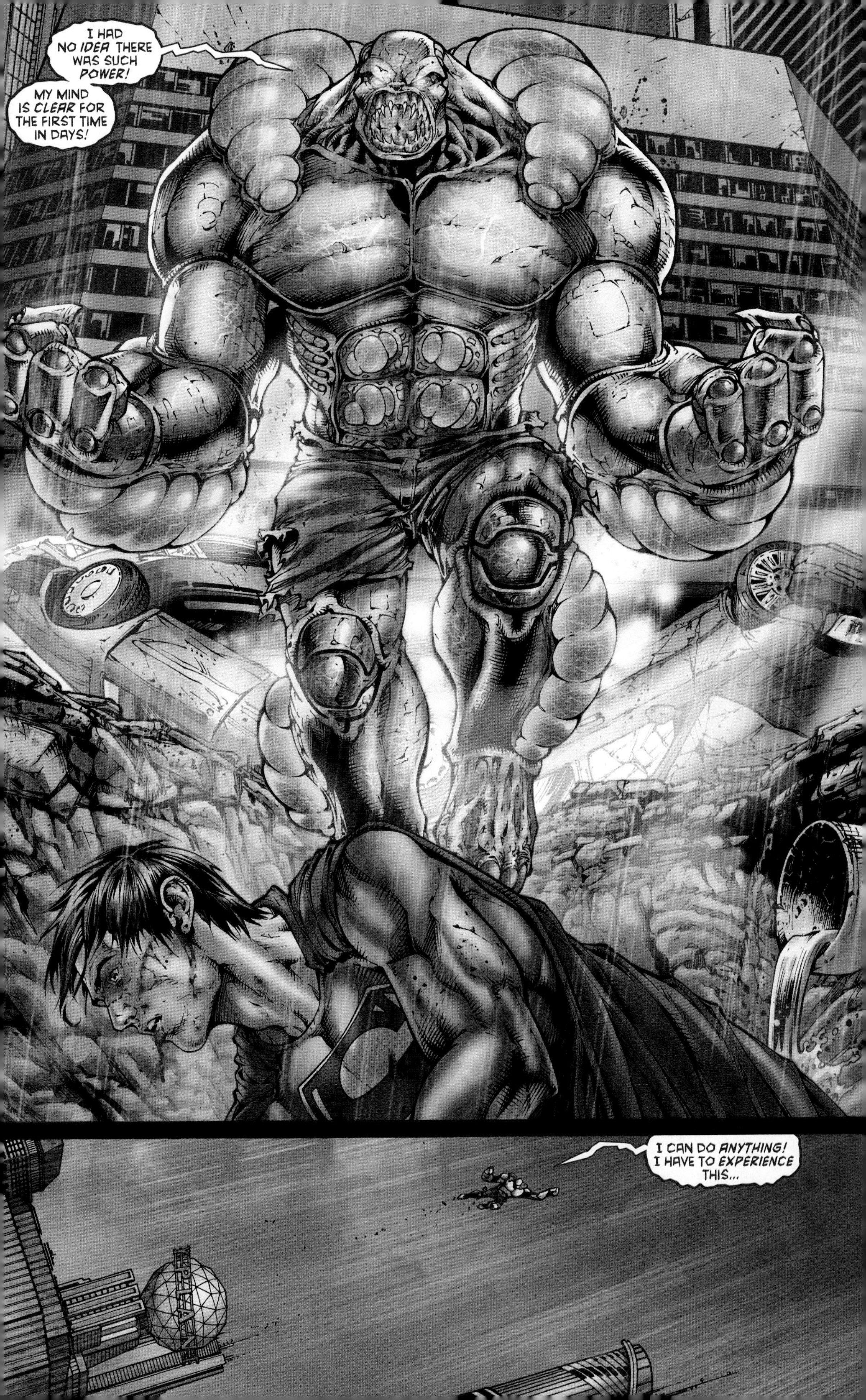
I HAD NO IDEA THERE WAS SUCH POWER!
MY MIND IS CLEAR FOR THE FIRST TIME IN DAYS!
I CAN DO ANYTHING! I HAVE TO EXPERIENCE THIS...

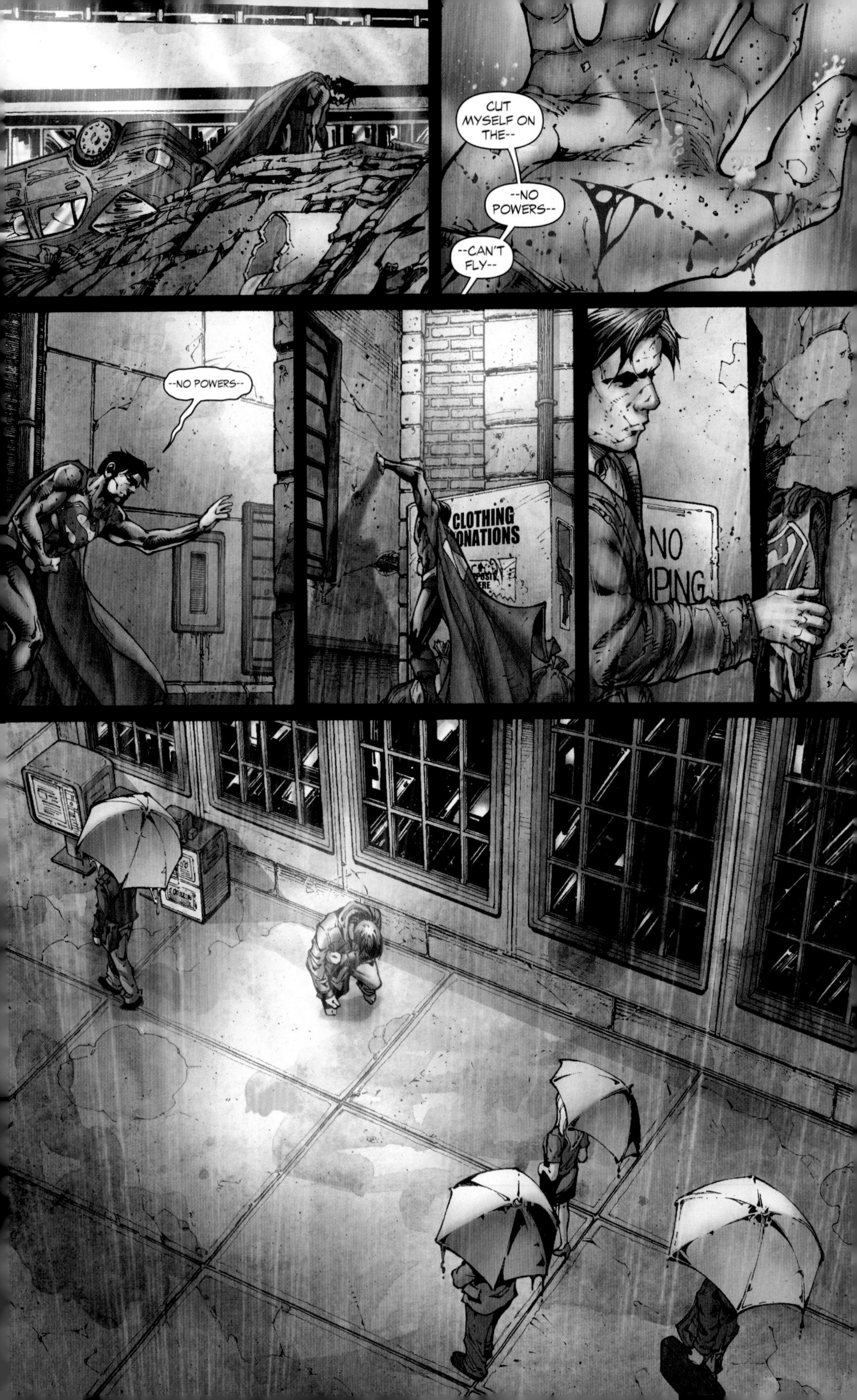
CUT MYSELF ON THE--
--NO POWERS--
--CAN'T FLY--
--NO POWERS--
CLOTHING DONATIONS
NO PING

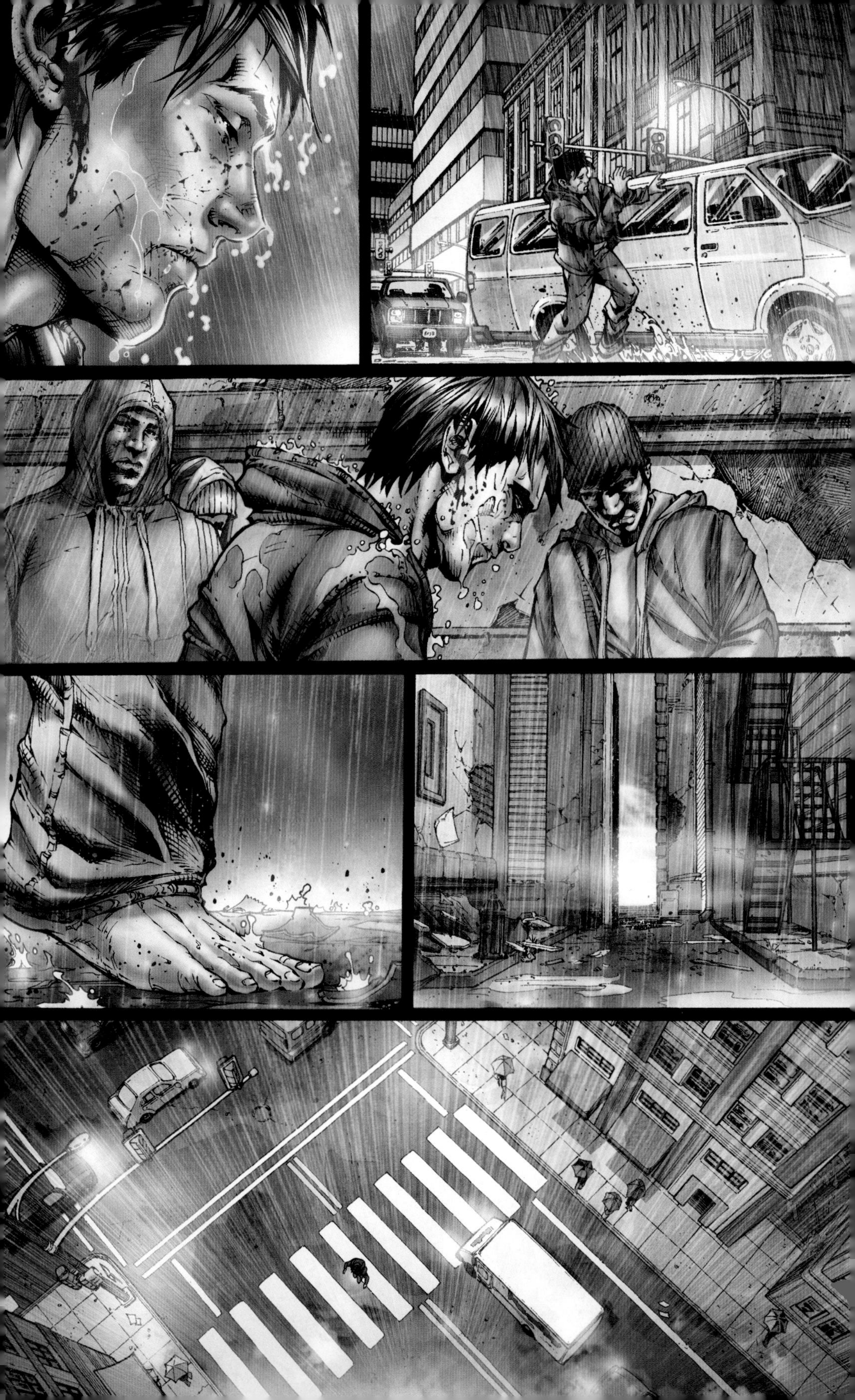

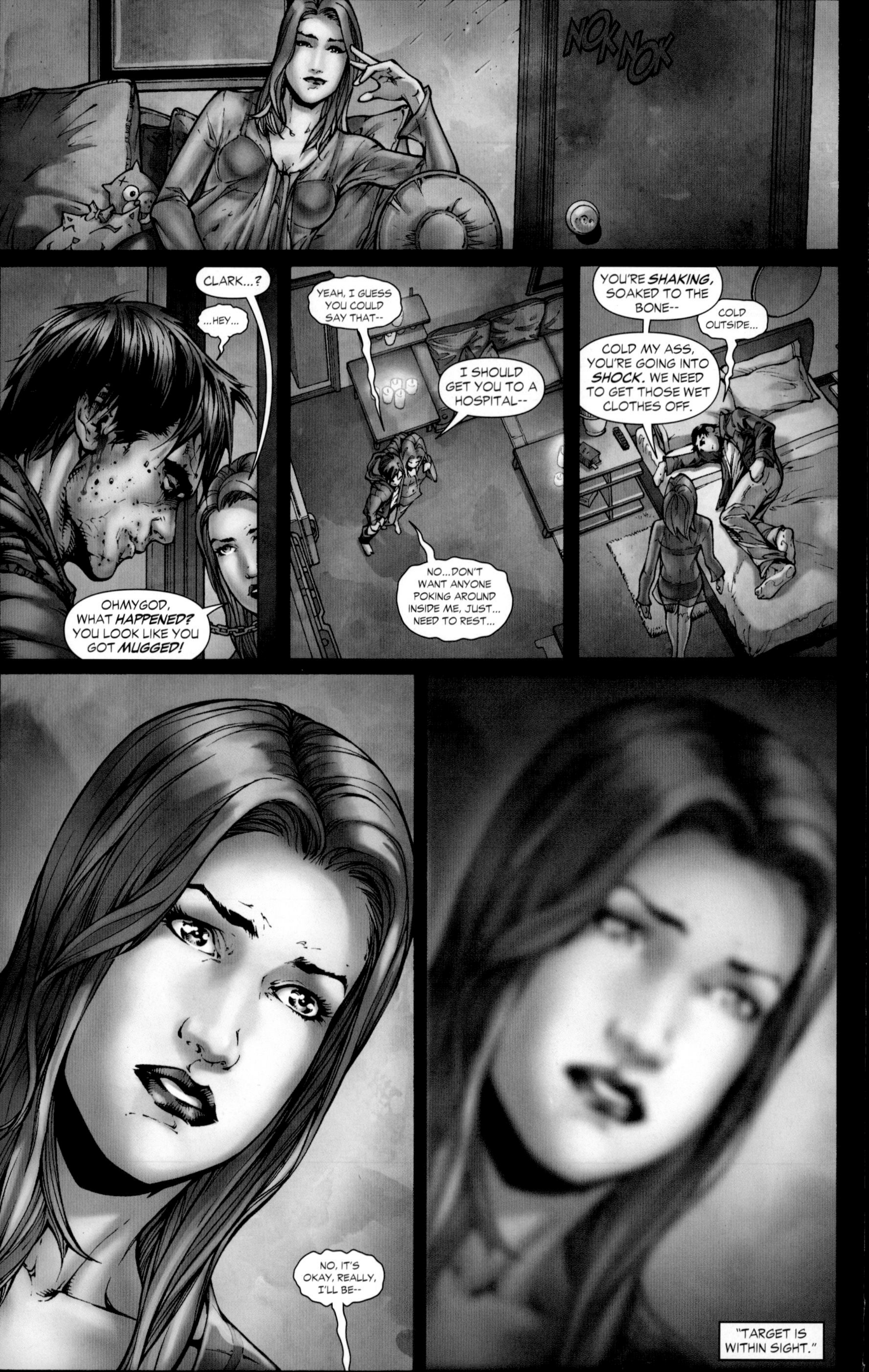
NOK NOK
CLARK...?
...HEY...
OHMYGOD, WHAT HAPPENED? YOU LOOK LIKE YOU GOT MUGGED!
YEAH, I GUESS YOU COULD SAY THAT--
I SHOULD GET YOU TO A HOSPITAL--
NO...DON'T WANT ANYONE POKING AROUND INSIDE ME, JUST... NEED TO REST...
YOU'RE SHAKING, SOAKED TO THE BONE--
COLD OUTSIDE...
COLD MY ASS, YOU'RE GOING INTO SHOCK. WE NEED TO GET THOSE WET CLOTHES OFF.
NO, IT'S OKAY, REALLY, I'LL BE--
"TARGET IS WITHIN SIGHT."

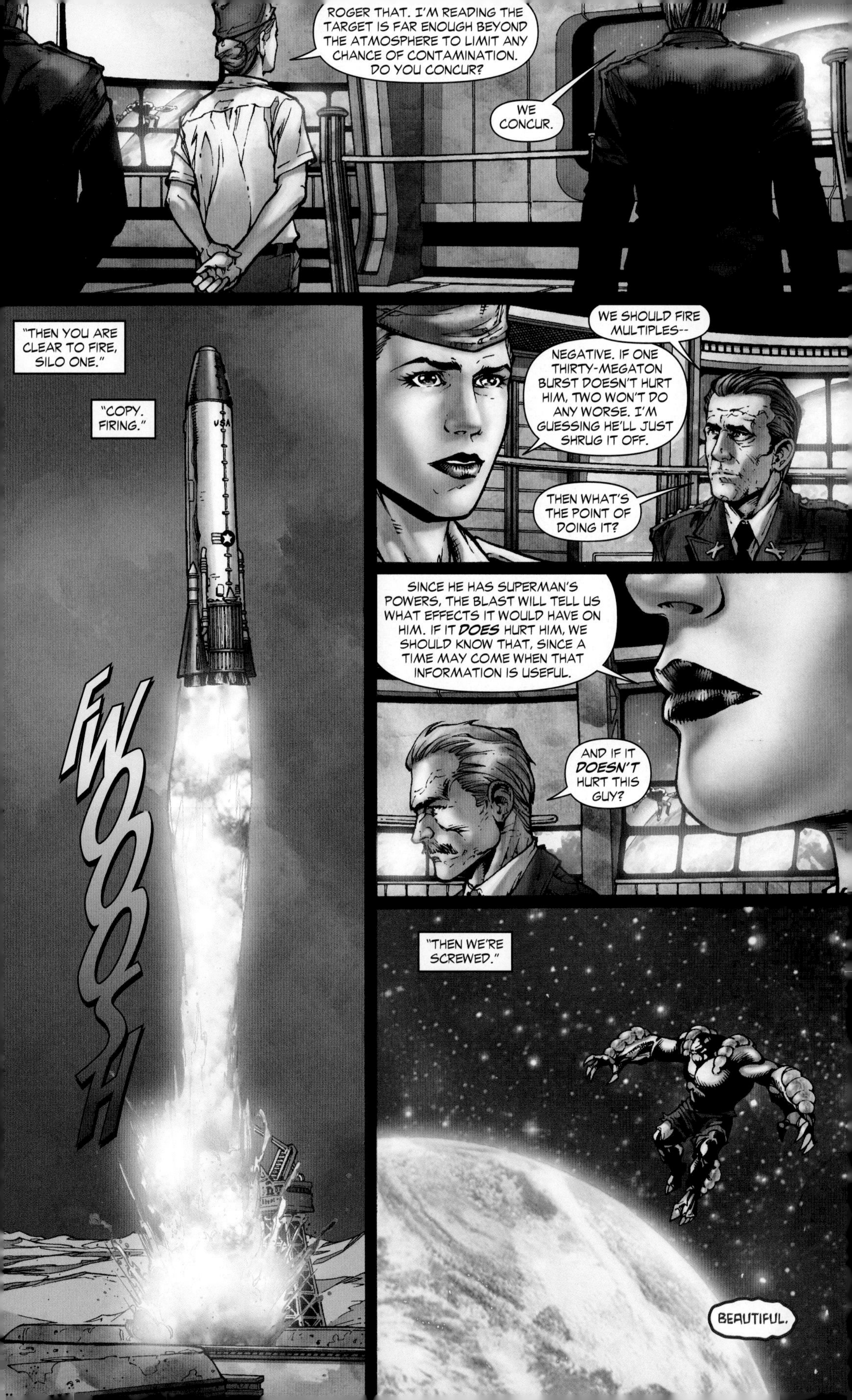
ROGER THAT. I'M READING THE TARGET IS FAR ENOUGH BEYOND THE ATMOSPHERE TO LIMIT ANY CHANCE OF CONTAMINATION. DO YOU CONCUR?
WE CONCUR.
"THEN YOU ARE CLEAR TO FIRE, SILO ONE."
"COPY. FIRING."
USA
FWOOOSH
WE SHOULD FIRE MULTIPLES--
NEGATIVE. IF ONE THIRTY-MEGATON BURST DOESN'T HURT HIM, TWO WON'T DO ANY WORSE. I'M GUESSING HE'LL JUST SHRUG IT OFF.
THEN WHAT'S THE POINT OF DOING IT?
SINCE HE HAS SUPERMAN'S POWERS, THE BLAST WILL TELL US WHAT EFFECTS IT WOULD HAVE ON HIM. IF IT DOES HURT HIM, WE SHOULD KNOW THAT, SINCE A TIME MAY COME WHEN THAT INFORMATION IS USEFUL.
AND IF IT DOESN'T HURT THIS GUY?
"THEN WE'RE SCREWED."
BEAUTIFUL.

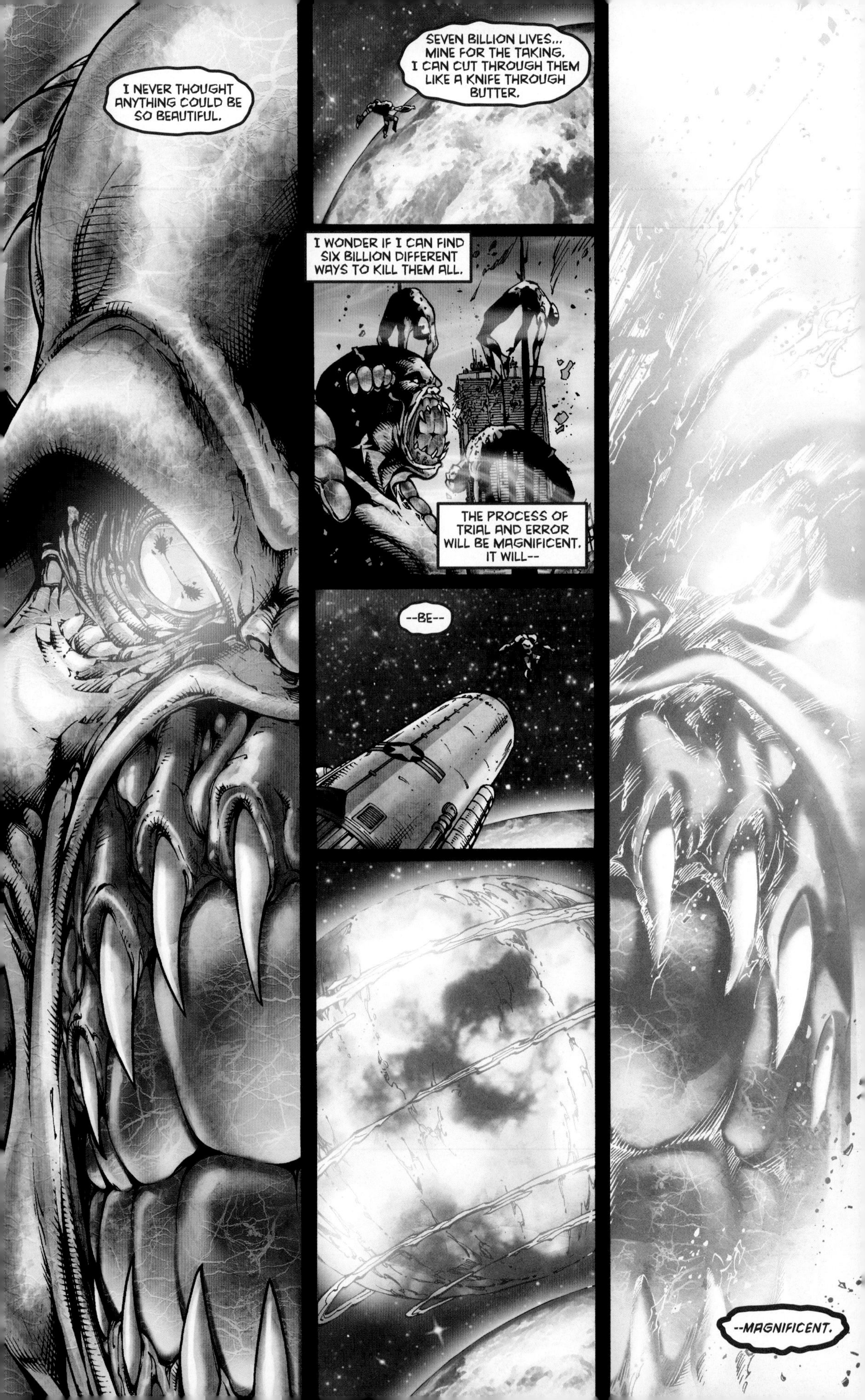
I NEVER THOUGHT ANYTHING COULD BE SO BEAUTIFUL.
SEVEN BILLION LIVES... MINE FOR THE TAKING. I CAN CUT THROUGH THEM LIKE A KNIFE THROUGH BUTTER.
I WONDER IF I CAN FIND SIX BILLION DIFFERENT WAYS TO KILL THEM ALL.
THE PROCESS OF TRIAL AND ERROR WILL BE MAGNIFICENT. IT WILL--
--BE--
--MAGNIFICENT.

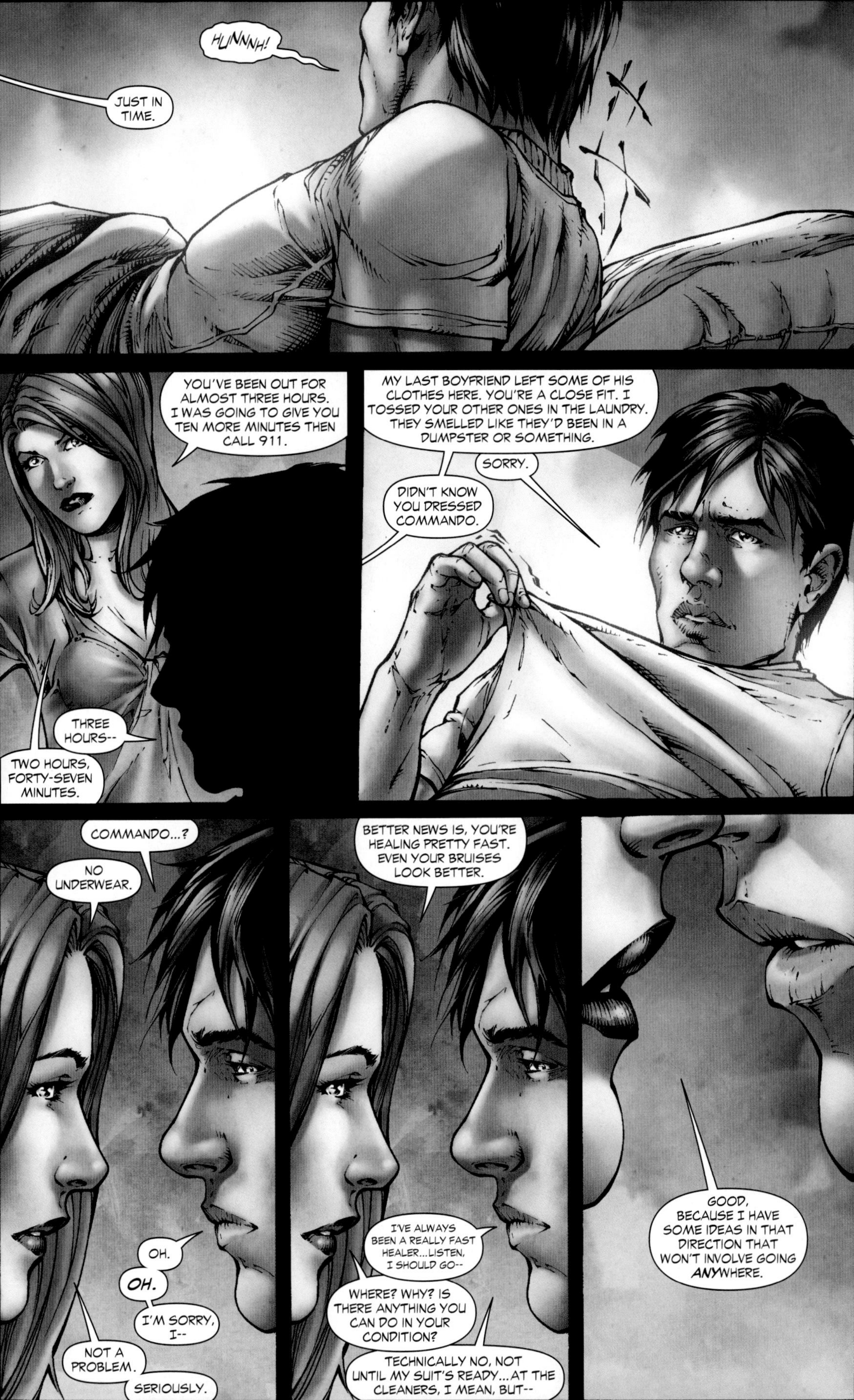
HUNNNH!
JUST IN TIME.
YOU'VE BEEN OUT FOR ALMOST THREE HOURS. I WAS GOING TO GIVE YOU TEN MORE MINUTES THEN CALL 911.
THREE HOURS--
TWO HOURS, FORTY-SEVEN MINUTES.
MY LAST BOYFRIEND LEFT SOME OF HIS CLOTHES HERE. YOU'RE A CLOSE FIT. I TOSSED YOUR OTHER ONES IN THE LAUNDRY. THEY SMELLED LIKE THEY'D BEEN IN A DUMPSTER OR SOMETHING.
SORRY.
DIDN'T KNOW YOU DRESSED COMMANDO.
COMMANDO...?
NO UNDERWEAR.
OH.
OH.
I'M SORRY, I--
NOT A PROBLEM.
SERIOUSLY.
BETTER NEWS IS, YOU'RE HEALING PRETTY FAST. EVEN YOUR BRUISES LOOK BETTER.
I'VE ALWAYS BEEN A REALLY FAST HEALER...LISTEN, I SHOULD GO--
WHERE? WHY? IS THERE ANYTHING YOU CAN DO IN YOUR CONDITION?
TECHNICALLY NO, NOT UNTIL MY SUIT'S READY...AT THE CLEANERS, I MEAN, BUT--
GOOD, BECAUSE I HAVE SOME IDEAS IN THAT DIRECTION THAT WON'T INVOLVE GOING ANYWHERE.

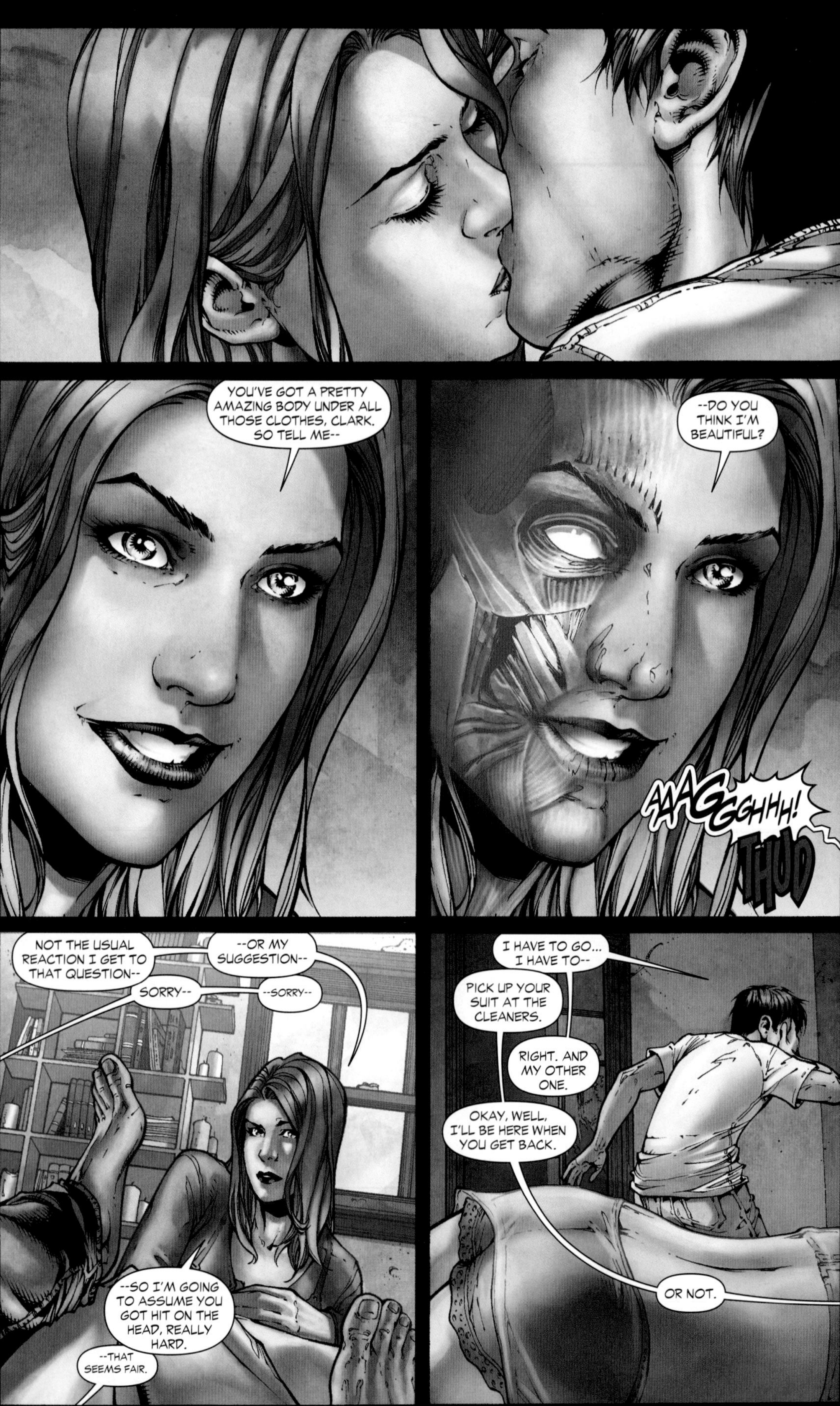

YOU'VE GOT A PRETTY AMAZING BODY UNDER ALL THOSE CLOTHES, CLARK. SO TELL ME--
--DO YOU THINK I'M BEAUTIFUL?
AAAGGGHHH!
THUD
NOT THE USUAL REACTION I GET TO THAT QUESTION--
--OR MY SUGGESTION--
SORRY--
--SORRY--
--SO I'M GOING TO ASSUME YOU GOT HIT ON THE HEAD, REALLY HARD.
--THAT SEEMS FAIR.
I HAVE TO GO... I HAVE TO--
PICK UP YOUR SUIT AT THE CLEANERS.
RIGHT. AND MY OTHER ONE.
OKAY, WELL, I'LL BE HERE WHEN YOU GET BACK.
OR NOT.

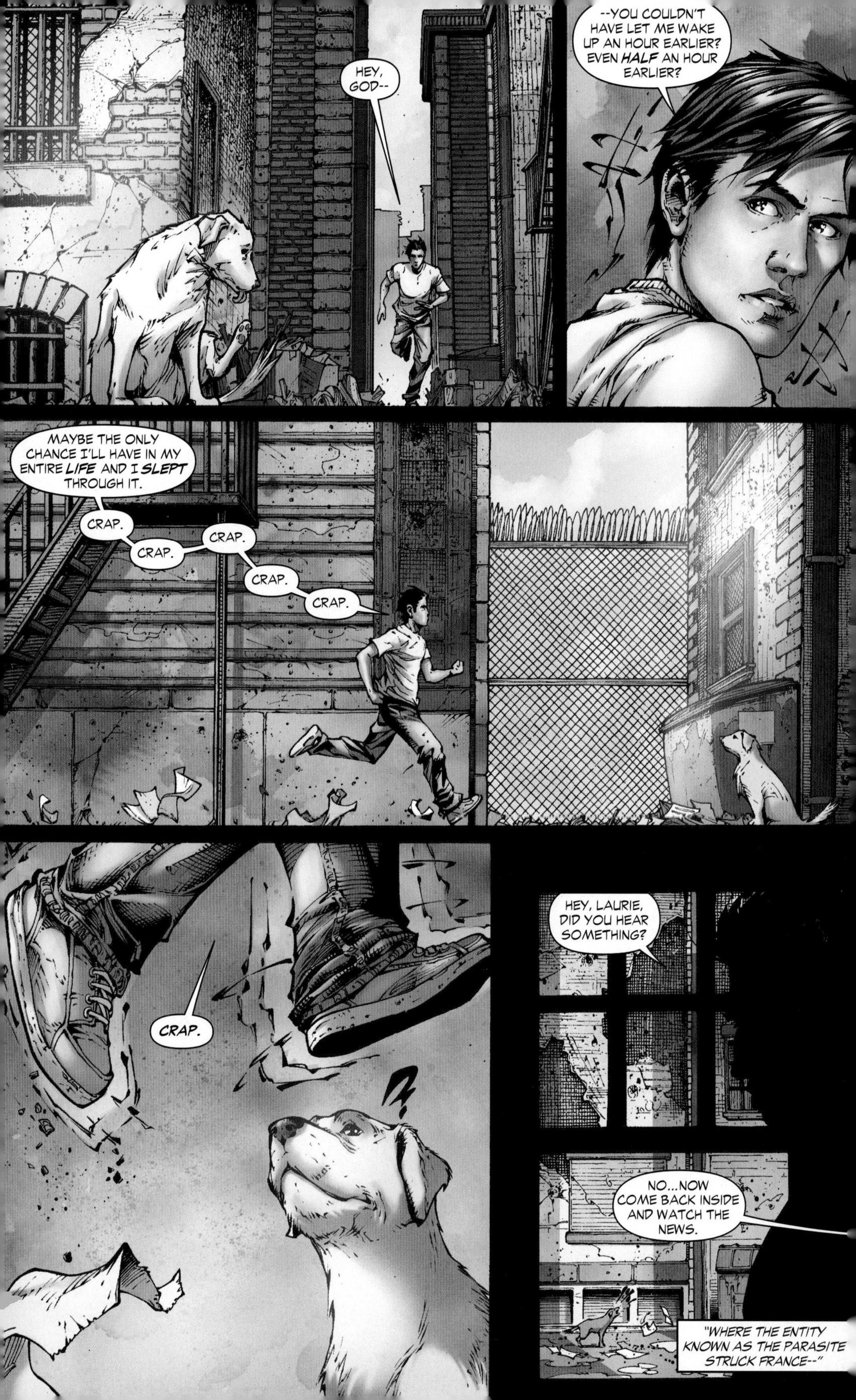
HEY, GOD--
--YOU COULDN'T HAVE LET ME WAKE UP AN HOUR EARLIER? EVEN HALF AN HOUR EARLIER?
MAYBE THE ONLY CHANCE I'LL HAVE IN MY ENTIRE LIFE AND I SLEPT THROUGH IT.
CRAP.
CRAP.
CRAP.
CRAP.
CRAP.
CRAP.
HEY, LAURIE, DID YOU HEAR SOMETHING?
NO...NOW COME BACK INSIDE AND WATCH THE NEWS.
"WHERE THE ENTITY KNOWN AS THE PARASITE STRUCK FRANCE--"

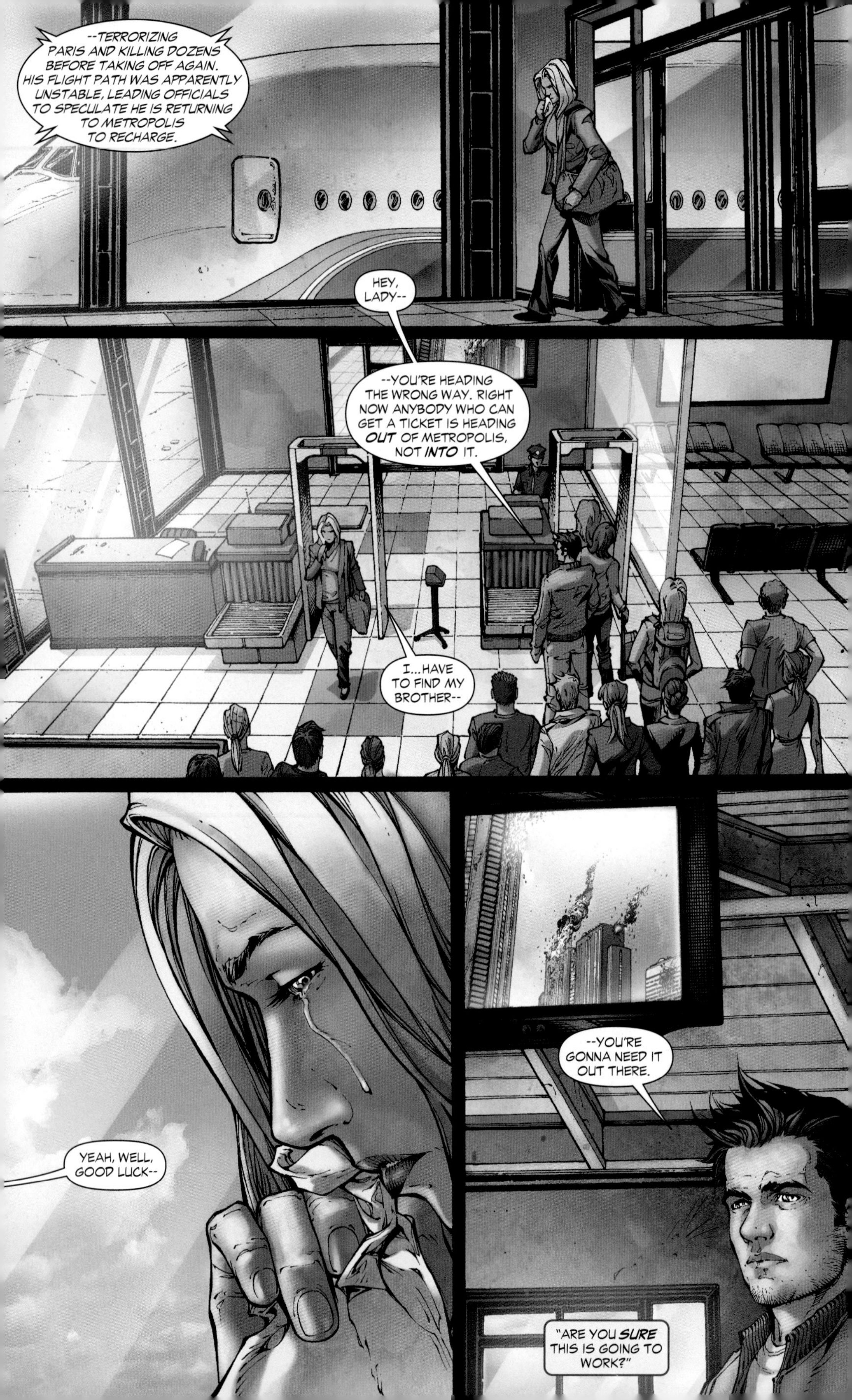
--TERRORIZING PARIS AND KILLING DOZENS BEFORE TAKING OFF AGAIN. HIS FLIGHT PATH WAS APPARENTLY UNSTABLE, LEADING OFFICIALS TO SPECULATE HE IS RETURNING TO METROPOLIS TO RECHARGE.
HEY, LADY--
--YOU'RE HEADING THE WRONG WAY. RIGHT NOW ANYBODY WHO CAN GET A TICKET IS HEADING OUT OF METROPOLIS, NOT INTO IT.
I...HAVE TO FIND MY BROTHER--
YEAH, WELL, GOOD LUCK--
--YOU'RE GONNA NEED IT OUT THERE.
"ARE YOU SURE THIS IS GOING TO WORK?"

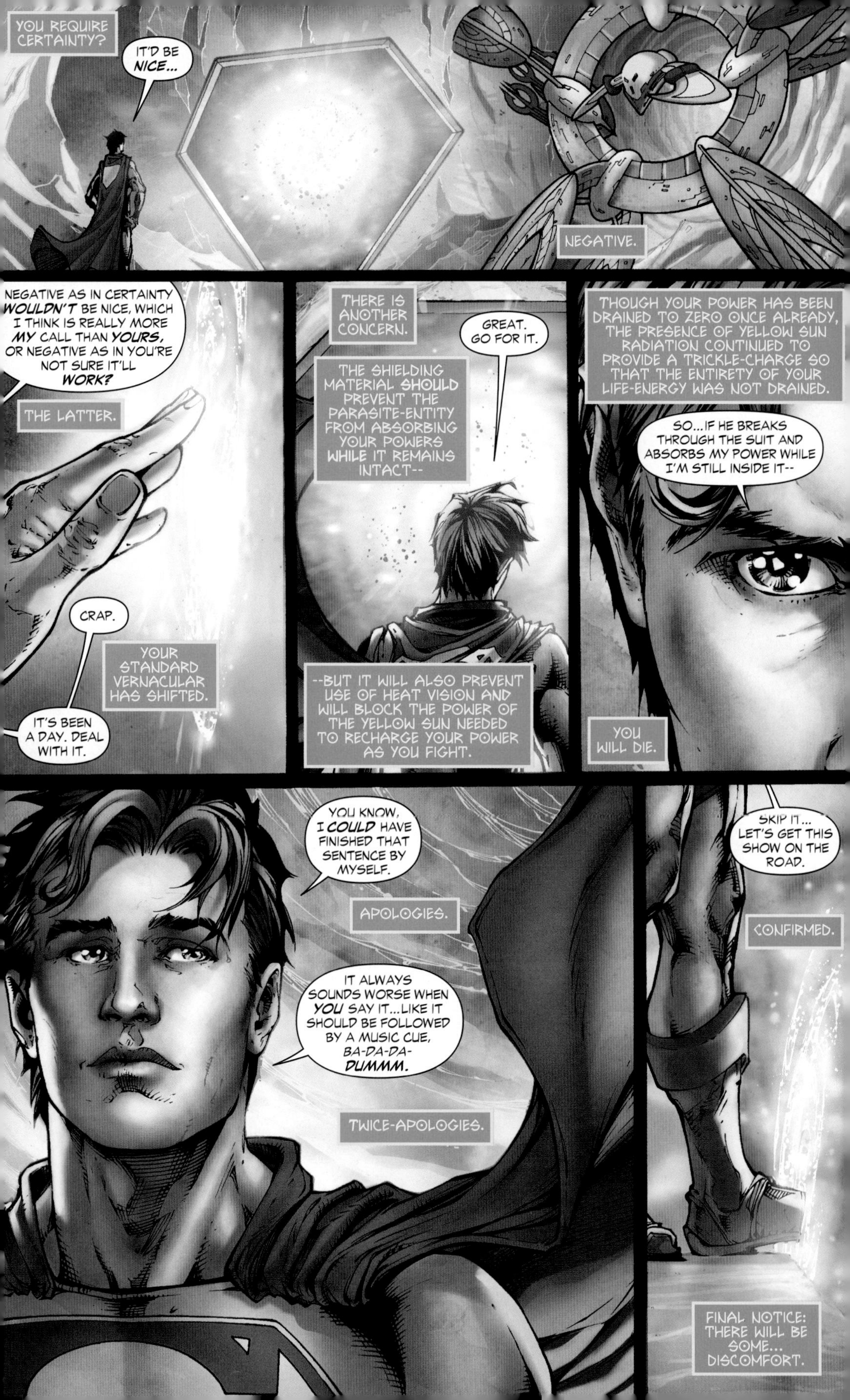
YOU REQUIRE CERTAINTY?
IT'D BE NICE...
NEGATIVE.
NEGATIVE AS IN CERTAINTY WOULDN'T BE NICE, WHICH I THINK IS REALLY MORE MY CALL THAN YOURS, OR NEGATIVE AS IN YOU'RE NOT SURE IT'LL WORK?
THE LATTER.
CRAP.
YOUR STANDARD VERNACULAR HAS SHIFTED.
IT'S BEEN A DAY. DEAL WITH IT.
THERE IS ANOTHER CONCERN.
GREAT. GO FOR IT.
THE SHIELDING MATERIAL SHOULD PREVENT THE PARASITE-ENTITY FROM ABSORBING YOUR POWERS WHILE IT REMAINS INTACT--
--BUT IT WILL ALSO PREVENT USE OF HEAT VISION AND WILL BLOCK THE POWER OF THE YELLOW SUN NEEDED TO RECHARGE YOUR POWER AS YOU FIGHT.
THOUGH YOUR POWER HAS BEEN DRAINED TO ZERO ONCE ALREADY, THE PRESENCE OF YELLOW SUN RADIATION CONTINUED TO PROVIDE A TRICKLE-CHARGE SO THAT THE ENTIRETY OF YOUR LIFE-ENERGY WAS NOT DRAINED.
SO...IF HE BREAKS THROUGH THE SUIT AND ABSORBS MY POWER WHILE I'M STILL INSIDE IT--
YOU WILL DIE.
YOU KNOW, I COULD HAVE FINISHED THAT SENTENCE BY MYSELF.
APOLOGIES.
IT ALWAYS SOUNDS WORSE WHEN YOU SAY IT...LIKE IT SHOULD BE FOLLOWED BY A MUSIC CUE, BA-DA-DA-DUMMM.
TWICE-APOLOGIES.
SKIP IT... LET'S GET THIS SHOW ON THE ROAD.
CONFIRMED.
FINAL NOTICE: THERE WILL BE SOME... DISCOMFORT.

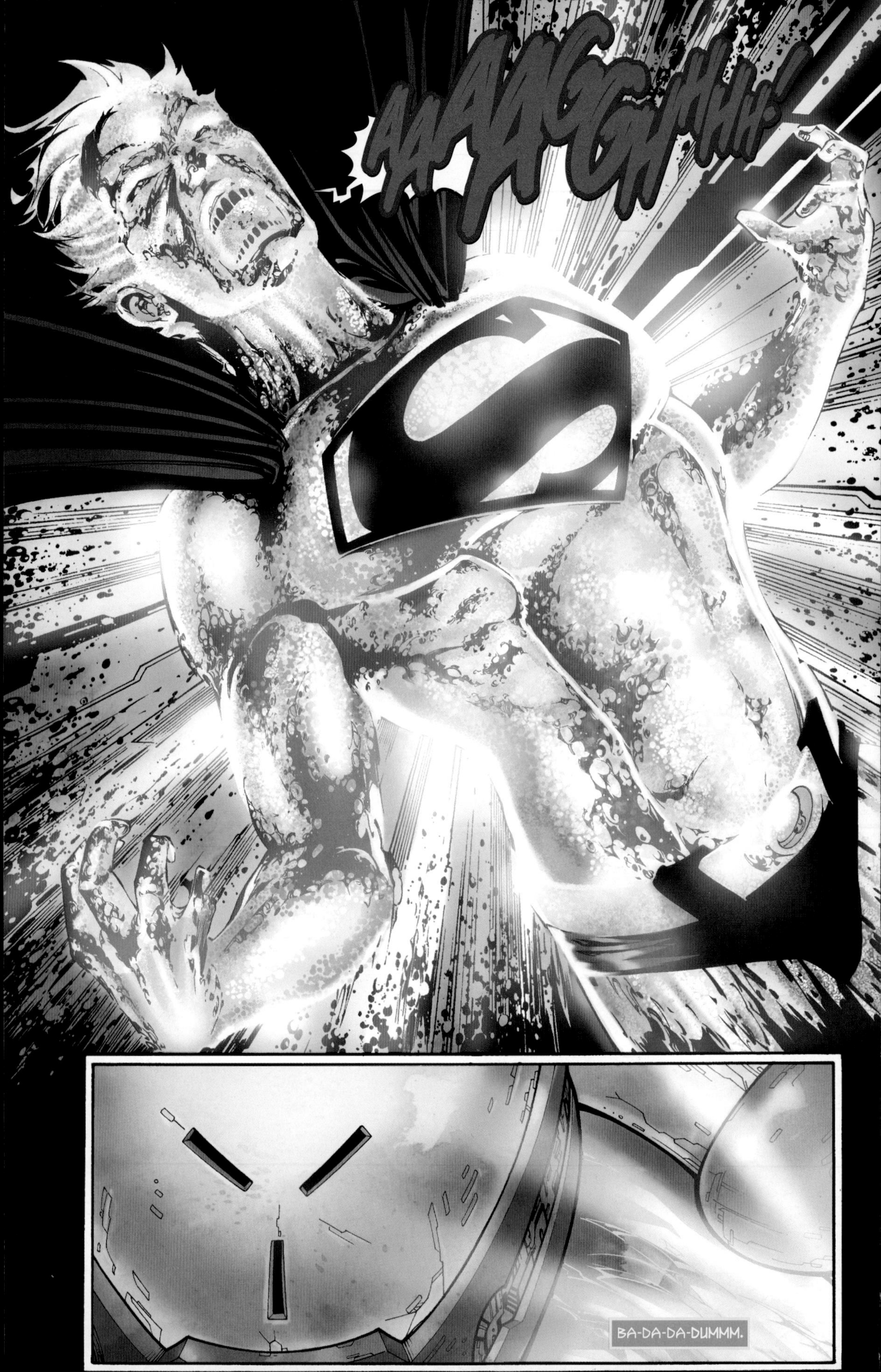
AAAAAGHHHH!
BA-DA-DA-DUMMM.

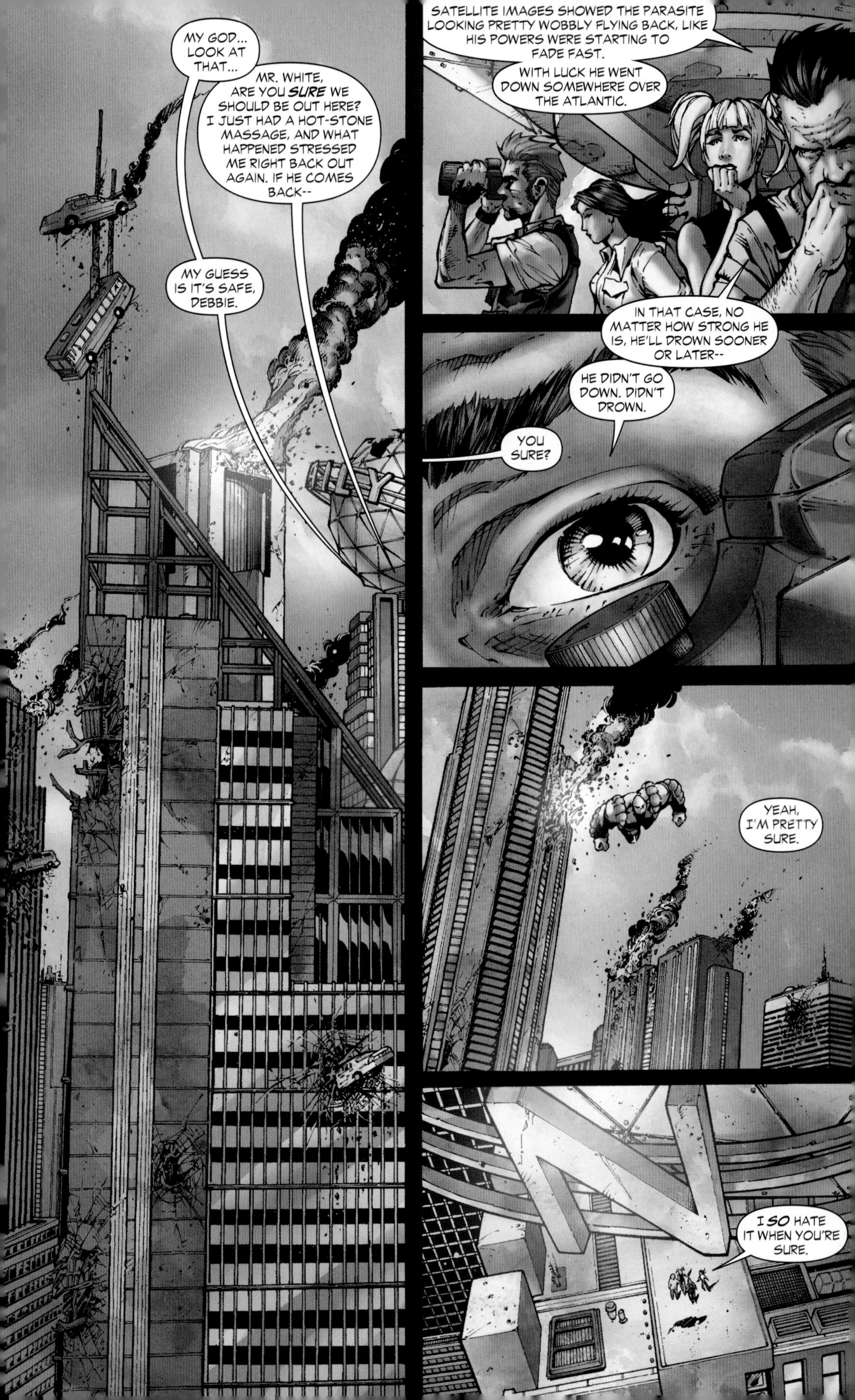
MY GOD... LOOK AT THAT...
MR. WHITE, ARE YOU SURE WE SHOULD BE OUT HERE? I JUST HAD A HOT-STONE MASSAGE, AND WHAT HAPPENED STRESSED ME RIGHT BACK OUT AGAIN. IF HE COMES BACK--
MY GUESS IS IT'S SAFE, DEBBIE.
SATELLITE IMAGES SHOWED THE PARASITE LOOKING PRETTY WOBBLY FLYING BACK, LIKE HIS POWERS WERE STARTING TO FADE FAST.
WITH LUCK HE WENT DOWN SOMEWHERE OVER THE ATLANTIC.
IN THAT CASE, NO MATTER HOW STRONG HE IS, HE'LL DROWN SOONER OR LATER--
HE DIDN'T GO DOWN. DIDN'T DROWN.
YOU SURE?
YEAH, I'M PRETTY SURE.
I SO HATE IT WHEN YOU'RE SURE.

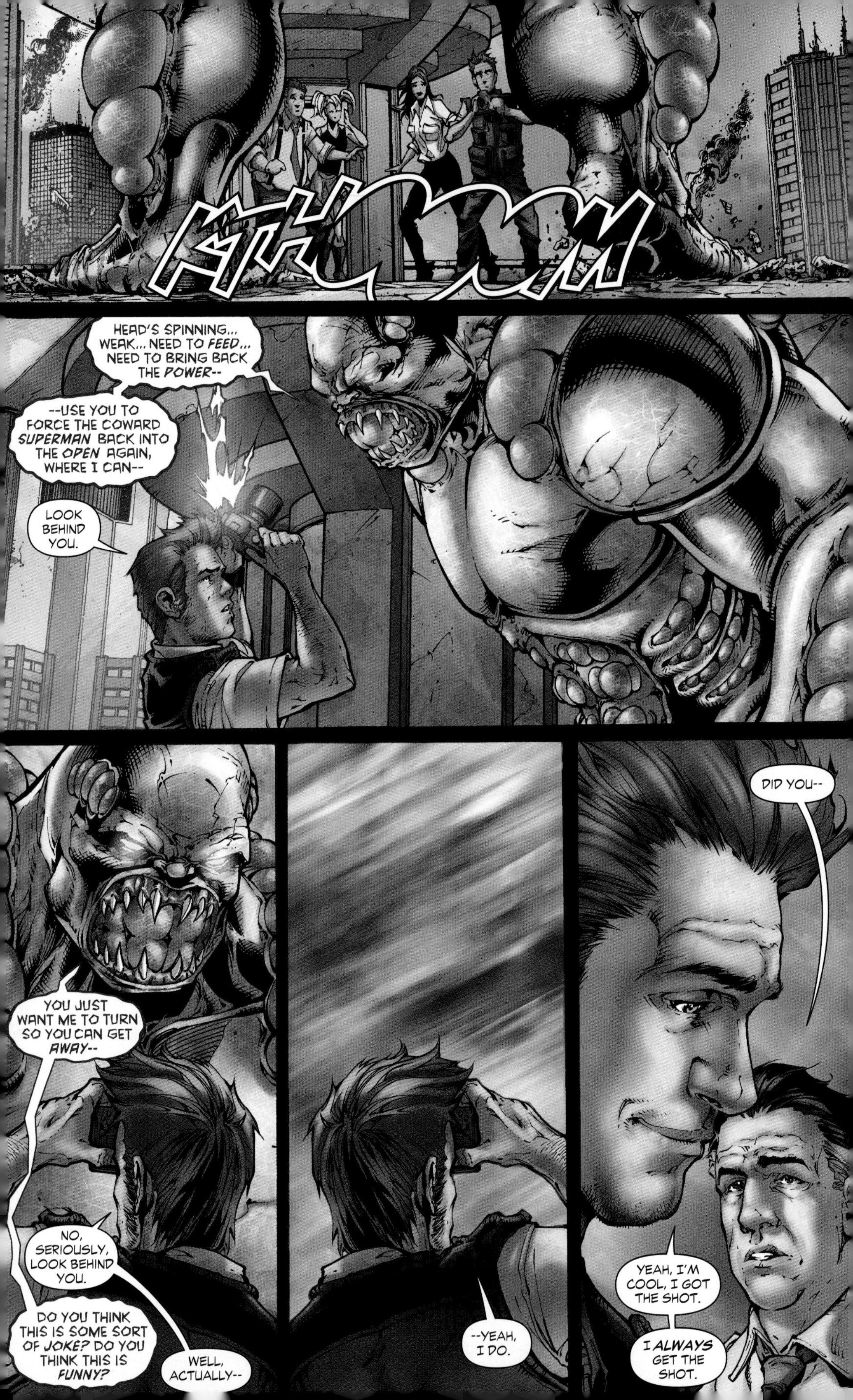
KATHOOM
HEAD'S SPINNING... WEAK... NEED TO FEED... NEED TO BRING BACK THE POWER--
--USE YOU TO FORCE THE COWARD SUPERMAN BACK INTO THE OPEN AGAIN, WHERE I CAN--
LOOK BEHIND YOU.
YOU JUST WANT ME TO TURN SO YOU CAN GET AWAY--
NO, SERIOUSLY, LOOK BEHIND YOU.
DO YOU THINK THIS IS SOME SORT OF JOKE? DO YOU THINK THIS IS FUNNY?
WELL, ACTUALLY--
--YEAH, I DO.
DID YOU--
YEAH, I'M COOL, I GOT THE SHOT.
I ALWAYS GET THE SHOT.

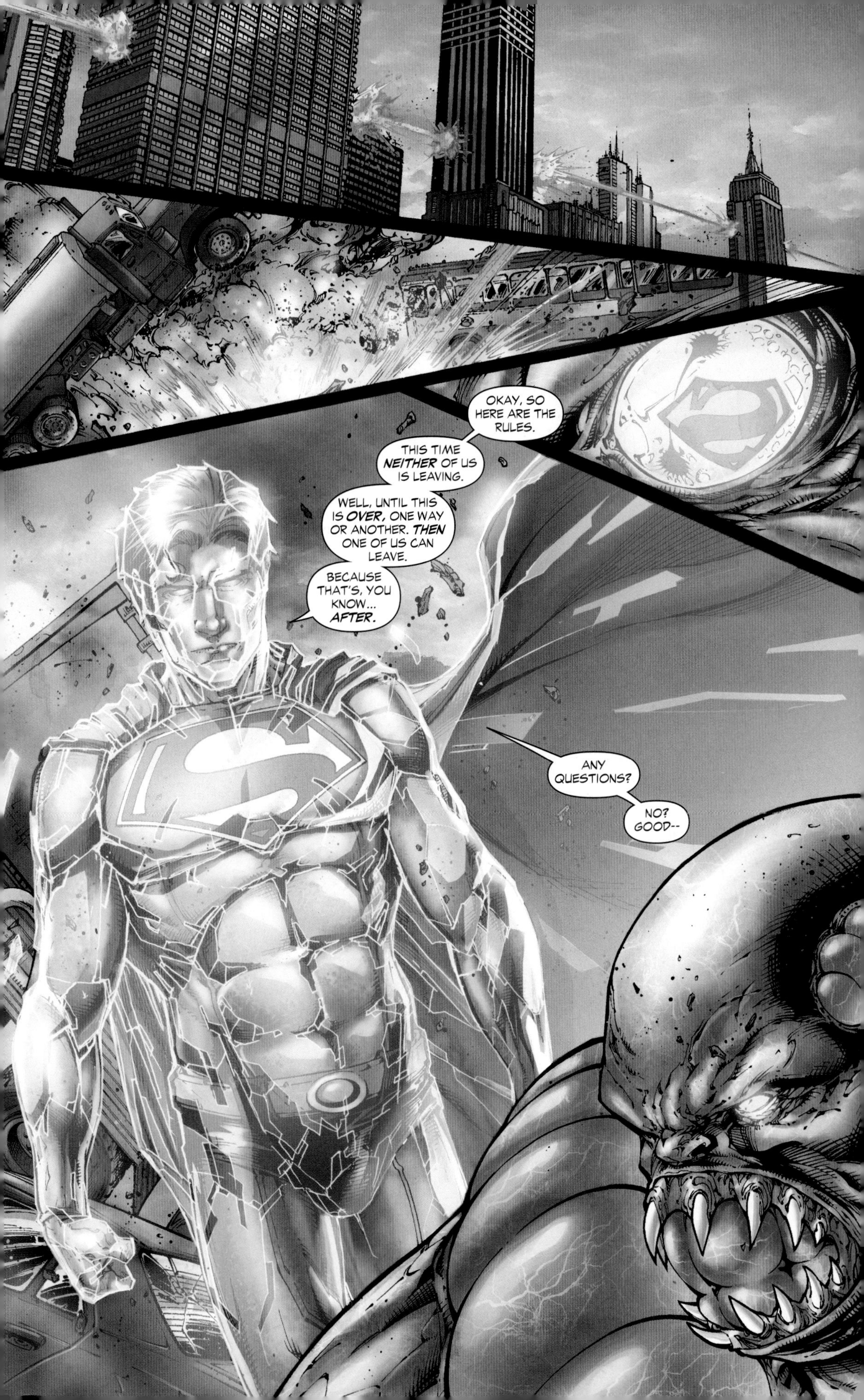

OKAY, SO HERE ARE THE RULES.
THIS TIME **NEITHER** OF US IS LEAVING.
WELL, UNTIL THIS IS **OVER,** ONE WAY OR ANOTHER. **THEN** ONE OF US CAN LEAVE.
BECAUSE THAT'S, YOU KNOW... **AFTER.**
ANY QUESTIONS?
NO? GOOD--

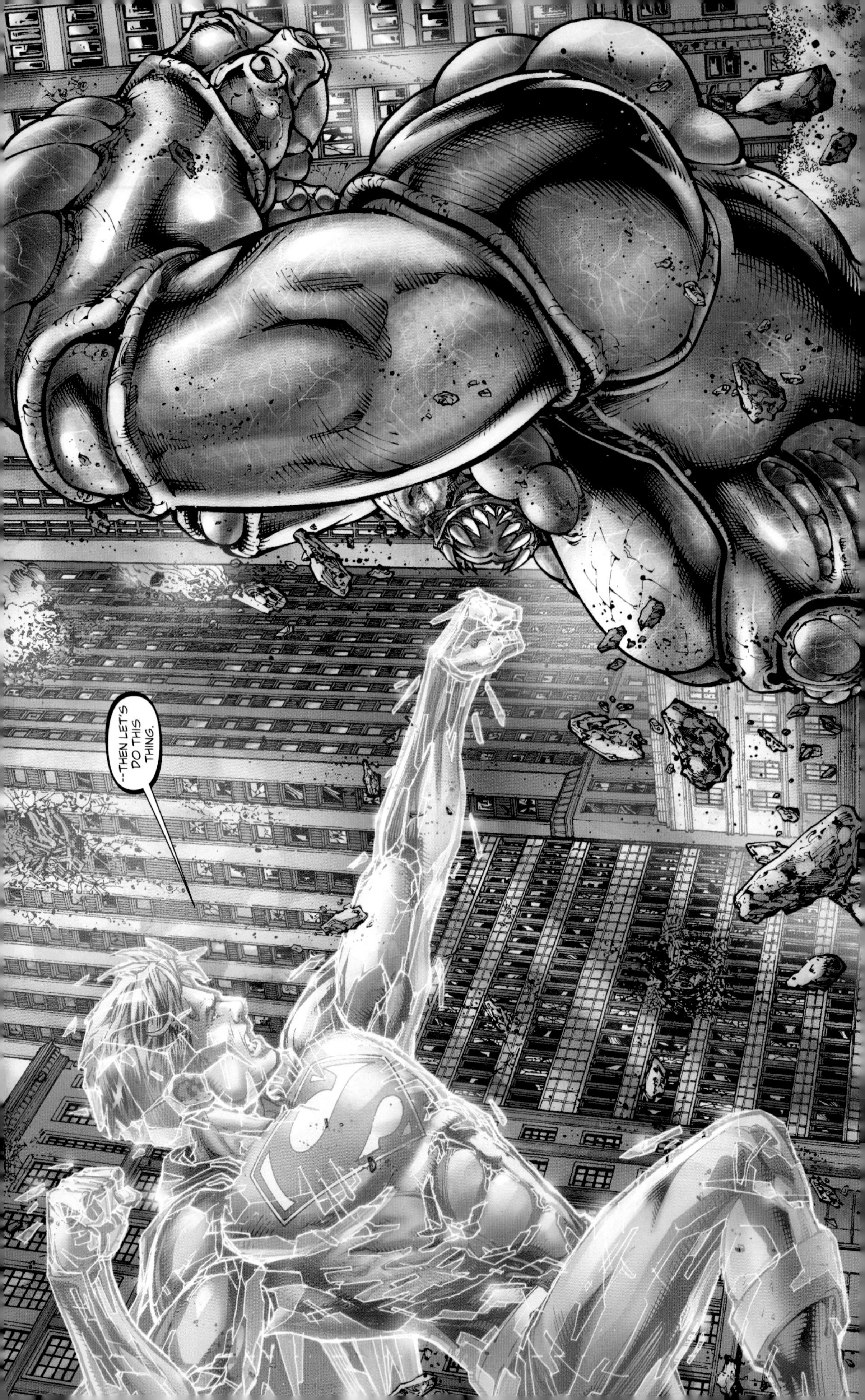
--THEN LET'S DO THIS THING.

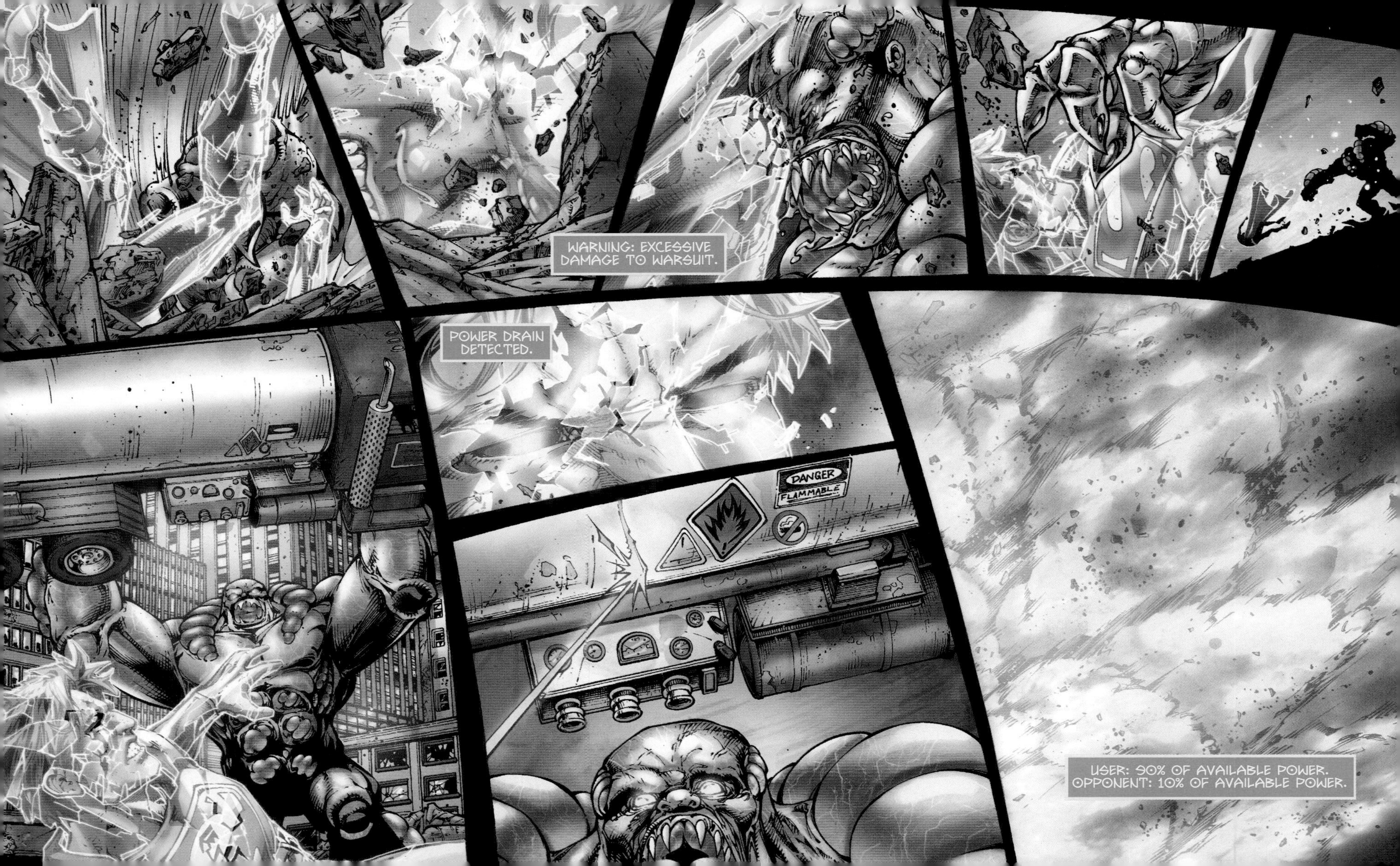
WARNING: EXCESSIVE DAMAGE TO WARSUIT.
POWER DRAIN DETECTED.
DANGER
FLAMMABLE
USER: 90% OF AVAILABLE POWER.
OPPONENT: 10% OF AVAILABLE POWER.

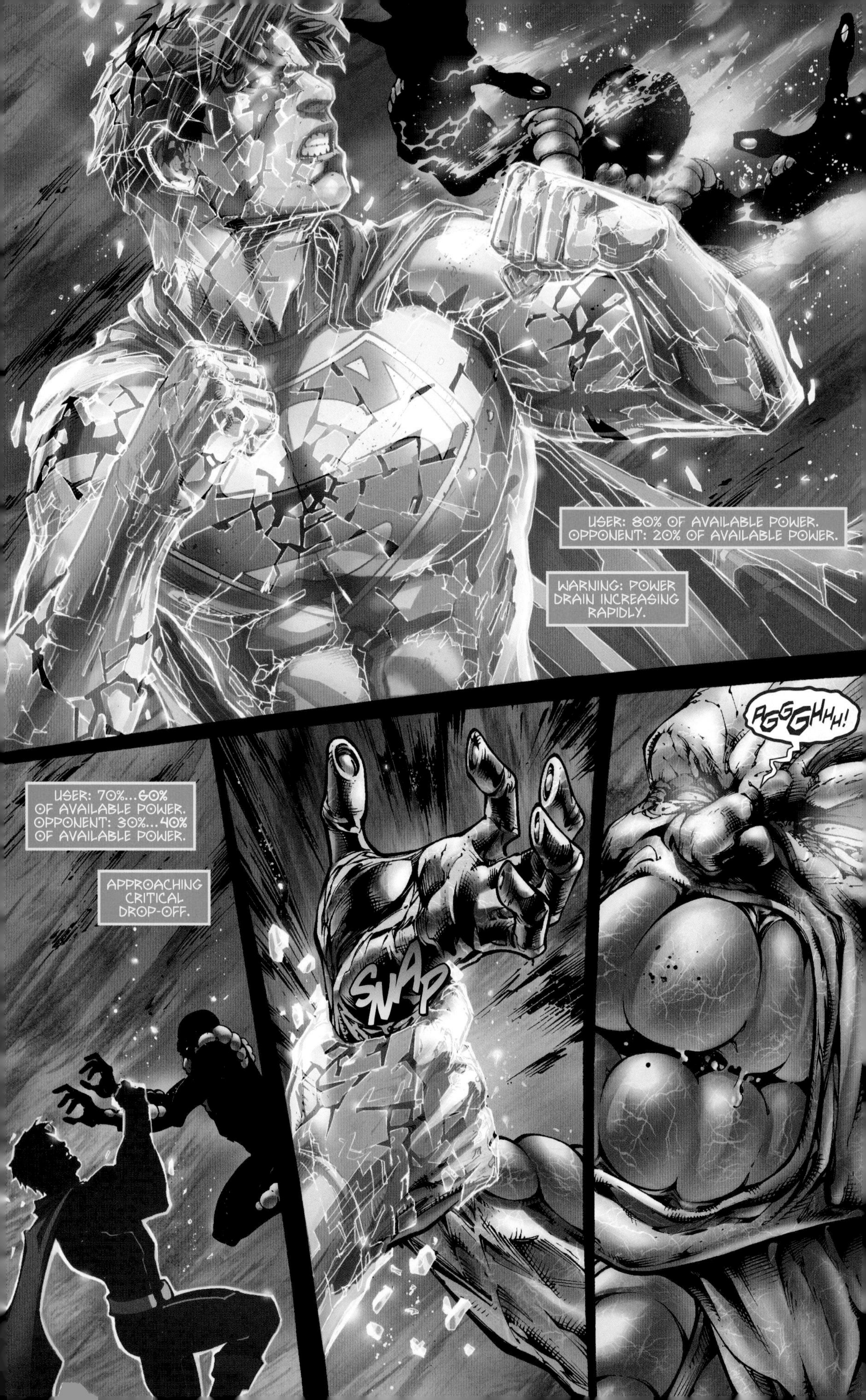
USER: 80% OF AVAILABLE POWER.
OPPONENT: 20% OF AVAILABLE POWER.
WARNING: POWER DRAIN INCREASING RAPIDLY.
USER: 70%...60% OF AVAILABLE POWER.
OPPONENT: 30%...40% OF AVAILABLE POWER.
APPROACHING CRITICAL DROP-OFF.
SNAP
AGGGHHH!

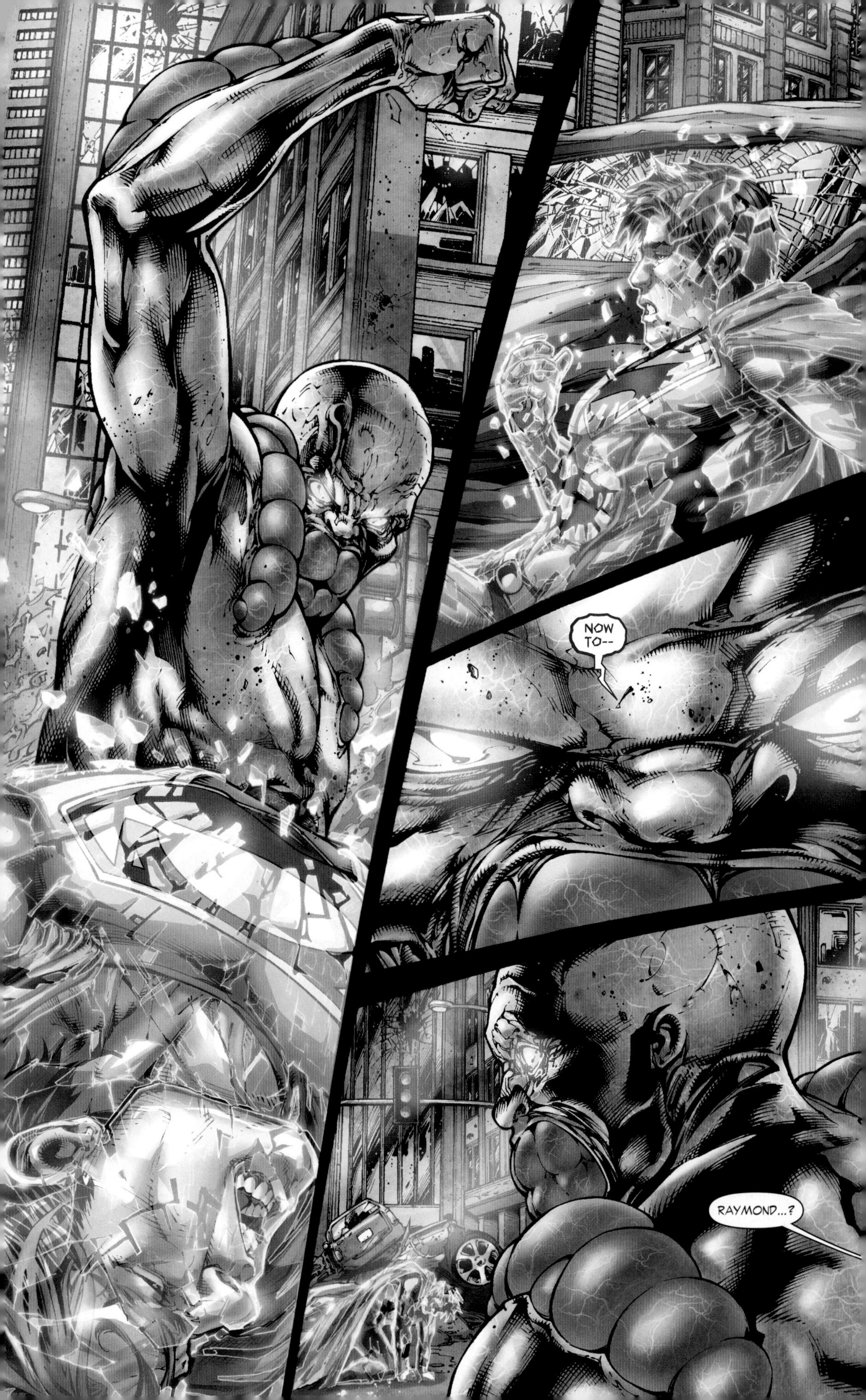
NOW TO--
RAYMOND...?

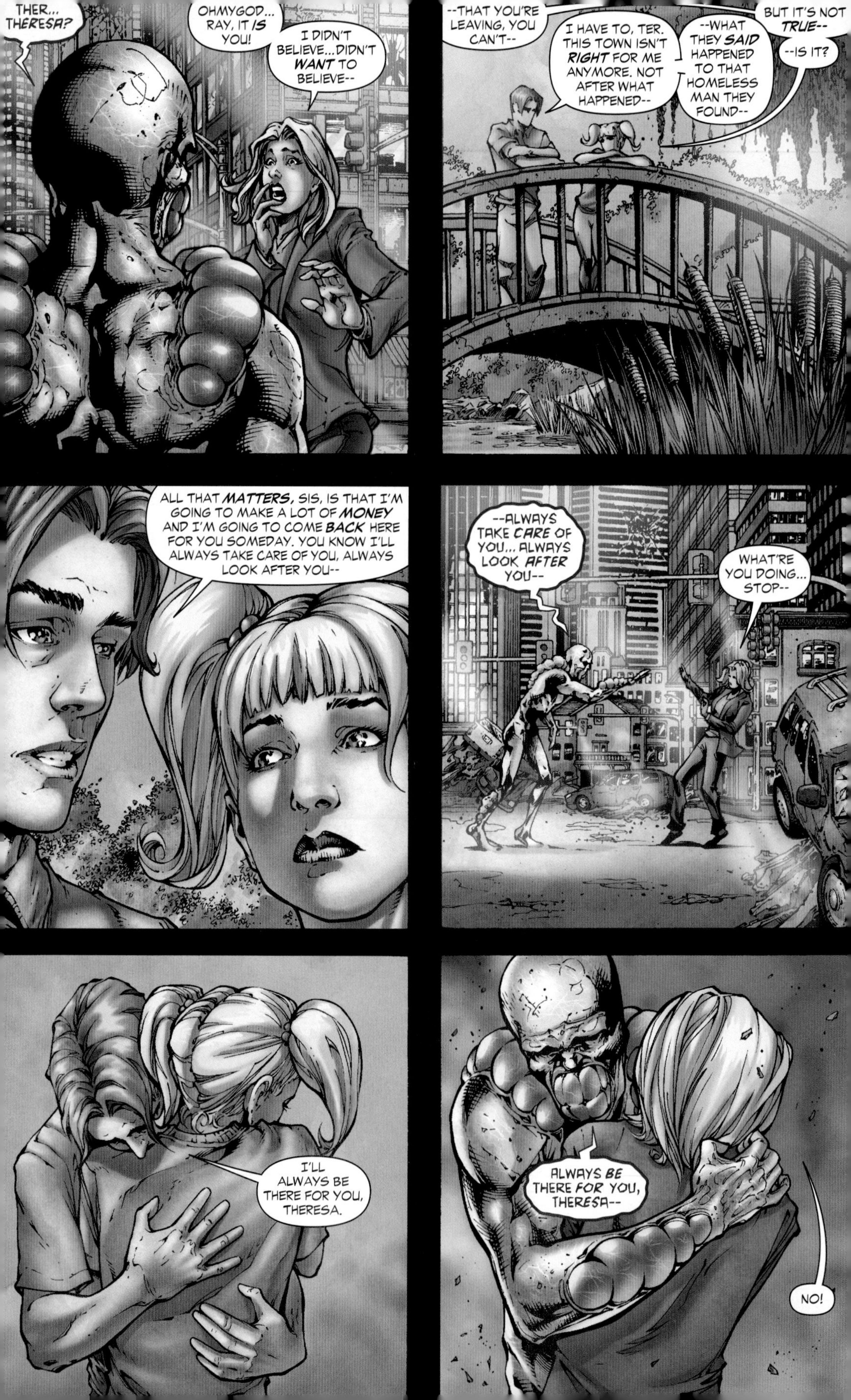
THER... THERESA?
OHMYGOD... RAY, IT IS YOU!
I DIDN'T BELIEVE...DIDN'T WANT TO BELIEVE--
--THAT YOU'RE LEAVING, YOU CAN'T--
I HAVE TO, TER. THIS TOWN ISN'T RIGHT FOR ME ANYMORE. NOT AFTER WHAT HAPPENED--
--WHAT THEY SAID HAPPENED TO THAT HOMELESS MAN THEY FOUND--
BUT IT'S NOT TRUE--
--IS IT?
ALL THAT MATTERS, SIS, IS THAT I'M GOING TO MAKE A LOT OF MONEY AND I'M GOING TO COME BACK HERE FOR YOU SOMEDAY. YOU KNOW I'LL ALWAYS TAKE CARE OF YOU, ALWAYS LOOK AFTER YOU--
--ALWAYS TAKE CARE OF YOU... ALWAYS LOOK AFTER YOU--
WHAT'RE YOU DOING... STOP--
I'LL ALWAYS BE THERE FOR YOU, THERESA.
ALWAYS BE THERE FOR YOU, THERESA--
NO!

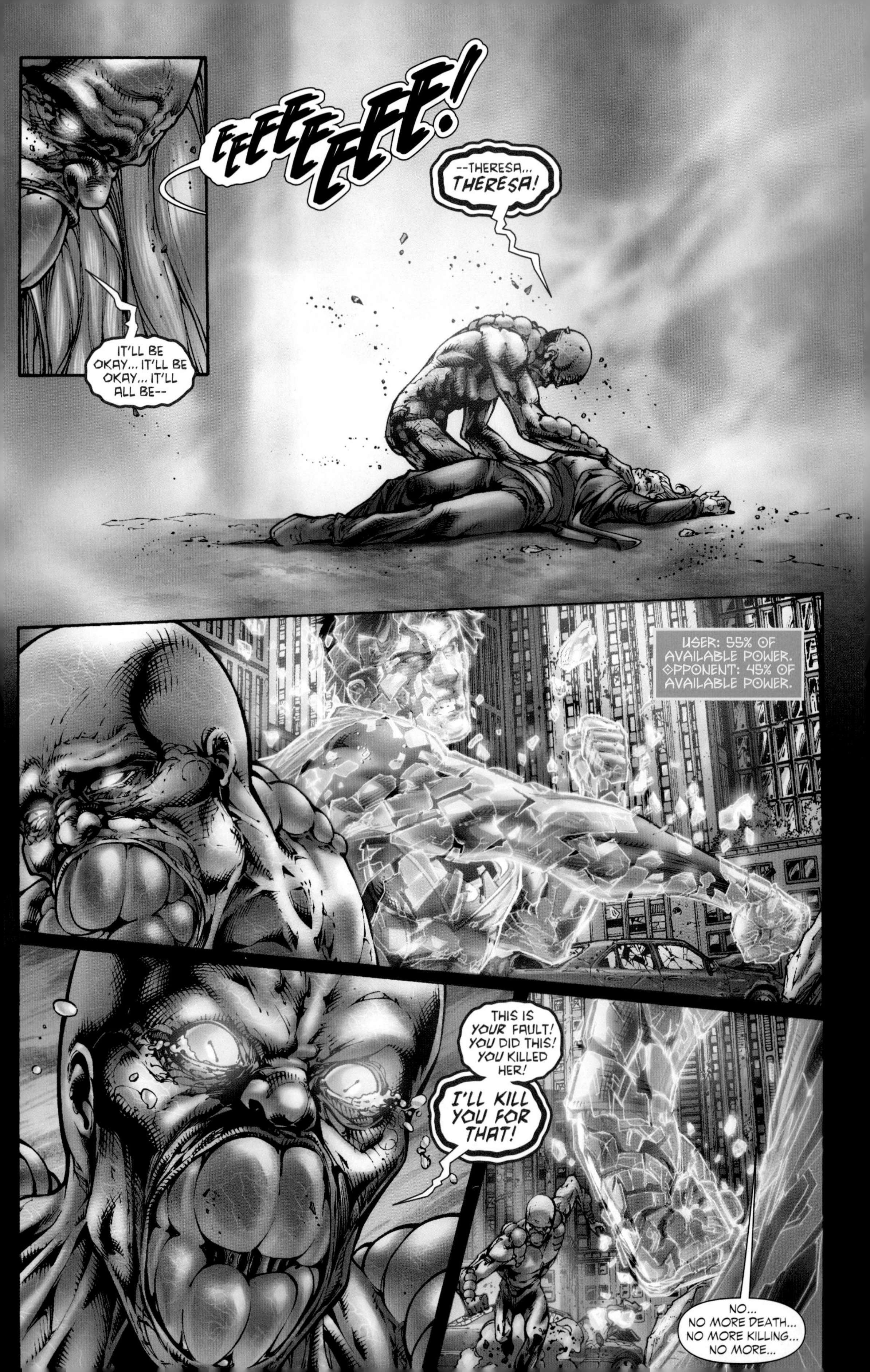
EEEEEEEEEEE!
--THERESA... THERESA!
IT'LL BE OKAY... IT'LL BE OKAY... IT'LL ALL BE--
USER: 55% OF AVAILABLE POWER. OPPONENT: 45% OF AVAILABLE POWER.
THIS IS YOUR FAULT! YOU DID THIS! YOU KILLED HER!
I'LL KILL YOU FOR THAT!
NO... NO MORE DEATH... NO MORE KILLING... NO MORE...

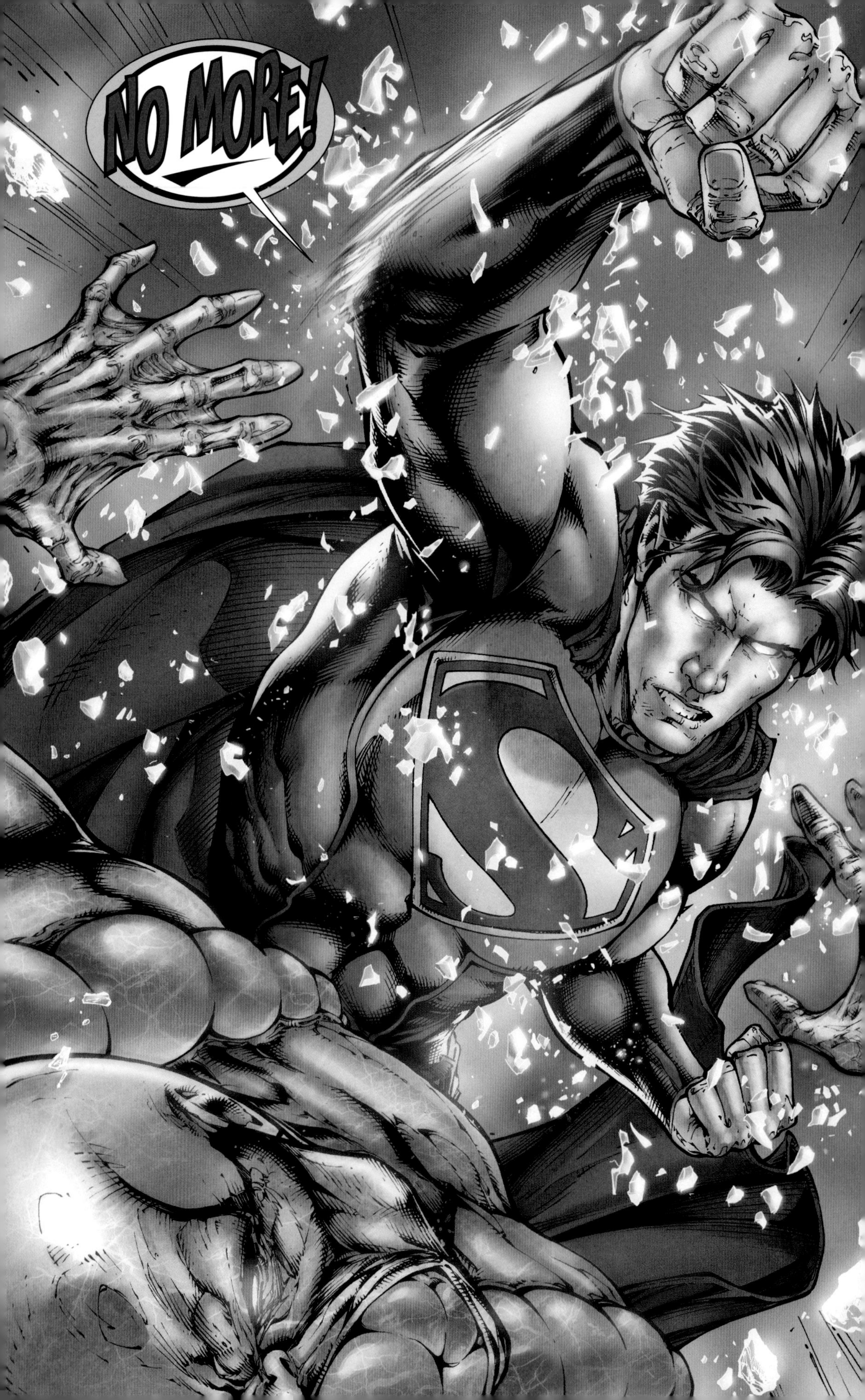
NO MORE!

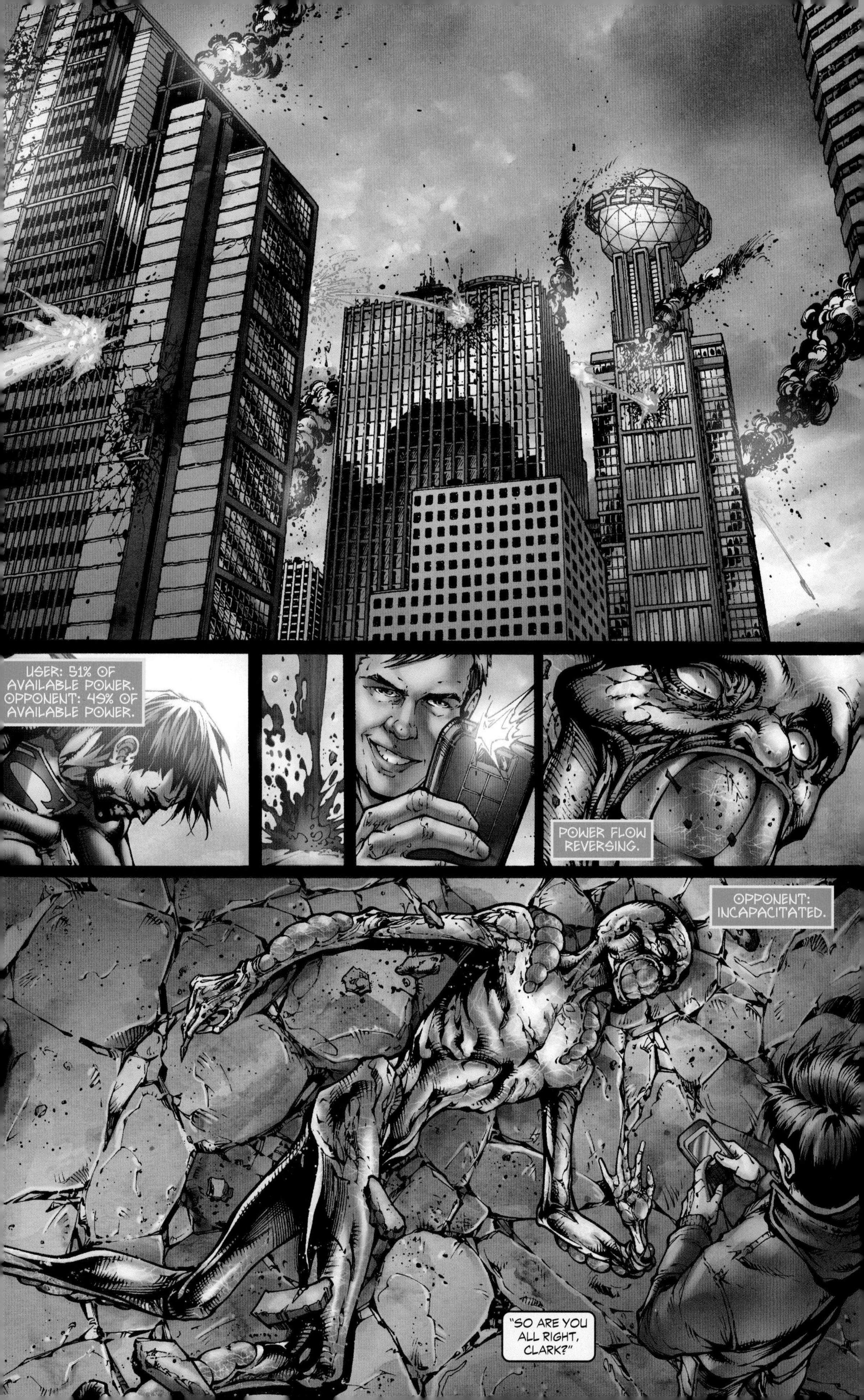
USER: 51% OF AVAILABLE POWER. OPPONENT: 49% OF AVAILABLE POWER.
POWER FLOW REVERSING.
OPPONENT: INCAPACITATED.
"SO ARE YOU ALL RIGHT, CLARK?"

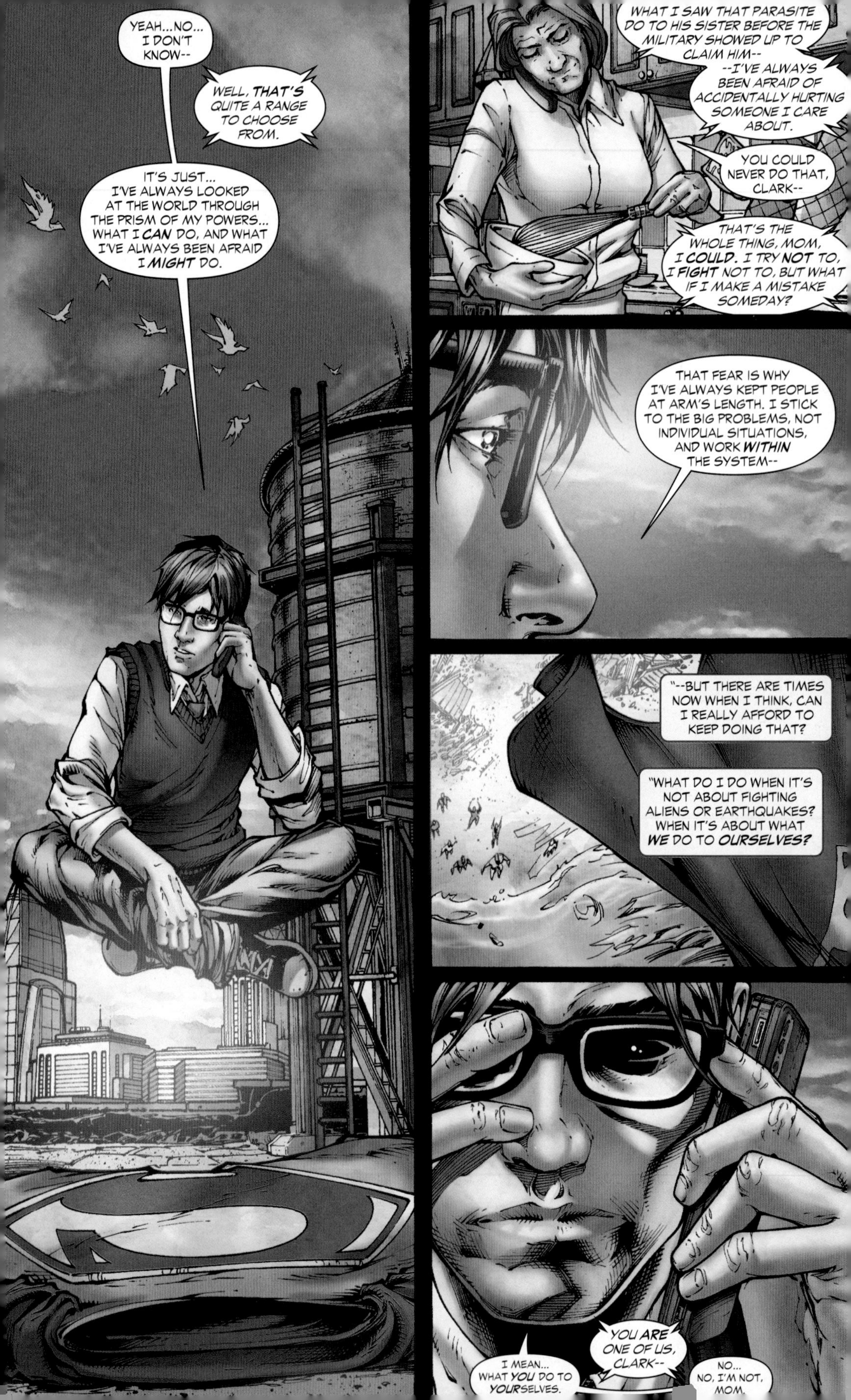
YEAH...NO... I DON'T KNOW--
WELL, THAT'S QUITE A RANGE TO CHOOSE FROM.
IT'S JUST... I'VE ALWAYS LOOKED AT THE WORLD THROUGH THE PRISM OF MY POWERS... WHAT I CAN DO, AND WHAT I'VE ALWAYS BEEN AFRAID I MIGHT DO.
WHAT I SAW THAT PARASITE DO TO HIS SISTER BEFORE THE MILITARY SHOWED UP TO CLAIM HIM--
--I'VE ALWAYS BEEN AFRAID OF ACCIDENTALLY HURTING SOMEONE I CARE ABOUT.
YOU COULD NEVER DO THAT, CLARK--
THAT'S THE WHOLE THING, MOM, I COULD. I TRY NOT TO, I FIGHT NOT TO, BUT WHAT IF I MAKE A MISTAKE SOMEDAY?
THAT FEAR IS WHY I'VE ALWAYS KEPT PEOPLE AT ARM'S LENGTH. I STICK TO THE BIG PROBLEMS, NOT INDIVIDUAL SITUATIONS, AND WORK WITHIN THE SYSTEM--
"--BUT THERE ARE TIMES NOW WHEN I THINK, CAN I REALLY AFFORD TO KEEP DOING THAT?
"WHAT DO I DO WHEN IT'S NOT ABOUT FIGHTING ALIENS OR EARTHQUAKES? WHEN IT'S ABOUT WHAT WE DO TO OURSELVES?
I MEAN... WHAT YOU DO TO YOURSELVES.
YOU ARE ONE OF US, CLARK--
NO... NO, I'M NOT, MOM.

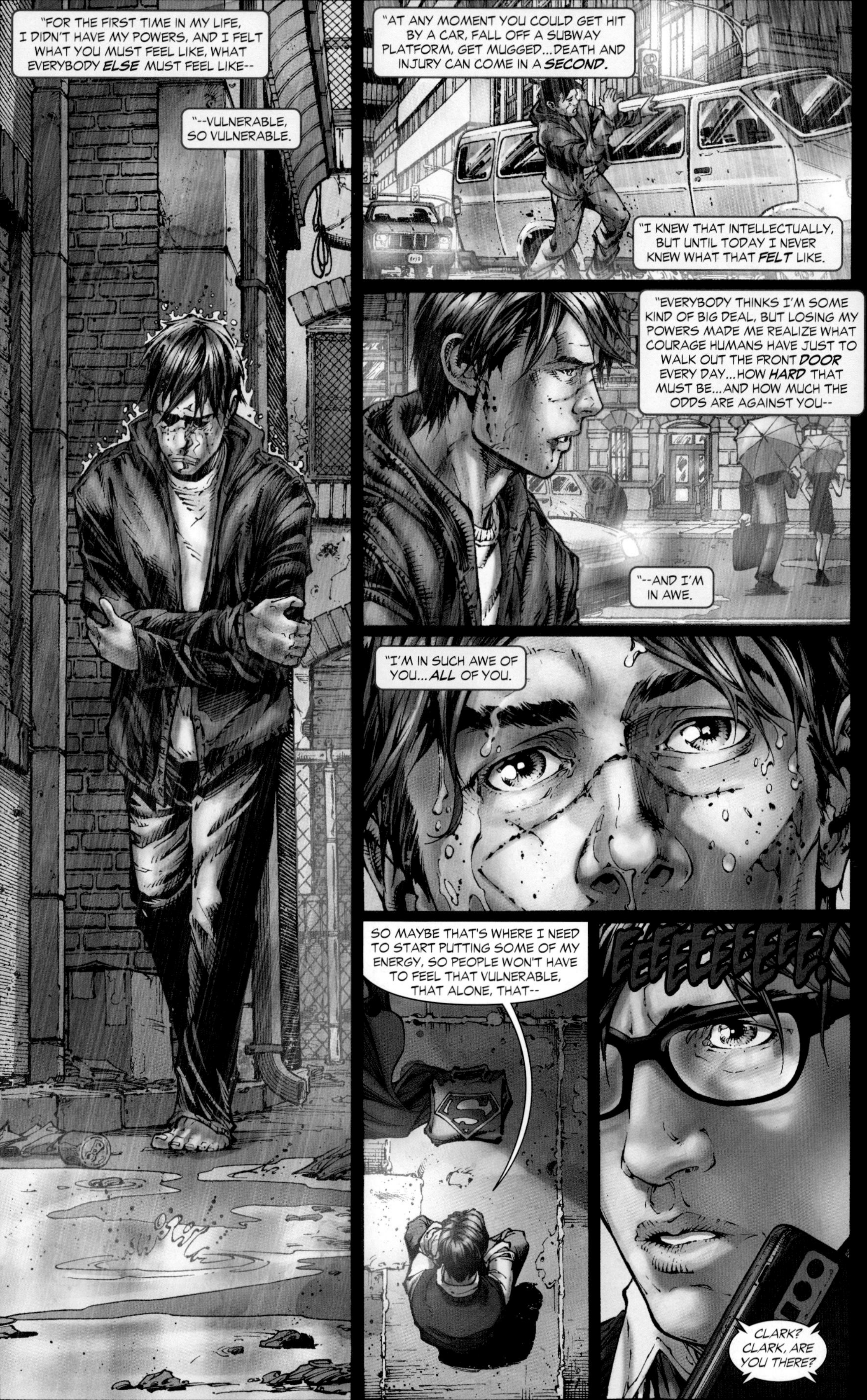
"FOR THE FIRST TIME IN MY LIFE, I DIDN'T HAVE MY POWERS, AND I FELT WHAT YOU MUST FEEL LIKE, WHAT EVERYBODY ELSE MUST FEEL LIKE--
"--VULNERABLE, SO VULNERABLE.
"AT ANY MOMENT YOU COULD GET HIT BY A CAR, FALL OFF A SUBWAY PLATFORM, GET MUGGED...DEATH AND INJURY CAN COME IN A SECOND.
"I KNEW THAT INTELLECTUALLY, BUT UNTIL TODAY I NEVER KNEW WHAT THAT FELT LIKE.
"EVERYBODY THINKS I'M SOME KIND OF BIG DEAL, BUT LOSING MY POWERS MADE ME REALIZE WHAT COURAGE HUMANS HAVE JUST TO WALK OUT THE FRONT DOOR EVERY DAY...HOW HARD THAT MUST BE...AND HOW MUCH THE ODDS ARE AGAINST YOU--
"--AND I'M IN AWE.
"I'M IN SUCH AWE OF YOU...ALL OF YOU.
SO MAYBE THAT'S WHERE I NEED TO START PUTTING SOME OF MY ENERGY, SO PEOPLE WON'T HAVE TO FEEL THAT VULNERABLE, THAT ALONE, THAT--
EEEEEEEEEE!
CLARK? CLARK, ARE YOU THERE?

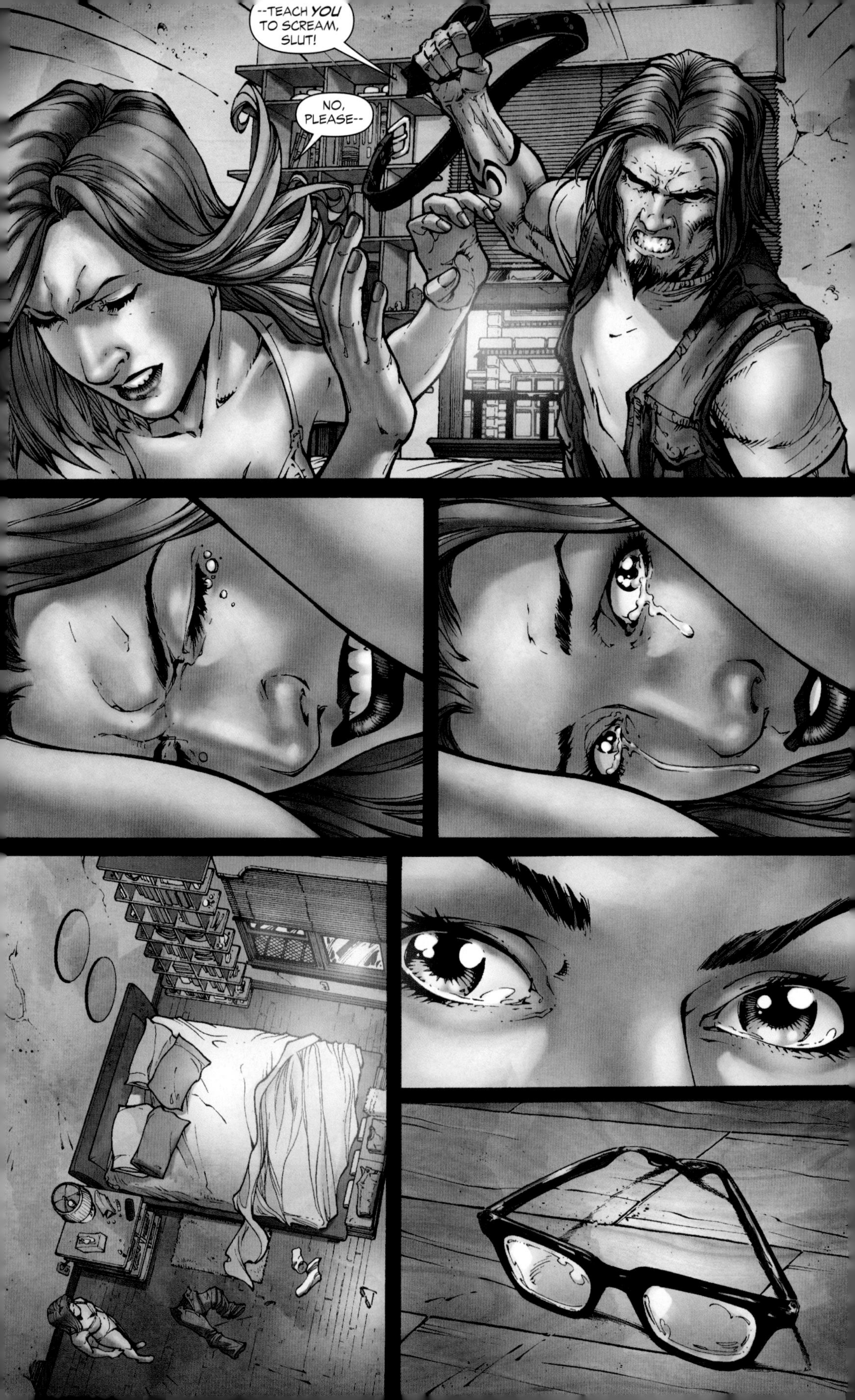
--TEACH YOU TO SCREAM, SLUT!
NO, PLEASE--

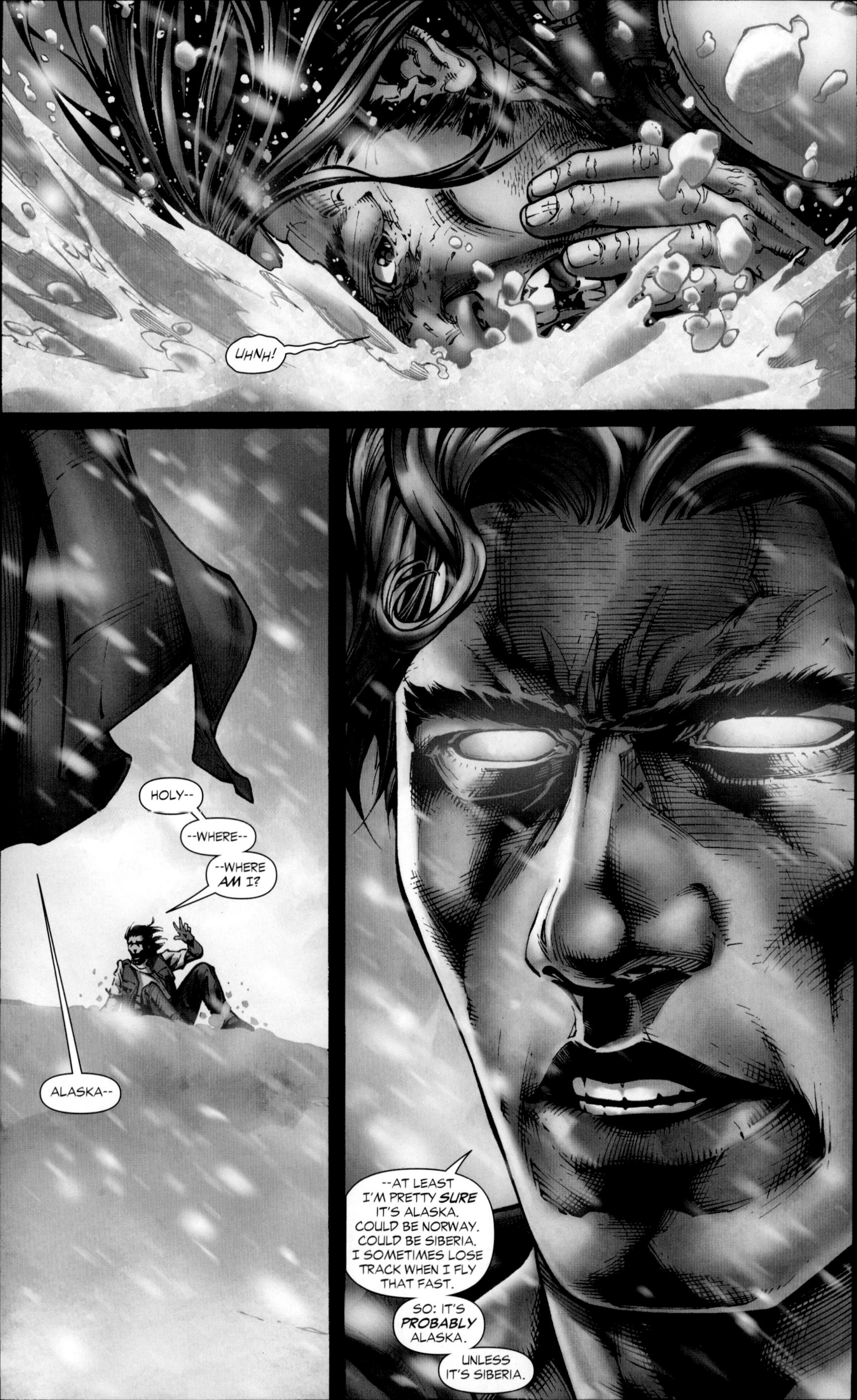
UHNH!
HOLY--
--WHERE--
--WHERE AM I?
ALASKA--
--AT LEAST I'M PRETTY SURE IT'S ALASKA. COULD BE NORWAY. COULD BE SIBERIA. I SOMETIMES LOSE TRACK WHEN I FLY THAT FAST.
SO: IT'S PROBABLY ALASKA.
UNLESS IT'S SIBERIA.

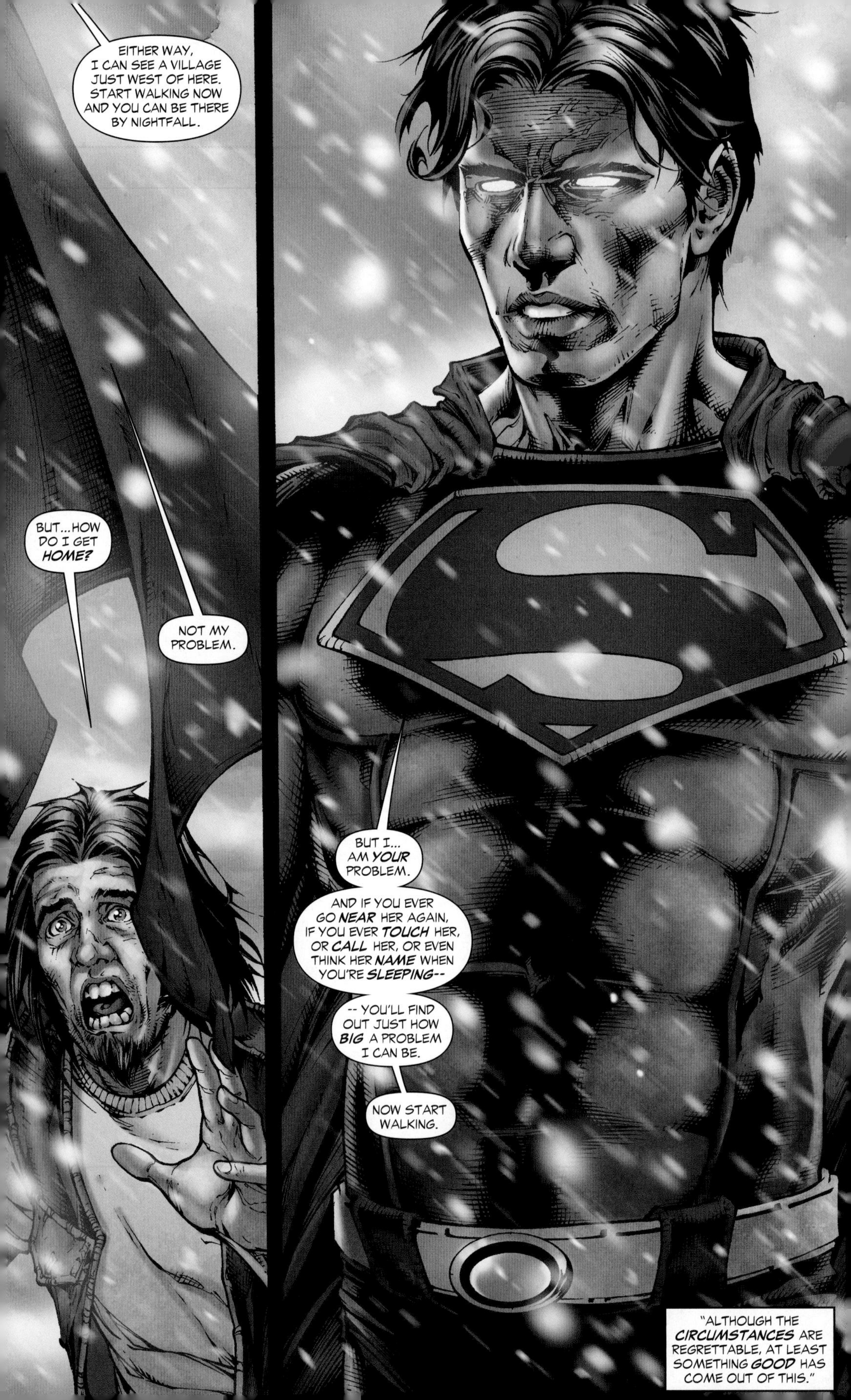
EITHER WAY, I CAN SEE A VILLAGE JUST WEST OF HERE. START WALKING NOW AND YOU CAN BE THERE BY NIGHTFALL.
BUT...HOW DO I GET *HOME?*
NOT MY PROBLEM.
BUT I... AM *YOUR* PROBLEM.
AND IF YOU EVER GO *NEAR* HER AGAIN, IF YOU EVER *TOUCH* HER, OR *CALL* HER, OR EVEN THINK HER *NAME* WHEN YOU'RE *SLEEPING*--
-- YOU'LL FIND OUT JUST HOW *BIG* A PROBLEM I CAN BE.
NOW START WALKING.
"ALTHOUGH THE *CIRCUMSTANCES* ARE REGRETTABLE, AT LEAST SOMETHING *GOOD* HAS COME OUT OF THIS."

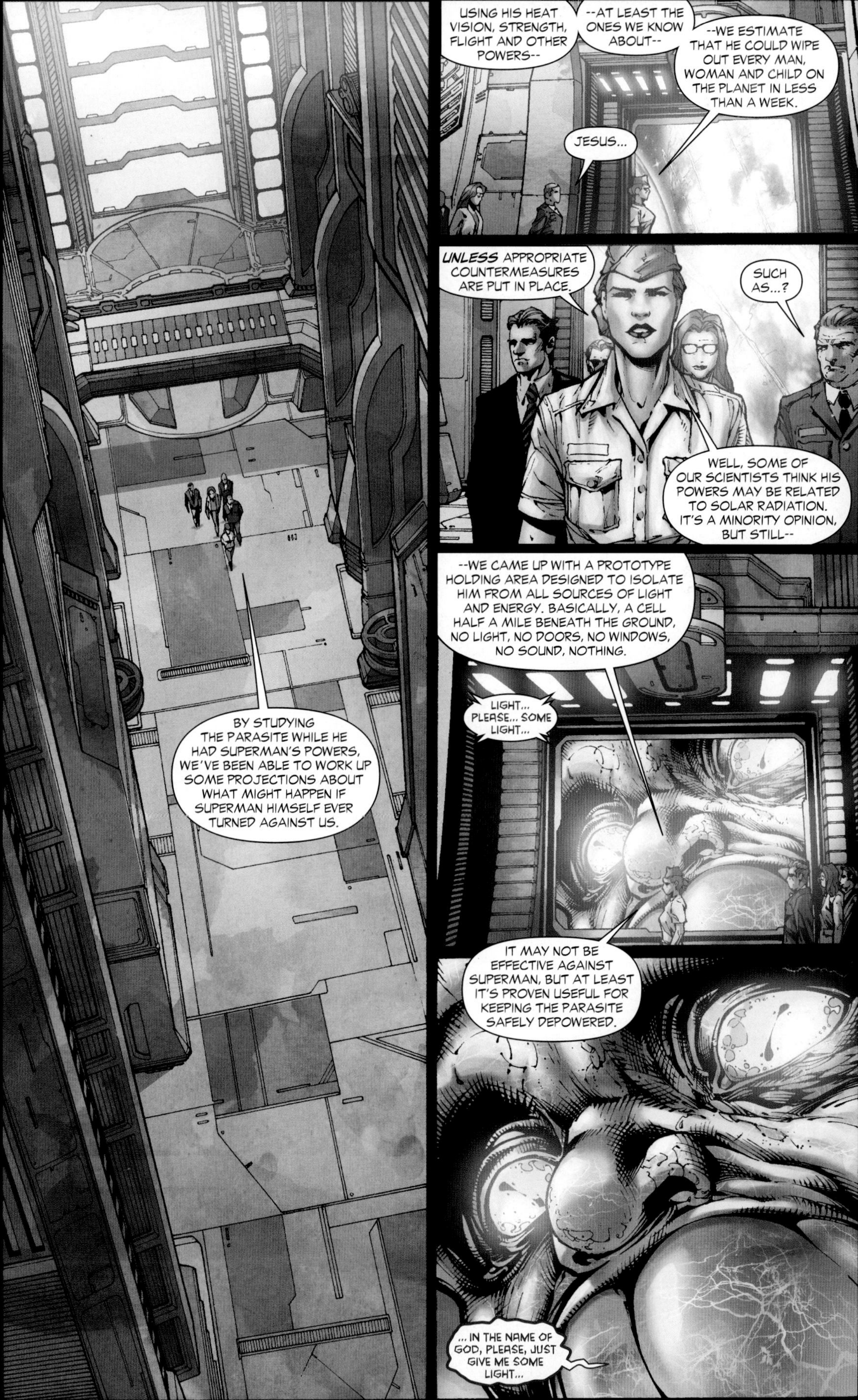
BY STUDYING THE PARASITE WHILE HE HAD SUPERMAN'S POWERS, WE'VE BEEN ABLE TO WORK UP SOME PROJECTIONS ABOUT WHAT MIGHT HAPPEN IF SUPERMAN HIMSELF EVER TURNED AGAINST US.
USING HIS HEAT VISION, STRENGTH, FLIGHT AND OTHER POWERS--
--AT LEAST THE ONES WE KNOW ABOUT--
--WE ESTIMATE THAT HE COULD WIPE OUT EVERY MAN, WOMAN AND CHILD ON THE PLANET IN LESS THAN A WEEK.
JESUS...
UNLESS APPROPRIATE COUNTERMEASURES ARE PUT IN PLACE.
SUCH AS...?
WELL, SOME OF OUR SCIENTISTS THINK HIS POWERS MAY BE RELATED TO SOLAR RADIATION. IT'S A MINORITY OPINION, BUT STILL--
--WE CAME UP WITH A PROTOTYPE HOLDING AREA DESIGNED TO ISOLATE HIM FROM ALL SOURCES OF LIGHT AND ENERGY. BASICALLY, A CELL HALF A MILE BENEATH THE GROUND, NO LIGHT, NO DOORS, NO WINDOWS, NO SOUND, NOTHING.
LIGHT... PLEASE... SOME LIGHT...
IT MAY NOT BE EFFECTIVE AGAINST SUPERMAN, BUT AT LEAST IT'S PROVEN USEFUL FOR KEEPING THE PARASITE SAFELY DEPOWERED.
...IN THE NAME OF GOD, PLEASE, JUST GIVE ME SOME LIGHT...

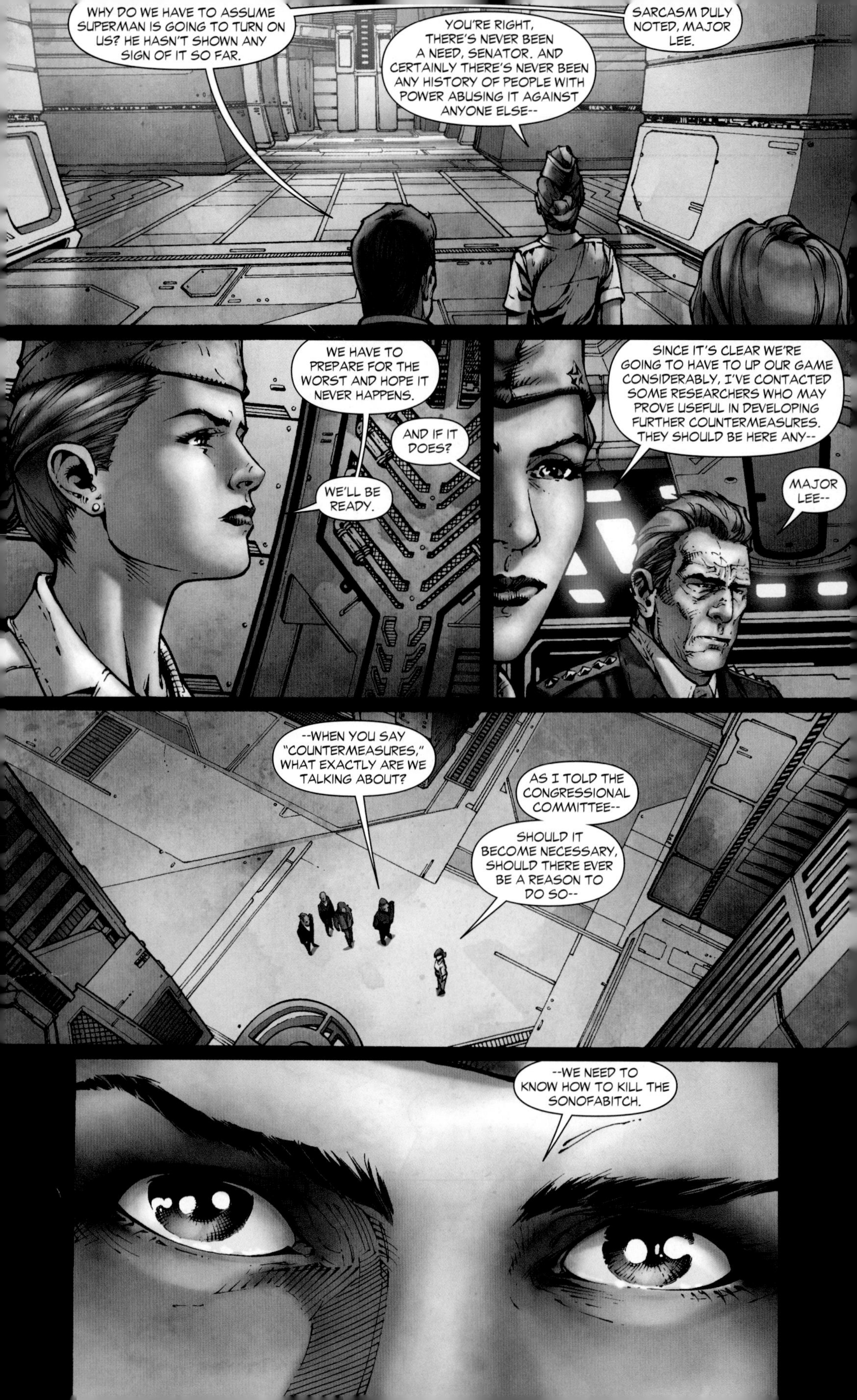
WHY DO WE HAVE TO ASSUME SUPERMAN IS GOING TO TURN ON US? HE HASN'T SHOWN ANY SIGN OF IT SO FAR.
YOU'RE RIGHT, THERE'S NEVER BEEN A NEED, SENATOR. AND CERTAINLY THERE'S NEVER BEEN ANY HISTORY OF PEOPLE WITH POWER ABUSING IT AGAINST ANYONE ELSE--
SARCASM DULY NOTED, MAJOR LEE.
WE HAVE TO PREPARE FOR THE WORST AND HOPE IT NEVER HAPPENS.
AND IF IT DOES?
WE'LL BE READY.
SINCE IT'S CLEAR WE'RE GOING TO HAVE TO UP OUR GAME CONSIDERABLY, I'VE CONTACTED SOME RESEARCHERS WHO MAY PROVE USEFUL IN DEVELOPING FURTHER COUNTERMEASURES. THEY SHOULD BE HERE ANY--
MAJOR LEE--
--WHEN YOU SAY "COUNTERMEASURES," WHAT EXACTLY ARE WE TALKING ABOUT?
AS I TOLD THE CONGRESSIONAL COMMITTEE--
SHOULD IT BECOME NECESSARY, SHOULD THERE EVER BE A REASON TO DO SO--
--WE NEED TO KNOW HOW TO KILL THE SONOFABITCH.

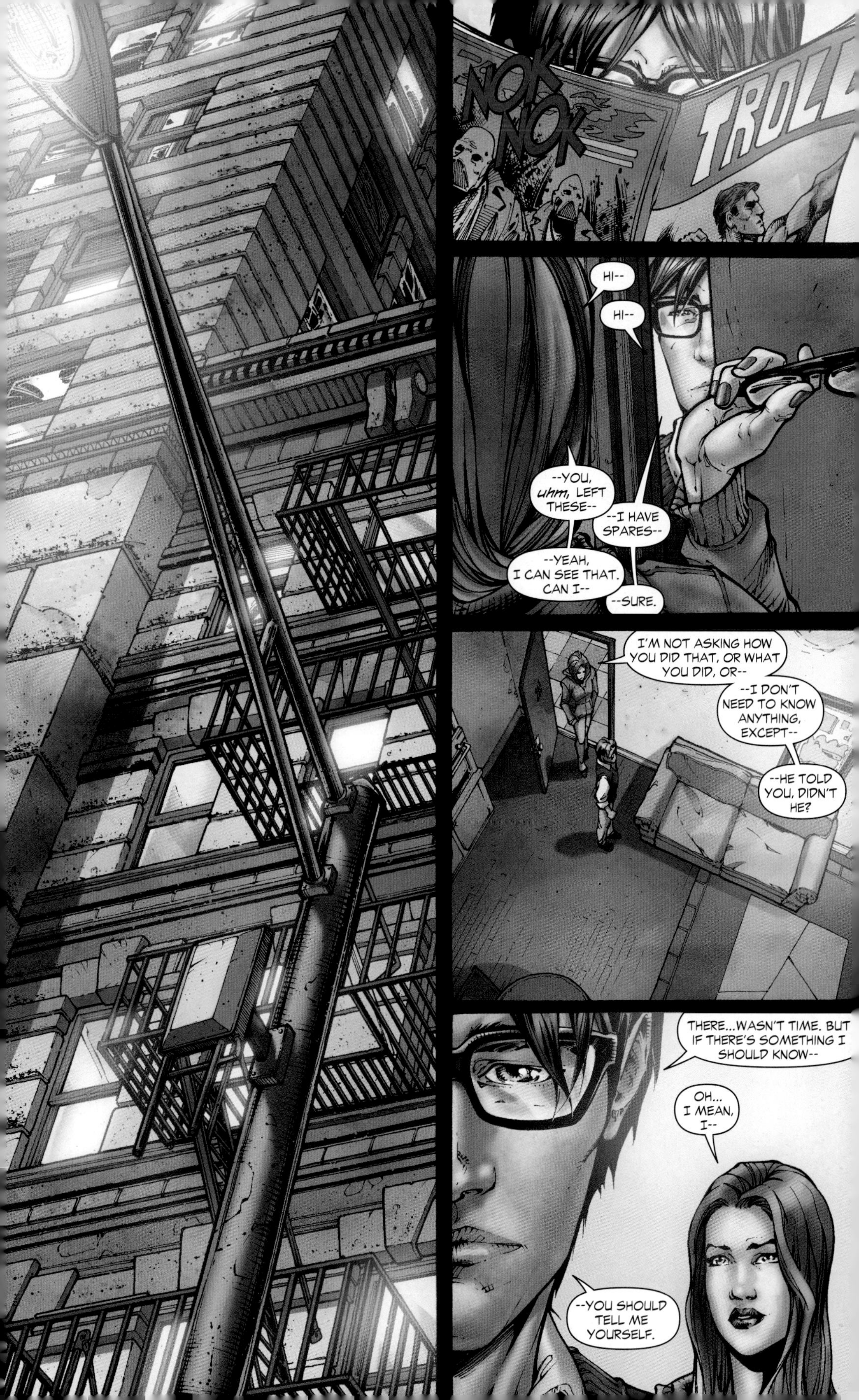
NOK NOK
TROLL
HI--
HI--
--YOU, *uhm*, LEFT THESE--
--I HAVE SPARES--
--YEAH, I CAN SEE THAT. CAN I--
--SURE.
I'M NOT ASKING HOW YOU DID THAT, OR WHAT YOU DID, OR--
--I DON'T NEED TO KNOW ANYTHING, EXCEPT--
--HE TOLD YOU, DIDN'T HE?
THERE...WASN'T TIME. BUT IF THERE'S SOMETHING I SHOULD KNOW--
OH... I MEAN, I--
--YOU SHOULD TELL ME YOURSELF.

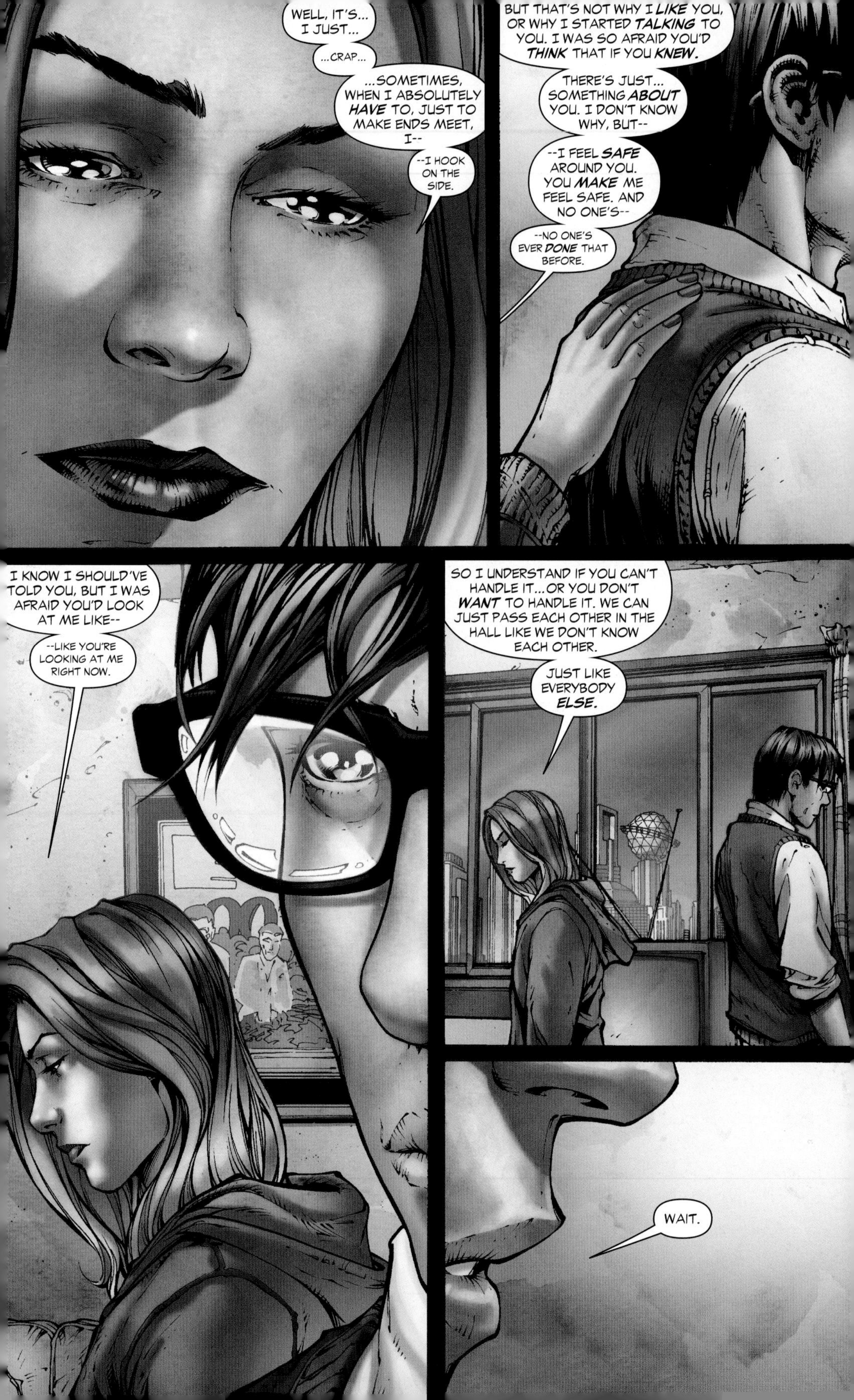
WELL, IT'S... I JUST...
...CRAP...
...SOMETIMES, WHEN I ABSOLUTELY HAVE TO, JUST TO MAKE ENDS MEET, I--
--I HOOK ON THE SIDE.
BUT THAT'S NOT WHY I LIKE YOU, OR WHY I STARTED TALKING TO YOU. I WAS SO AFRAID YOU'D THINK THAT IF YOU KNEW.
THERE'S JUST... SOMETHING ABOUT YOU. I DON'T KNOW WHY, BUT--
--I FEEL SAFE AROUND YOU. YOU MAKE ME FEEL SAFE. AND NO ONE'S--
--NO ONE'S EVER DONE THAT BEFORE.
I KNOW I SHOULD'VE TOLD YOU, BUT I WAS AFRAID YOU'D LOOK AT ME LIKE--
--LIKE YOU'RE LOOKING AT ME RIGHT NOW.
SO I UNDERSTAND IF YOU CAN'T HANDLE IT...OR YOU DON'T WANT TO HANDLE IT. WE CAN JUST PASS EACH OTHER IN THE HALL LIKE WE DON'T KNOW EACH OTHER.
JUST LIKE EVERYBODY ELSE.
WAIT.

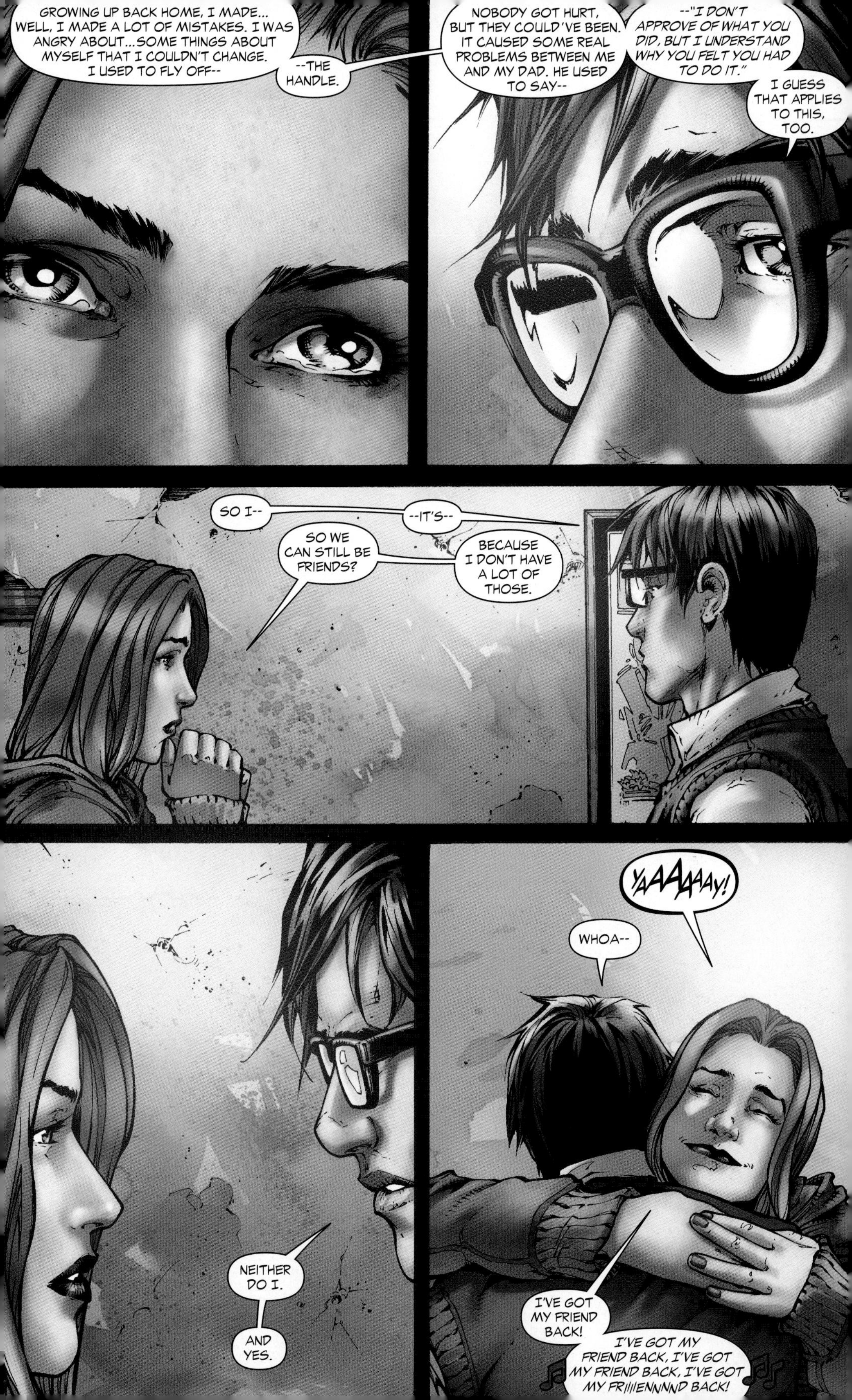
GROWING UP BACK HOME, I MADE... WELL, I MADE A LOT OF MISTAKES. I WAS ANGRY ABOUT...SOME THINGS ABOUT MYSELF THAT I COULDN'T CHANGE. I USED TO FLY OFF--
--THE HANDLE.
NOBODY GOT HURT, BUT THEY COULD'VE BEEN. IT CAUSED SOME REAL PROBLEMS BETWEEN ME AND MY DAD. HE USED TO SAY--
--"I DON'T APPROVE OF WHAT YOU DID, BUT I UNDERSTAND WHY YOU FELT YOU HAD TO DO IT."
I GUESS THAT APPLIES TO THIS, TOO.
SO I--
--IT'S--
SO WE CAN STILL BE FRIENDS?
BECAUSE I DON'T HAVE A LOT OF THOSE.
NEITHER DO I.
AND YES.
YAAAAAAY!
WHOA--
I'VE GOT MY FRIEND BACK!
I'VE GOT MY FRIEND BACK, I'VE GOT MY FRIEND BACK, I'VE GOT MY FRIIIIENNNND BACK!

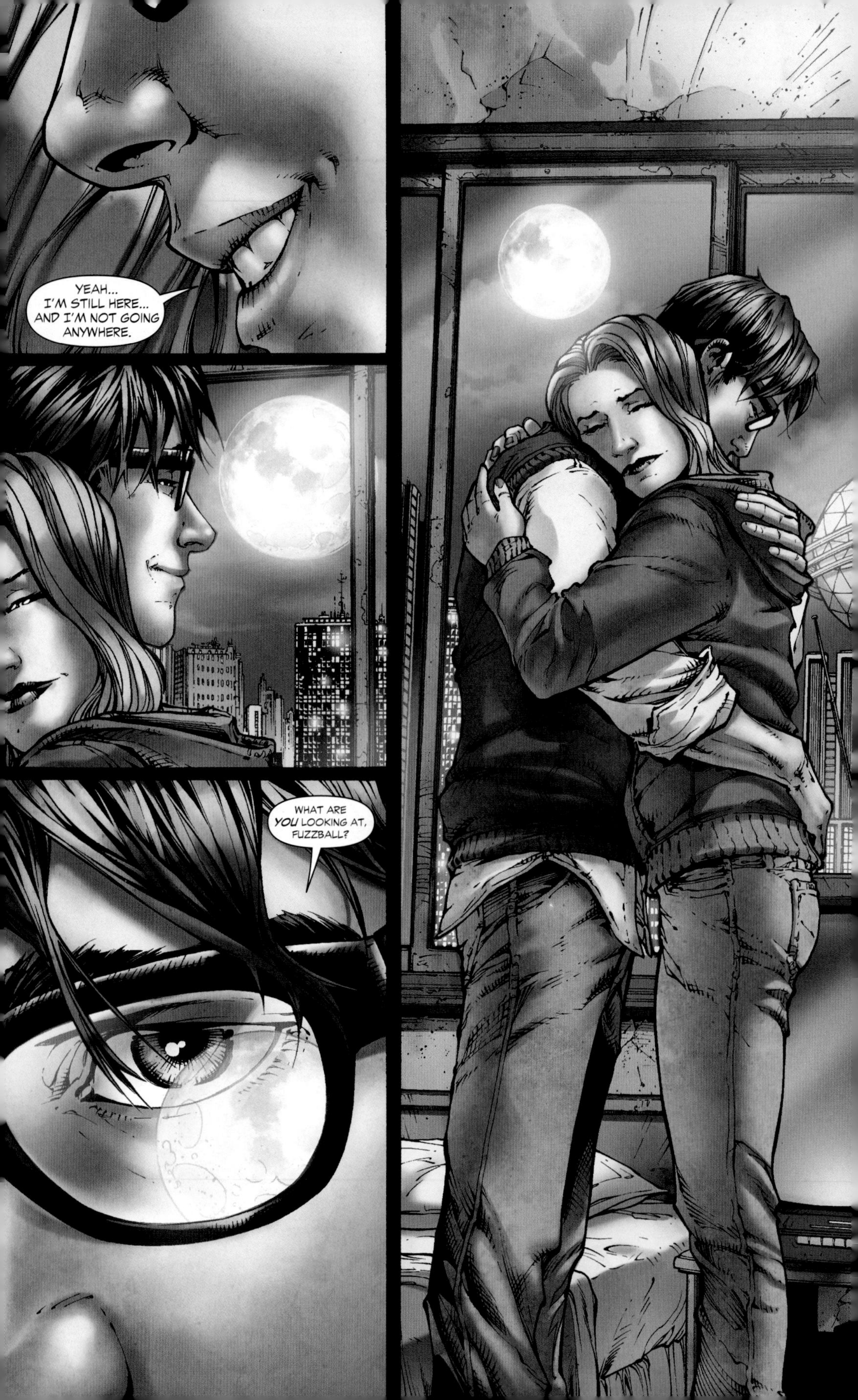
YEAH... I'M STILL HERE... AND I'M NOT GOING ANYWHERE.
WHAT ARE YOU LOOKING AT, FUZZBALL?

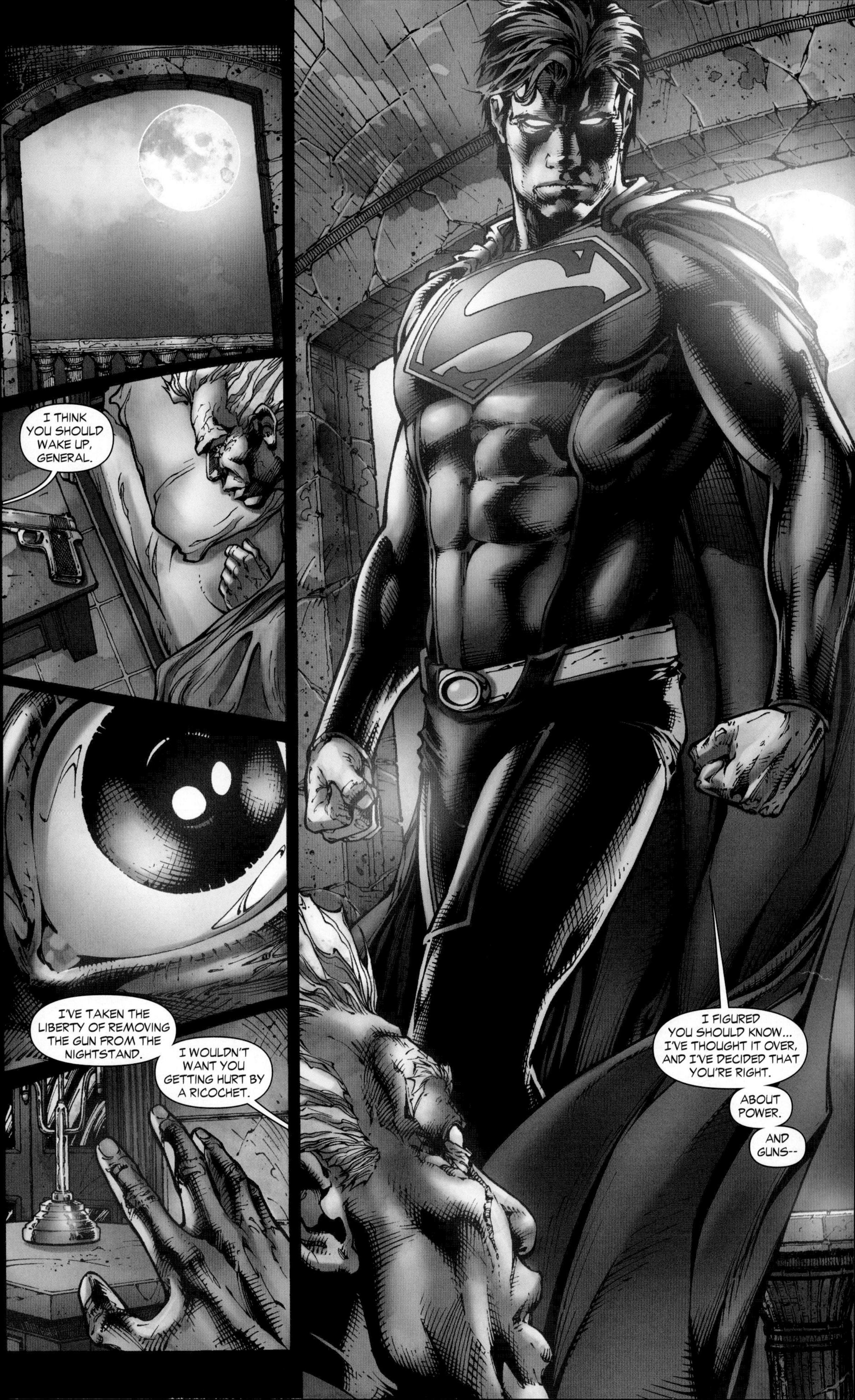
I THINK YOU SHOULD WAKE UP, GENERAL.
I'VE TAKEN THE LIBERTY OF REMOVING THE GUN FROM THE NIGHTSTAND.
I WOULDN'T WANT YOU GETTING HURT BY A RICOCHET.
I FIGURED YOU SHOULD KNOW... I'VE THOUGHT IT OVER, AND I'VE DECIDED THAT YOU'RE RIGHT.
ABOUT POWER.
AND GUNS--

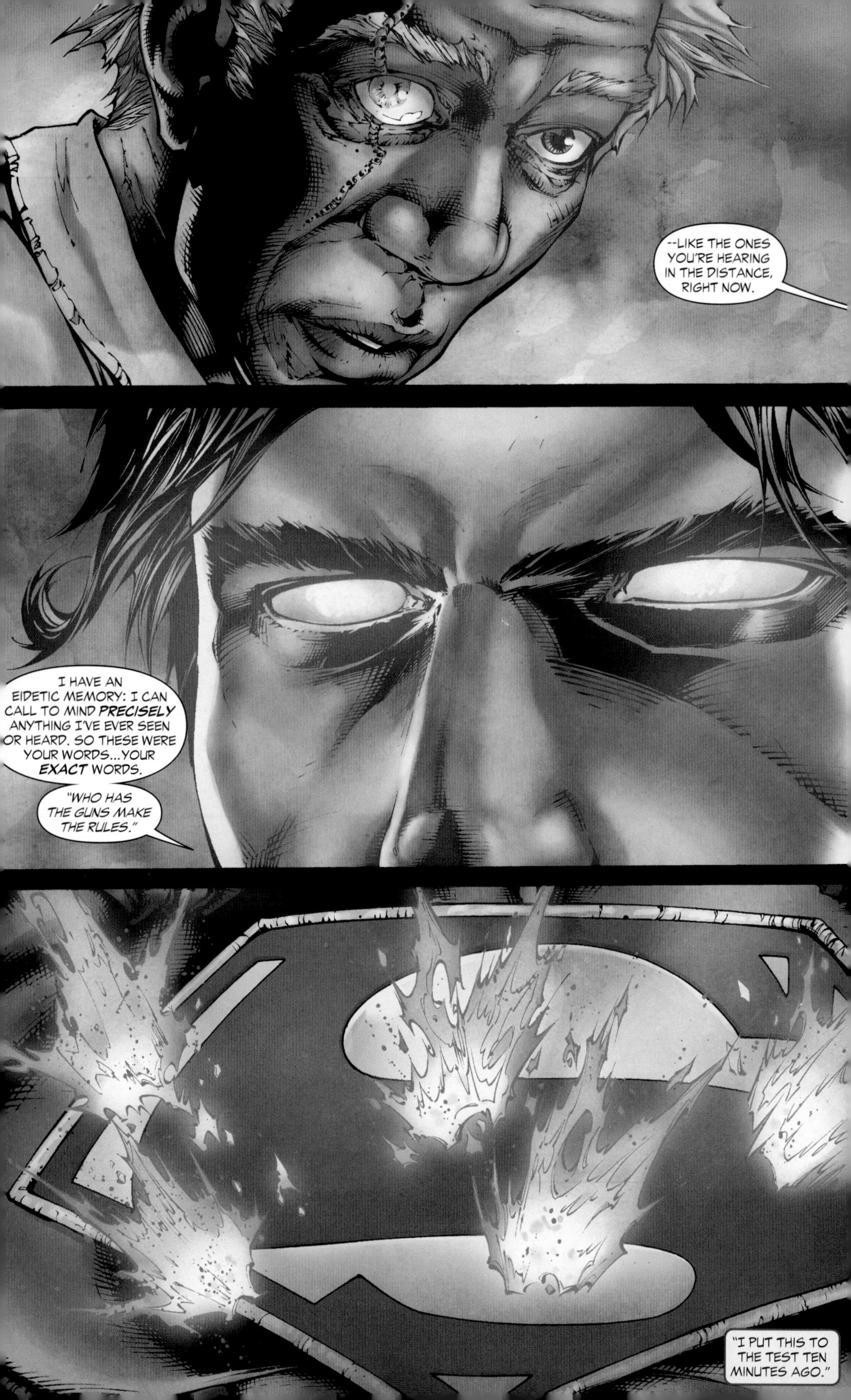
--LIKE THE ONES YOU'RE HEARING IN THE DISTANCE, RIGHT NOW.
I HAVE AN EIDETIC MEMORY: I CAN CALL TO MIND **PRECISELY** ANYTHING I'VE EVER SEEN OR HEARD. SO THESE WERE YOUR WORDS...YOUR **EXACT** WORDS.
"WHO HAS THE GUNS MAKE THE RULES."
"I PUT THIS TO THE TEST TEN MINUTES AGO."

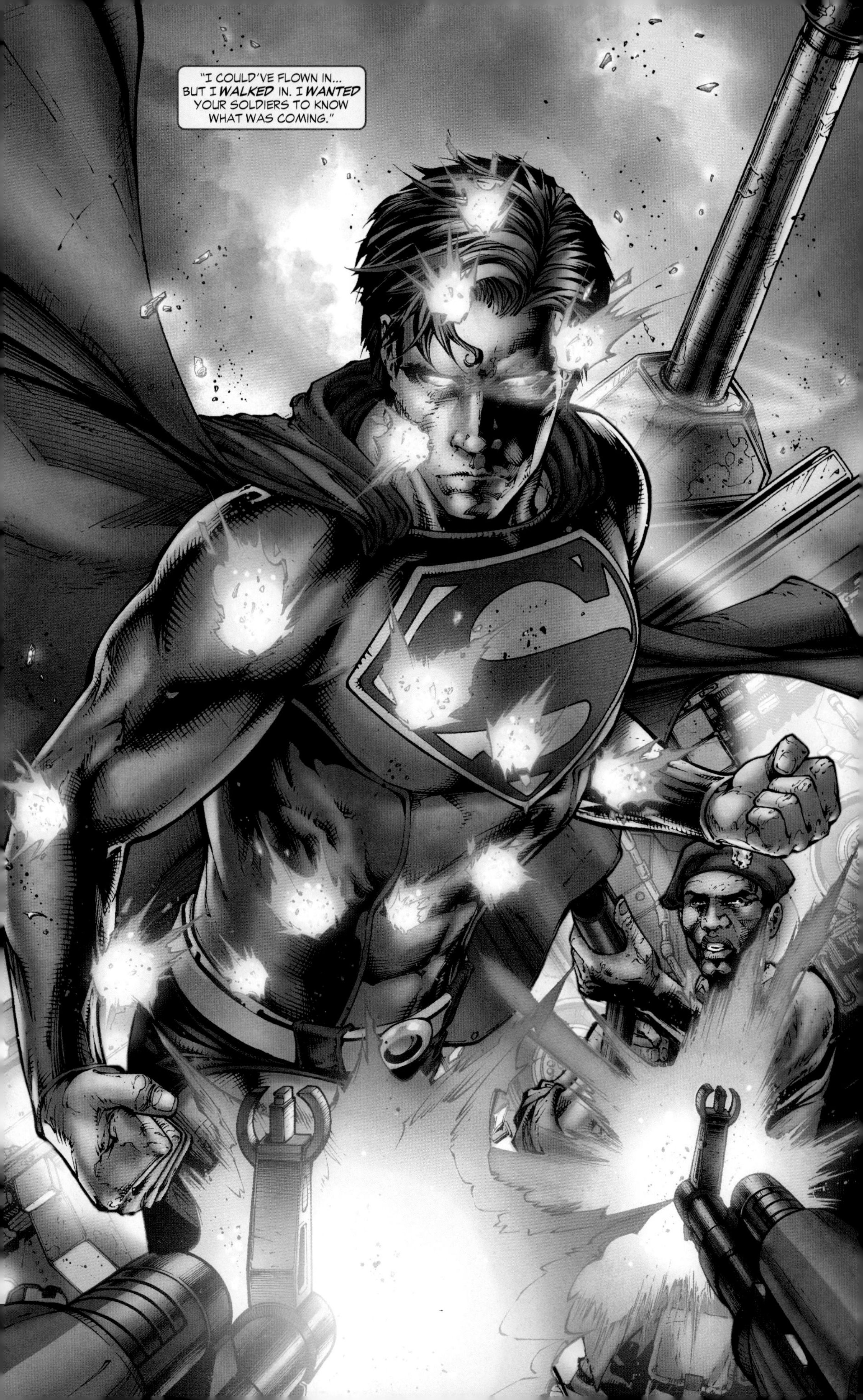
"I COULD'VE FLOWN IN... BUT I WALKED IN. I WANTED YOUR SOLDIERS TO KNOW WHAT WAS COMING."

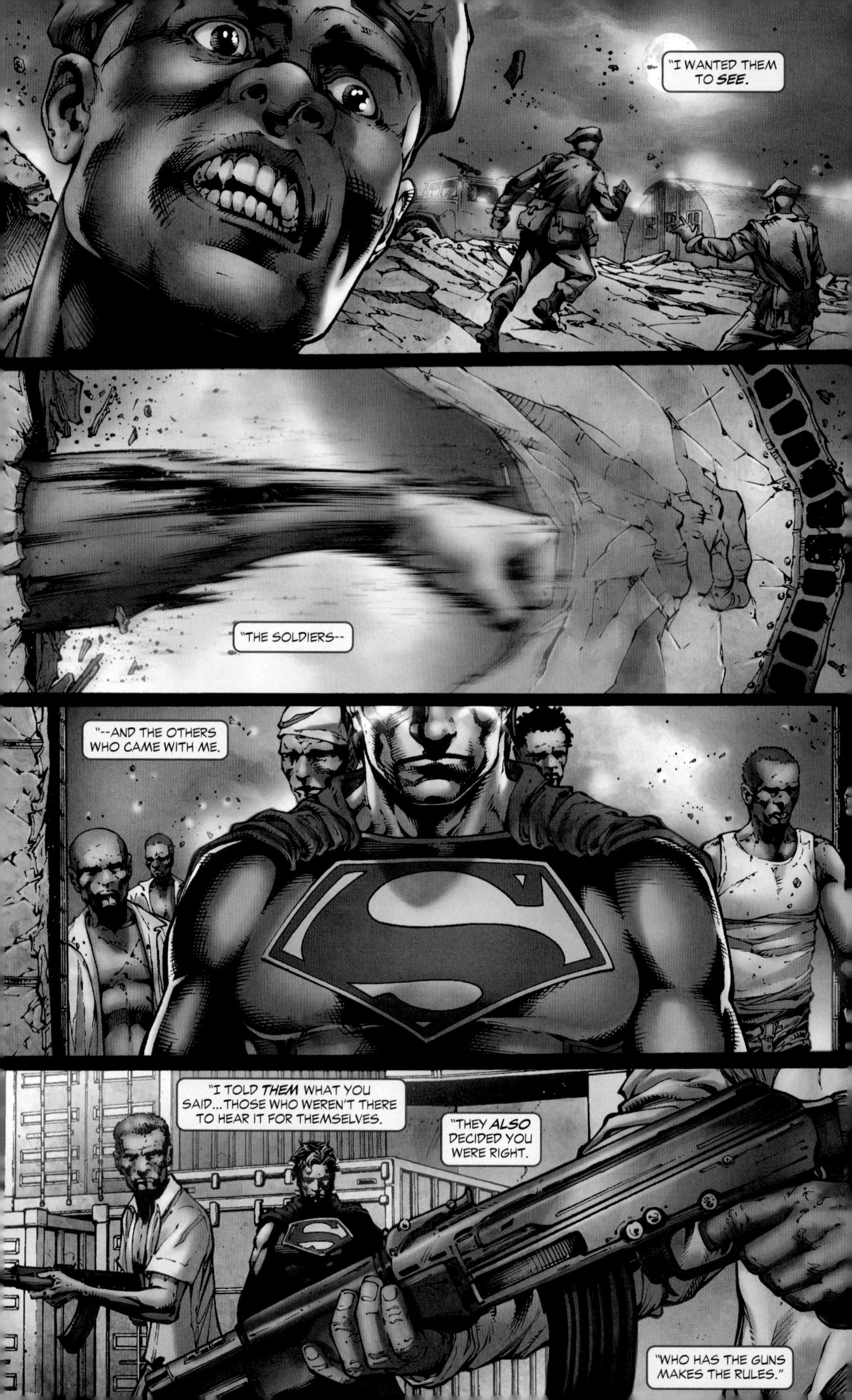
"I WANTED THEM TO SEE.
"THE SOLDIERS--
"--AND THE OTHERS WHO CAME WITH ME.
"I TOLD THEM WHAT YOU SAID...THOSE WHO WEREN'T THERE TO HEAR IT FOR THEMSELVES.
"THEY ALSO DECIDED YOU WERE RIGHT.
"WHO HAS THE GUNS MAKES THE RULES."

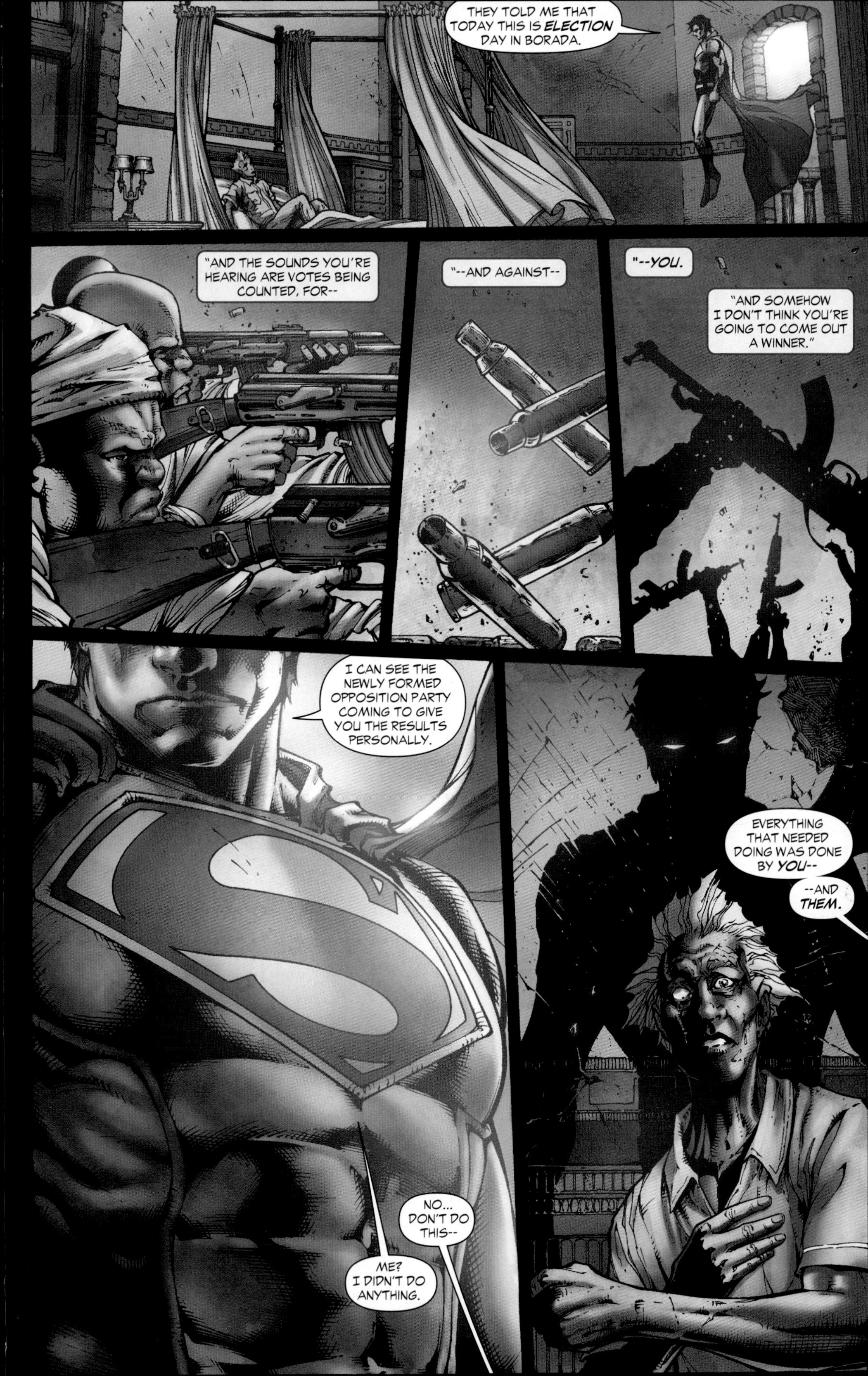
THEY TOLD ME THAT TODAY THIS IS ELECTION DAY IN BORADA.
"AND THE SOUNDS YOU'RE HEARING ARE VOTES BEING COUNTED, FOR--
"--AND AGAINST--
"--YOU.
"AND SOMEHOW I DON'T THINK YOU'RE GOING TO COME OUT A WINNER."
I CAN SEE THE NEWLY FORMED OPPOSITION PARTY COMING TO GIVE YOU THE RESULTS PERSONALLY.
EVERYTHING THAT NEEDED DOING WAS DONE BY YOU--
--AND THEM.
NO... DON'T DO THIS--
ME? I DIDN'T DO ANYTHING.

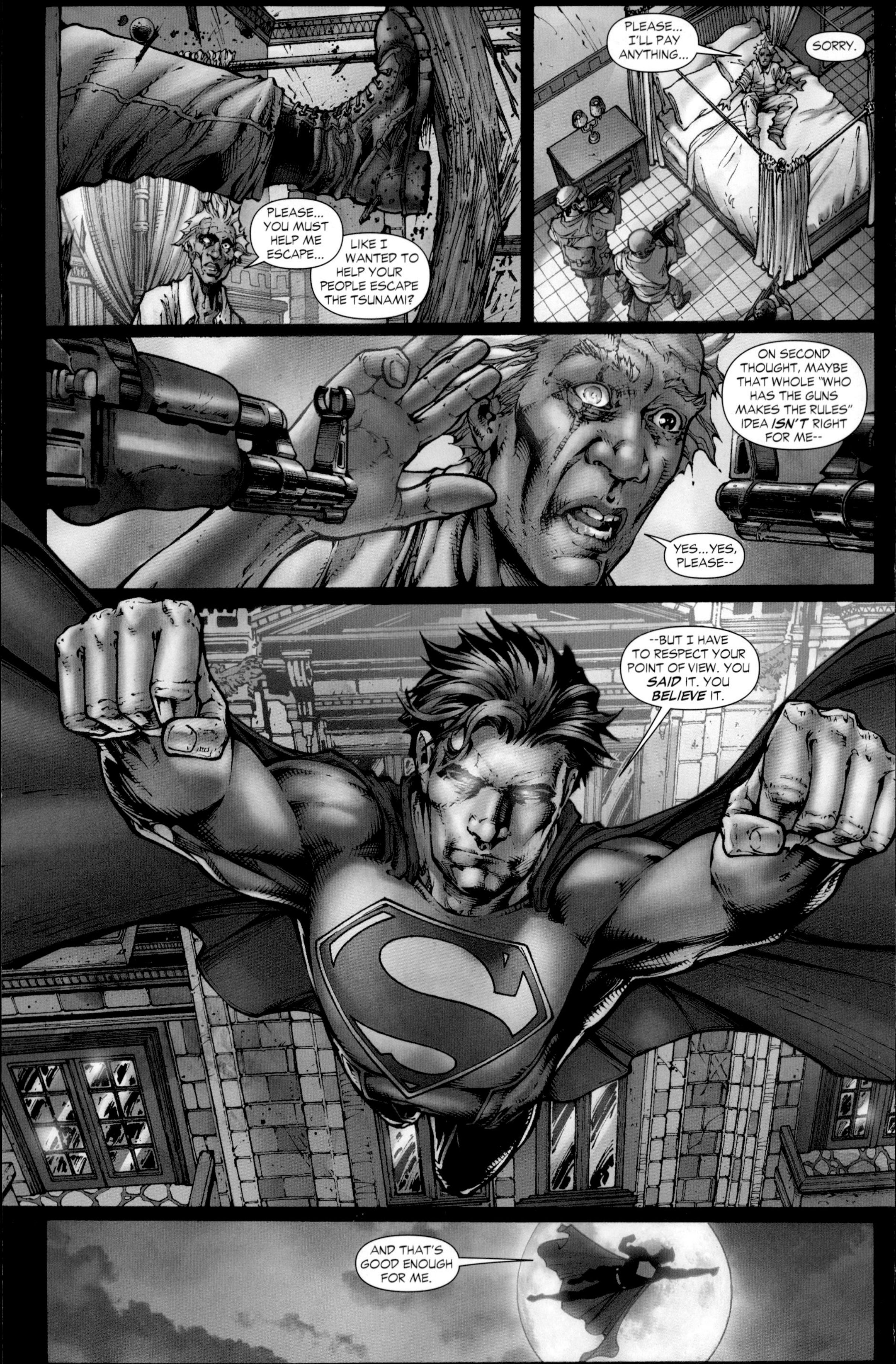
PLEASE... YOU MUST HELP ME ESCAPE...
LIKE I WANTED TO HELP YOUR PEOPLE ESCAPE THE TSUNAMI?
PLEASE... I'LL PAY ANYTHING...
SORRY.
ON SECOND THOUGHT, MAYBE THAT WHOLE "WHO HAS THE GUNS MAKES THE RULES" IDEA *ISN'T* RIGHT FOR ME--
YES...YES, PLEASE--
--BUT I HAVE TO RESPECT YOUR POINT OF VIEW. YOU *SAID* IT. YOU *BELIEVE* IT.
AND THAT'S GOOD ENOUGH FOR ME.

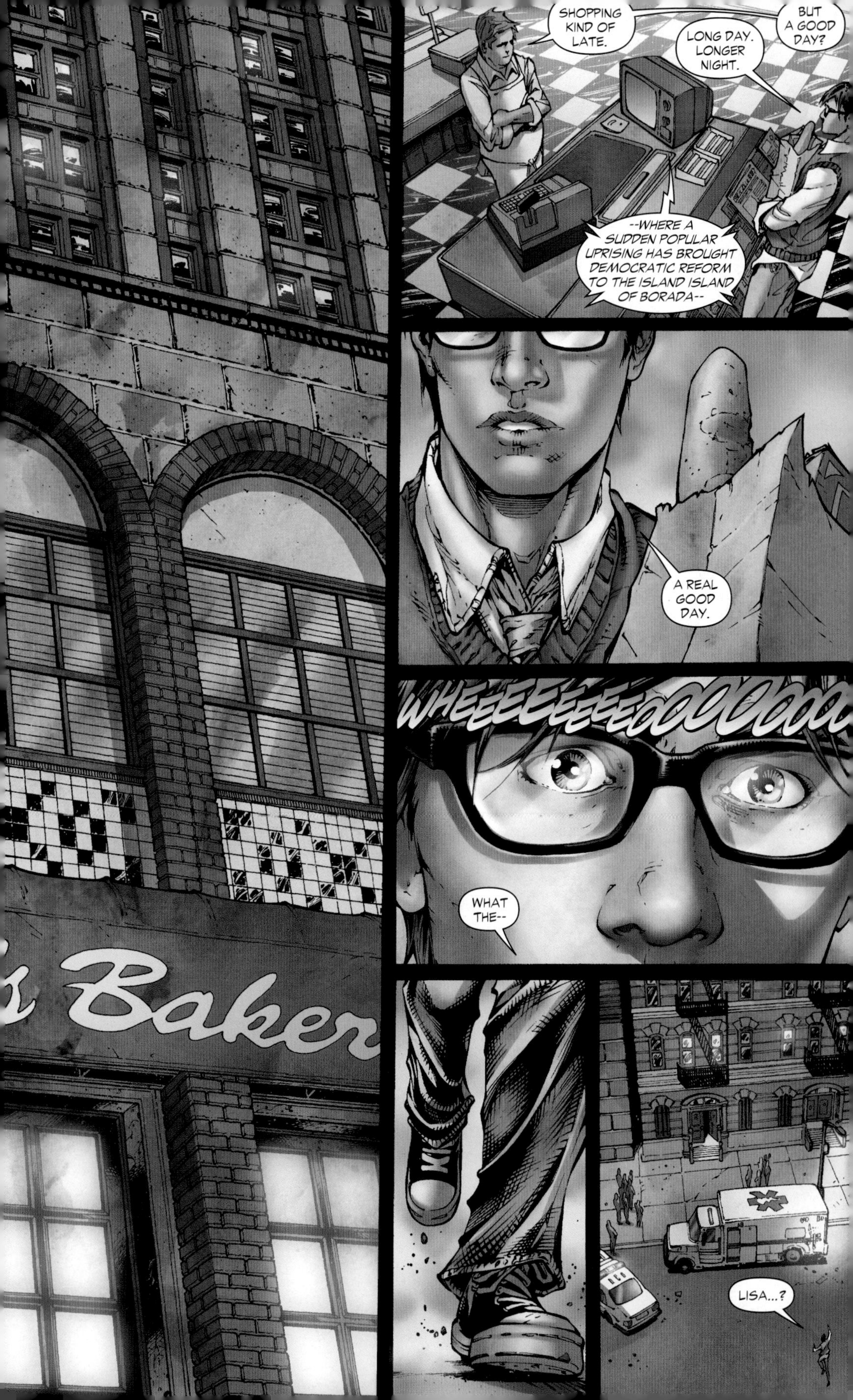

SHOPPING KIND OF LATE.
LONG DAY. LONGER NIGHT.
BUT A GOOD DAY?
--WHERE A SUDDEN POPULAR UPRISING HAS BROUGHT DEMOCRATIC REFORM TO THE ISLAND ISLAND OF BORADA--
A REAL GOOD DAY.
WHEEEEEEEEOOOOOOaa
WHAT THE--
LISA...?

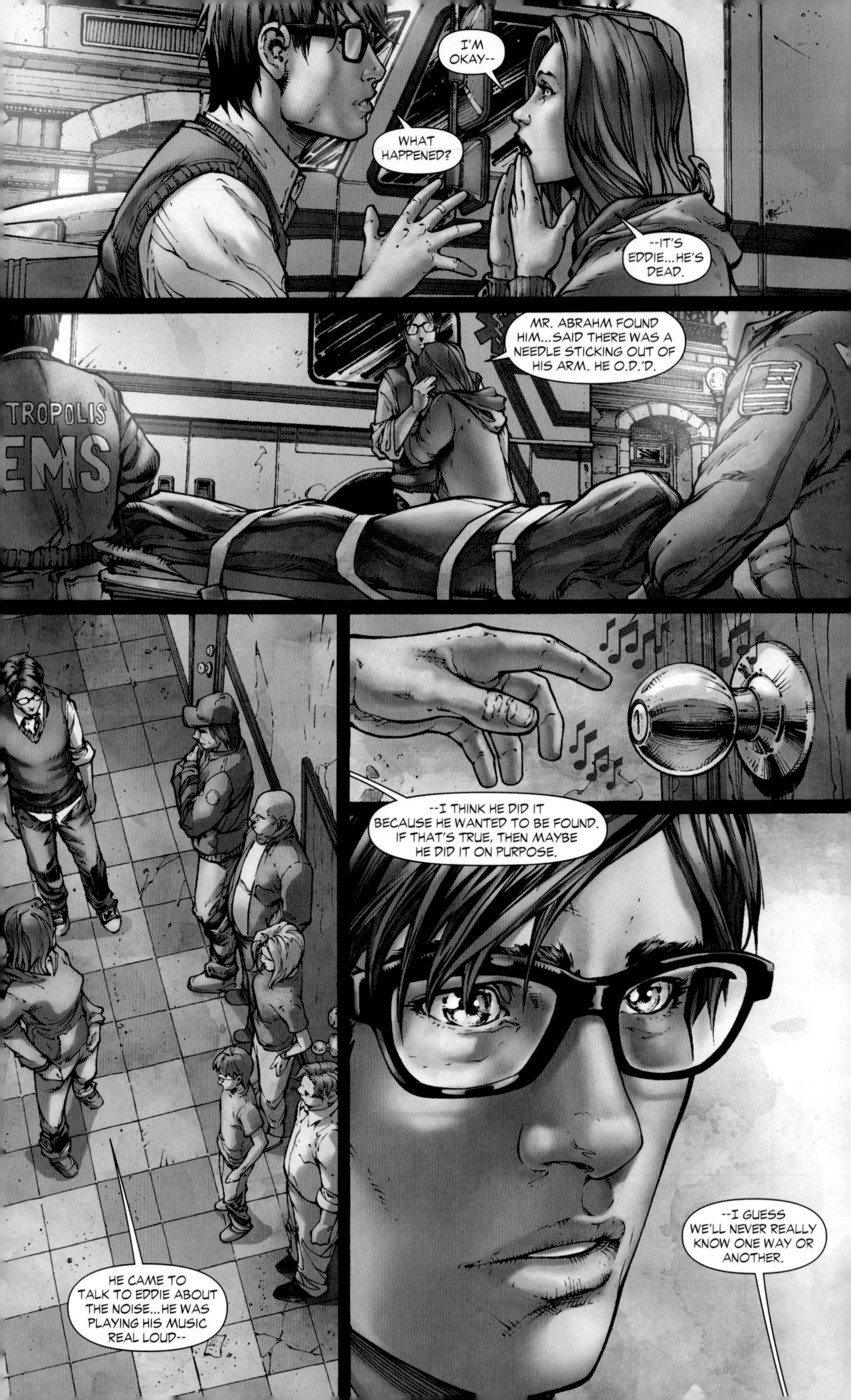
I'M OKAY--
WHAT HAPPENED?
--IT'S EDDIE...HE'S DEAD.
MR. ABRAHM FOUND HIM...SAID THERE WAS A NEEDLE STICKING OUT OF HIS ARM. HE O.D.'D.
TROPOLIS EMS
HE CAME TO TALK TO EDDIE ABOUT THE NOISE...HE WAS PLAYING HIS MUSIC REAL LOUD--
--I THINK HE DID IT BECAUSE HE WANTED TO BE FOUND. IF THAT'S TRUE, THEN MAYBE HE DID IT ON PURPOSE.
--I GUESS WE'LL NEVER REALLY KNOW ONE WAY OR ANOTHER.

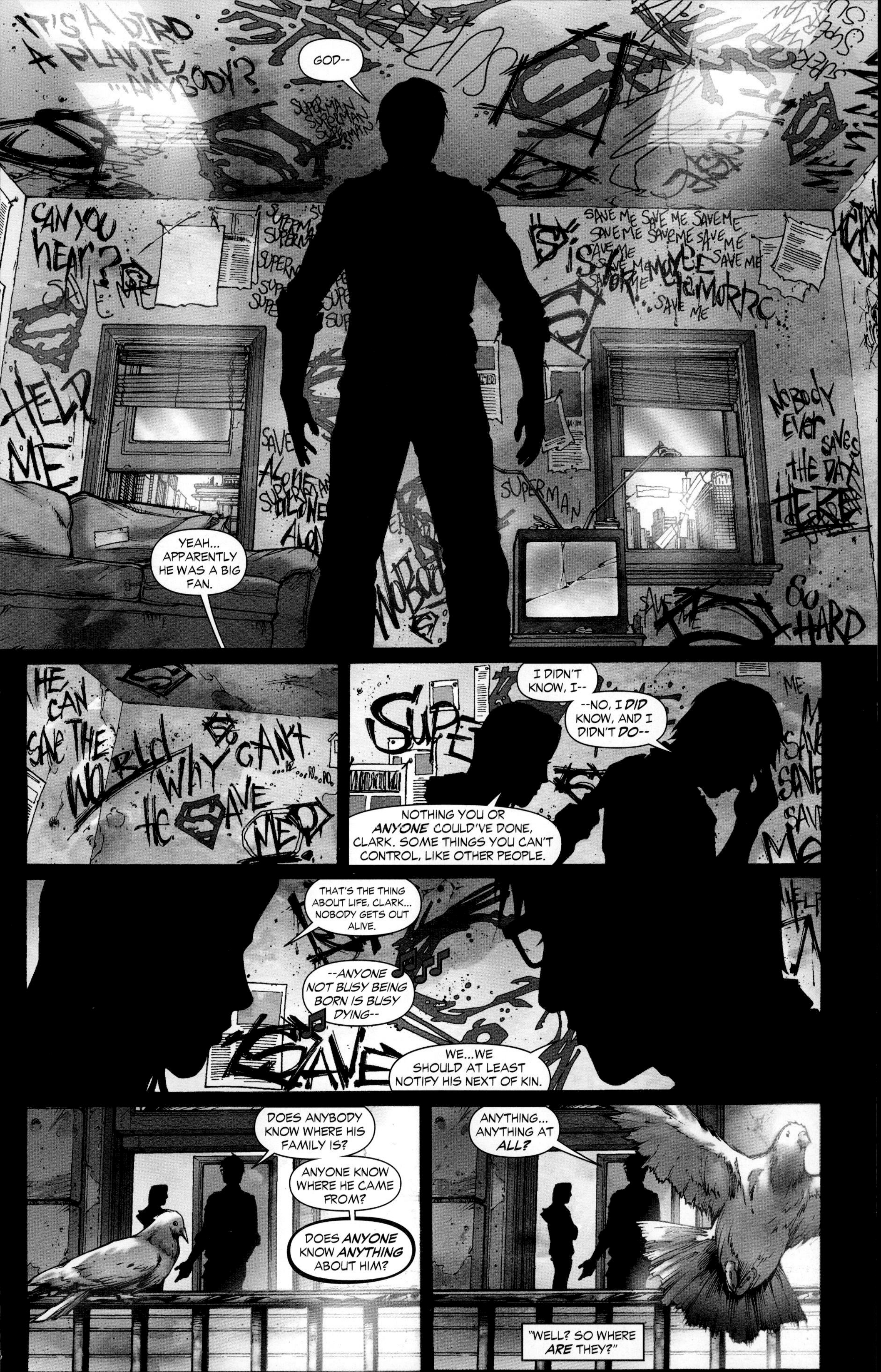

IT'S A BIRD
A PLANE
...ANYBODY?
GOD--
SAVE ME SAVE ME SAVE ME
CAN YOU
hear?
HELP
ME
NOBODY
EVER
SAVES
THE DAY
HERE
YEAH... APPARENTLY HE WAS A BIG FAN.
SO HARD
HE CAN
SAVE THE
WORLD
WHY CAN'T
HE SAVE
ME
I DIDN'T KNOW, I--
--NO, I DID KNOW, AND I DIDN'T DO--
NOTHING YOU OR ANYONE COULD'VE DONE, CLARK. SOME THINGS YOU CAN'T CONTROL, LIKE OTHER PEOPLE.
THAT'S THE THING ABOUT LIFE, CLARK... NOBODY GETS OUT ALIVE.
--ANYONE NOT BUSY BEING BORN IS BUSY DYING--
SAVE
WE...WE SHOULD AT LEAST NOTIFY HIS NEXT OF KIN.
DOES ANYBODY KNOW WHERE HIS FAMILY IS?
ANYONE KNOW WHERE HE CAME FROM?
DOES ANYONE KNOW ANYTHING ABOUT HIM?
ANYTHING... ANYTHING AT ALL?
"WELL? SO WHERE ARE THEY?"

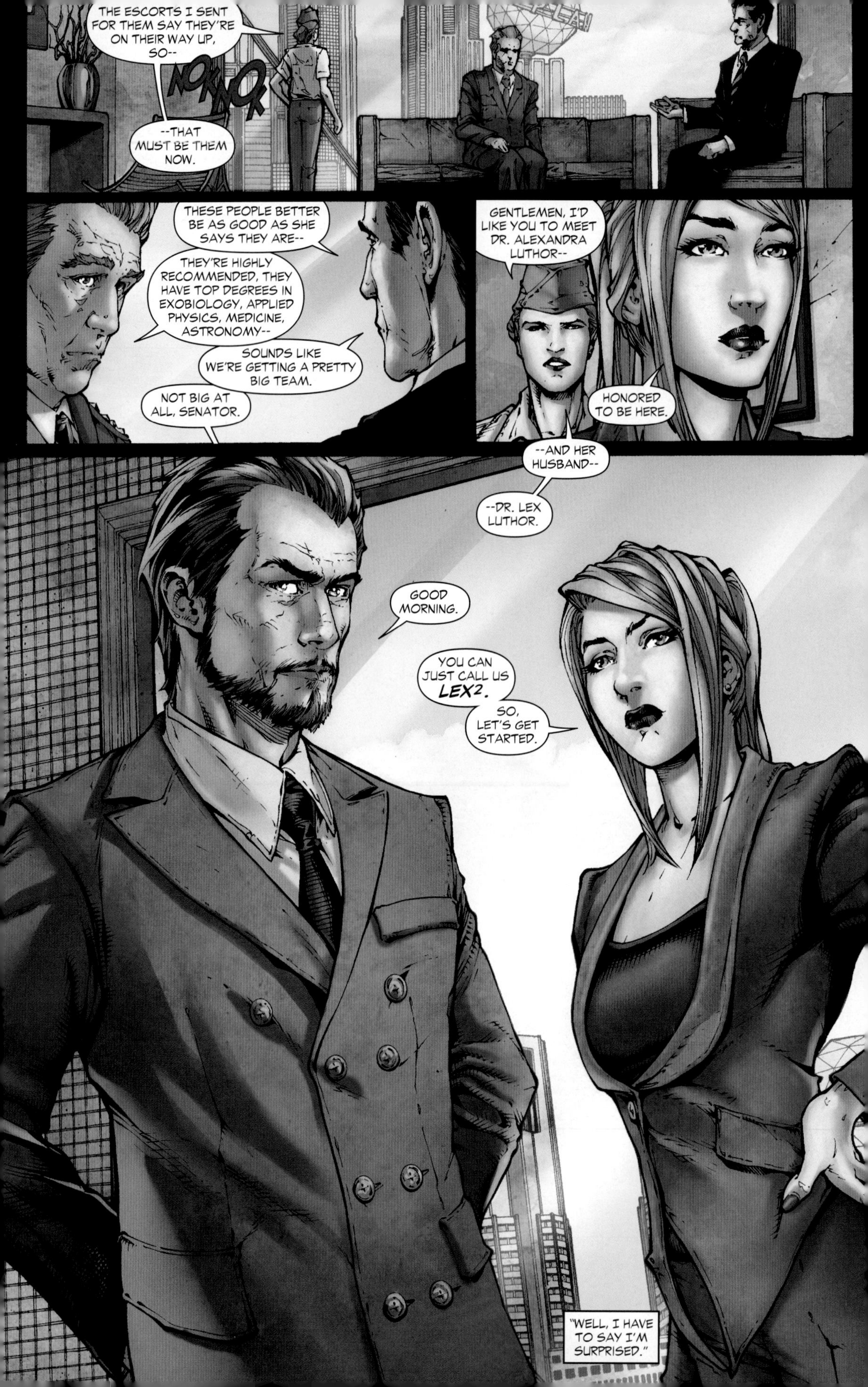
THE ESCORTS I SENT FOR THEM SAY THEY'RE ON THEIR WAY UP, SO--
NOKNOK
--THAT MUST BE THEM NOW.
THESE PEOPLE BETTER BE AS GOOD AS SHE SAYS THEY ARE--
THEY'RE HIGHLY RECOMMENDED, THEY HAVE TOP DEGREES IN EXOBIOLOGY, APPLIED PHYSICS, MEDICINE, ASTRONOMY--
SOUNDS LIKE WE'RE GETTING A PRETTY BIG TEAM.
NOT BIG AT ALL, SENATOR.
GENTLEMEN, I'D LIKE YOU TO MEET DR. ALEXANDRA LUTHOR--
HONORED TO BE HERE.
--AND HER HUSBAND--
--DR. LEX LUTHOR.
GOOD MORNING.
YOU CAN JUST CALL US LEX2.
SO, LET'S GET STARTED.
"WELL, I HAVE TO SAY I'M SURPRISED."

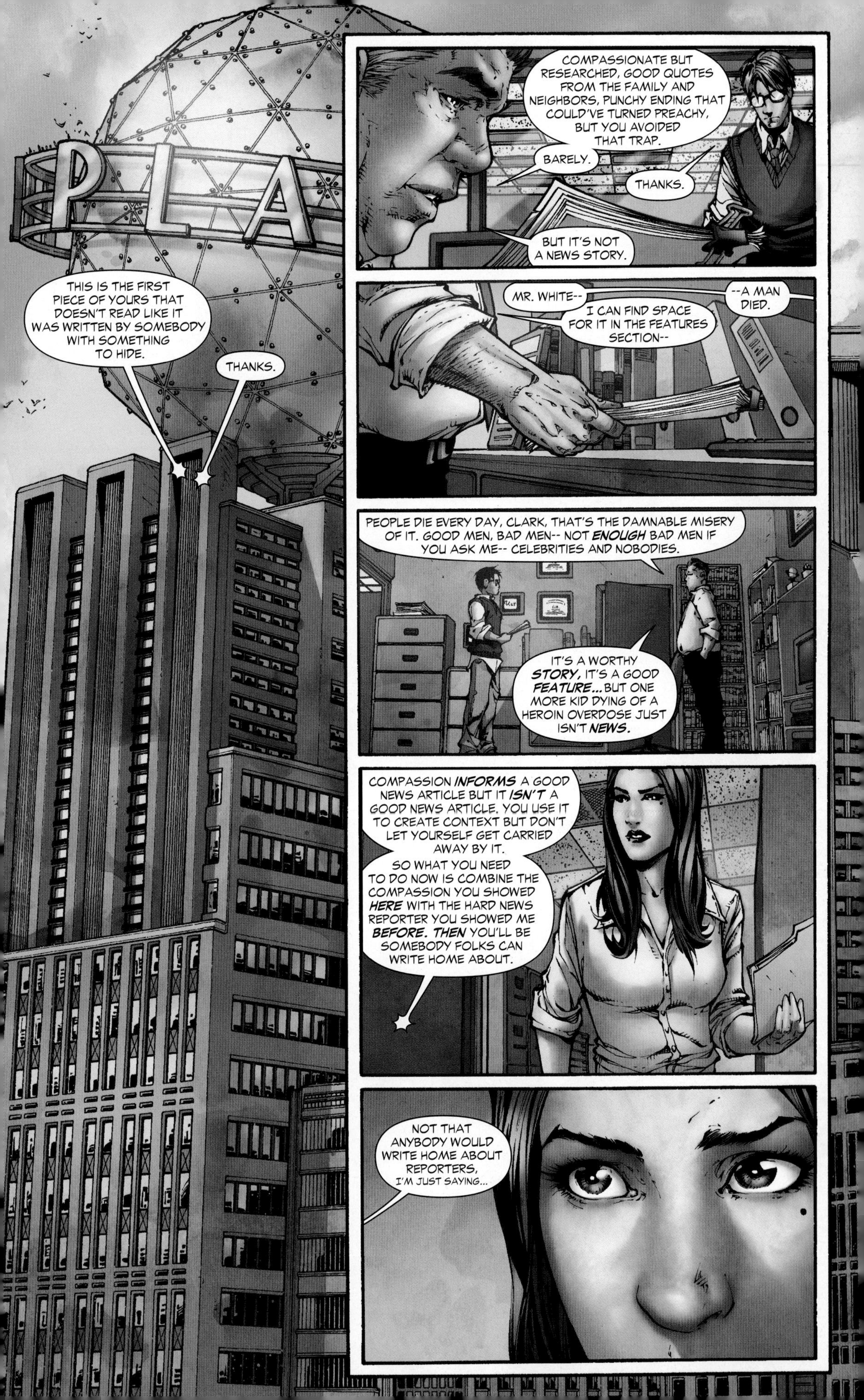
PLA
THIS IS THE FIRST PIECE OF YOURS THAT DOESN'T READ LIKE IT WAS WRITTEN BY SOMEBODY WITH SOMETHING TO HIDE.
THANKS.
COMPASSIONATE BUT RESEARCHED, GOOD QUOTES FROM THE FAMILY AND NEIGHBORS, PUNCHY ENDING THAT COULD'VE TURNED PREACHY, BUT YOU AVOIDED THAT TRAP.
BARELY.
THANKS.
BUT IT'S NOT A NEWS STORY.
MR. WHITE--
I CAN FIND SPACE FOR IT IN THE FEATURES SECTION--
--A MAN DIED.
PEOPLE DIE EVERY DAY, CLARK, THAT'S THE DAMNABLE MISERY OF IT. GOOD MEN, BAD MEN-- NOT ENOUGH BAD MEN IF YOU ASK ME-- CELEBRITIES AND NOBODIES.
IT'S A WORTHY STORY, IT'S A GOOD FEATURE... BUT ONE MORE KID DYING OF A HEROIN OVERDOSE JUST ISN'T NEWS.
COMPASSION INFORMS A GOOD NEWS ARTICLE BUT IT ISN'T A GOOD NEWS ARTICLE. YOU USE IT TO CREATE CONTEXT BUT DON'T LET YOURSELF GET CARRIED AWAY BY IT.
SO WHAT YOU NEED TO DO NOW IS COMBINE THE COMPASSION YOU SHOWED HERE WITH THE HARD NEWS REPORTER YOU SHOWED ME BEFORE. THEN YOU'LL BE SOMEBODY FOLKS CAN WRITE HOME ABOUT.
NOT THAT ANYBODY WOULD WRITE HOME ABOUT REPORTERS, I'M JUST SAYING...

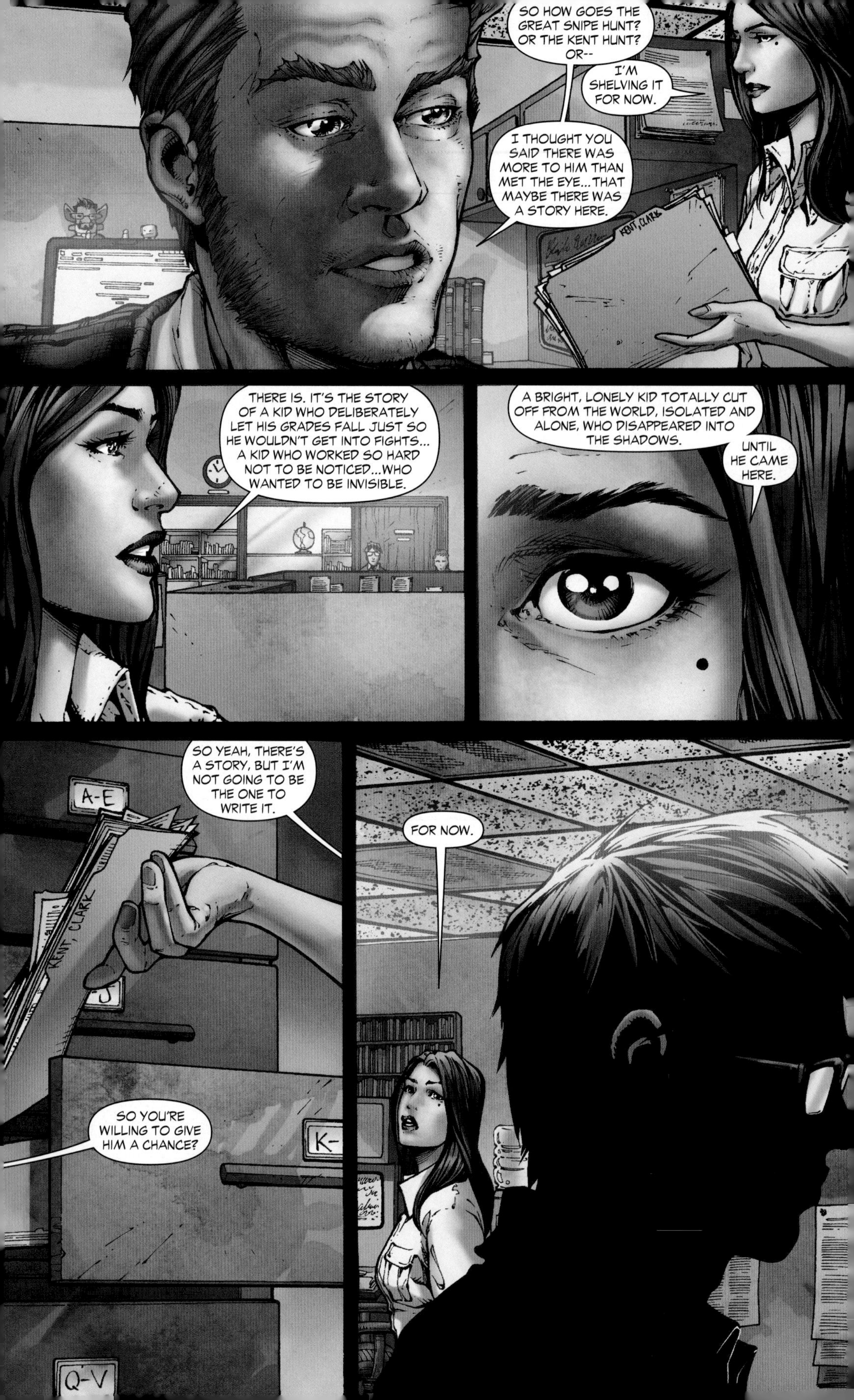
SO HOW GOES THE GREAT SNIPE HUNT? OR THE KENT HUNT? OR--
I'M SHELVING IT FOR NOW.
I THOUGHT YOU SAID THERE WAS MORE TO HIM THAN MET THE EYE...THAT MAYBE THERE WAS A STORY HERE.
KENT, CLARK
THERE IS. IT'S THE STORY OF A KID WHO DELIBERATELY LET HIS GRADES FALL JUST SO HE WOULDN'T GET INTO FIGHTS... A KID WHO WORKED SO HARD NOT TO BE NOTICED...WHO WANTED TO BE INVISIBLE.
A BRIGHT, LONELY KID TOTALLY CUT OFF FROM THE WORLD, ISOLATED AND ALONE, WHO DISAPPEARED INTO THE SHADOWS.
UNTIL HE CAME HERE.
SO YEAH, THERE'S A STORY, BUT I'M NOT GOING TO BE THE ONE TO WRITE IT.
A-E
KENT, CLARK
FOR NOW.
SO YOU'RE WILLING TO GIVE HIM A CHANCE?
K-
Q-V

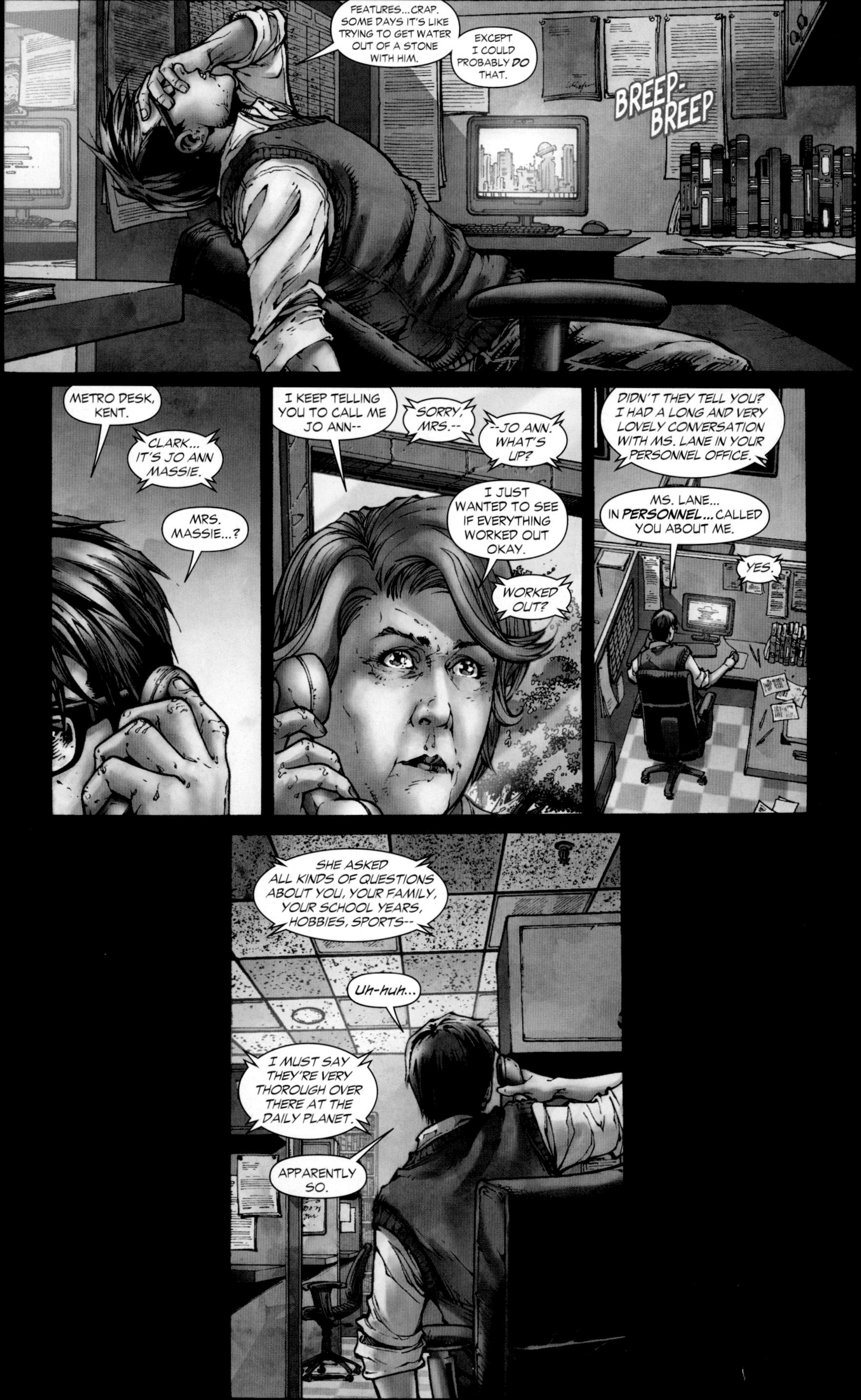
FEATURES...CRAP. SOME DAYS IT'S LIKE TRYING TO GET WATER OUT OF A STONE WITH HIM.
EXCEPT I COULD PROBABLY DO THAT.
BREEP-BREEP
METRO DESK, KENT.
CLARK... IT'S JO ANN MASSIE.
MRS. MASSIE...?
I KEEP TELLING YOU TO CALL ME JO ANN--
SORRY, MRS.--
--JO ANN. WHAT'S UP?
I JUST WANTED TO SEE IF EVERYTHING WORKED OUT OKAY.
WORKED OUT?
DIDN'T THEY TELL YOU? I HAD A LONG AND VERY LOVELY CONVERSATION WITH MS. LANE IN YOUR PERSONNEL OFFICE.
MS. LANE... IN PERSONNEL... CALLED YOU ABOUT ME.
YES.
SHE ASKED ALL KINDS OF QUESTIONS ABOUT YOU, YOUR FAMILY, YOUR SCHOOL YEARS, HOBBIES, SPORTS--
Uh-huh...
I MUST SAY THEY'RE VERY THOROUGH OVER THERE AT THE DAILY PLANET.
APPARENTLY SO.

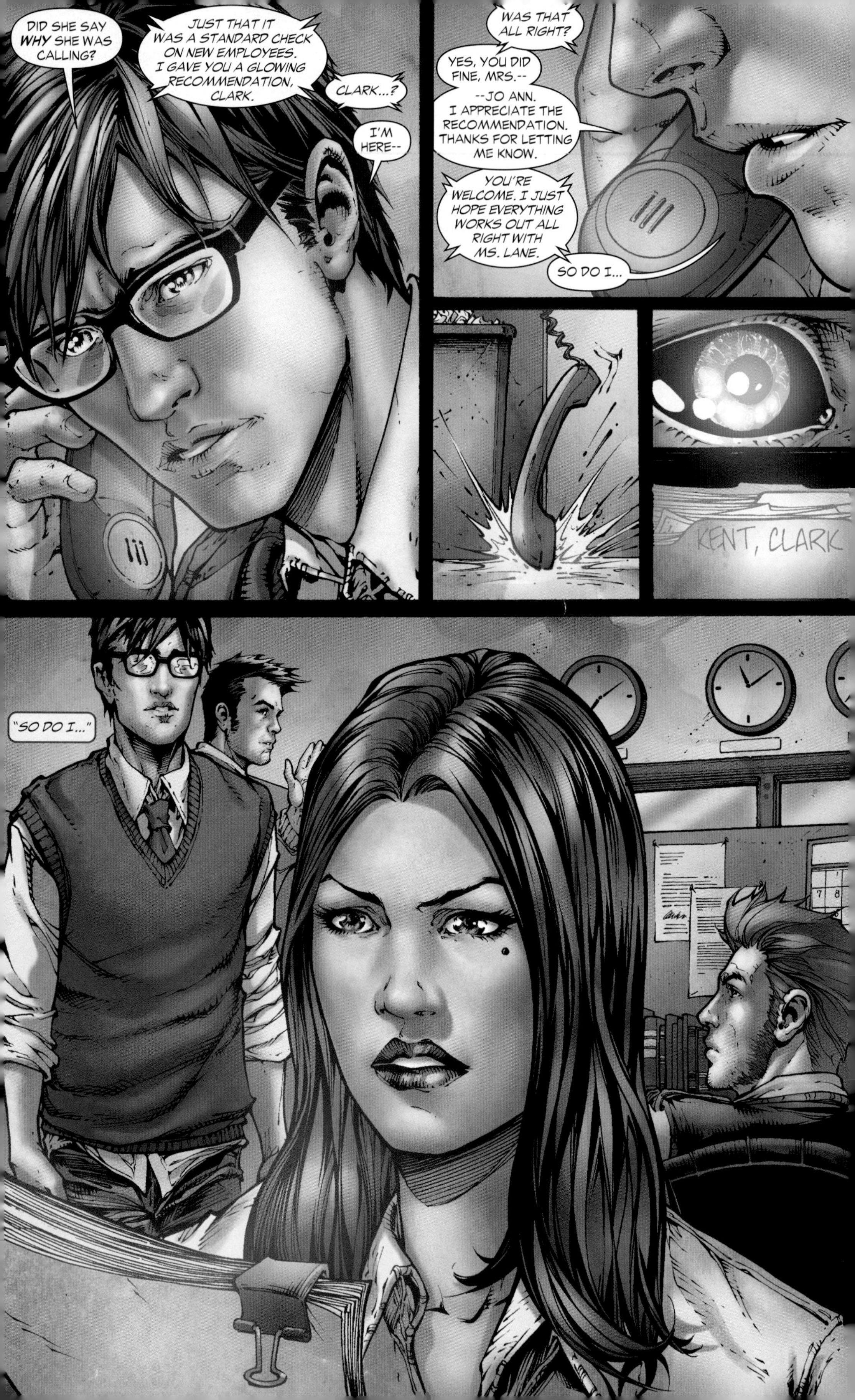
DID SHE SAY **WHY** SHE WAS CALLING?
JUST THAT IT WAS A STANDARD CHECK ON NEW EMPLOYEES. I GAVE YOU A GLOWING RECOMMENDATION, CLARK.
CLARK...?
I'M HERE--
WAS THAT ALL RIGHT?
YES, YOU DID FINE, MRS.--
--JO ANN. I APPRECIATE THE RECOMMENDATION. THANKS FOR LETTING ME KNOW.
YOU'RE WELCOME. I JUST HOPE EVERYTHING WORKS OUT ALL RIGHT WITH MS. LANE.
SO DO I...
KENT, CLARK
"SO DO I..."

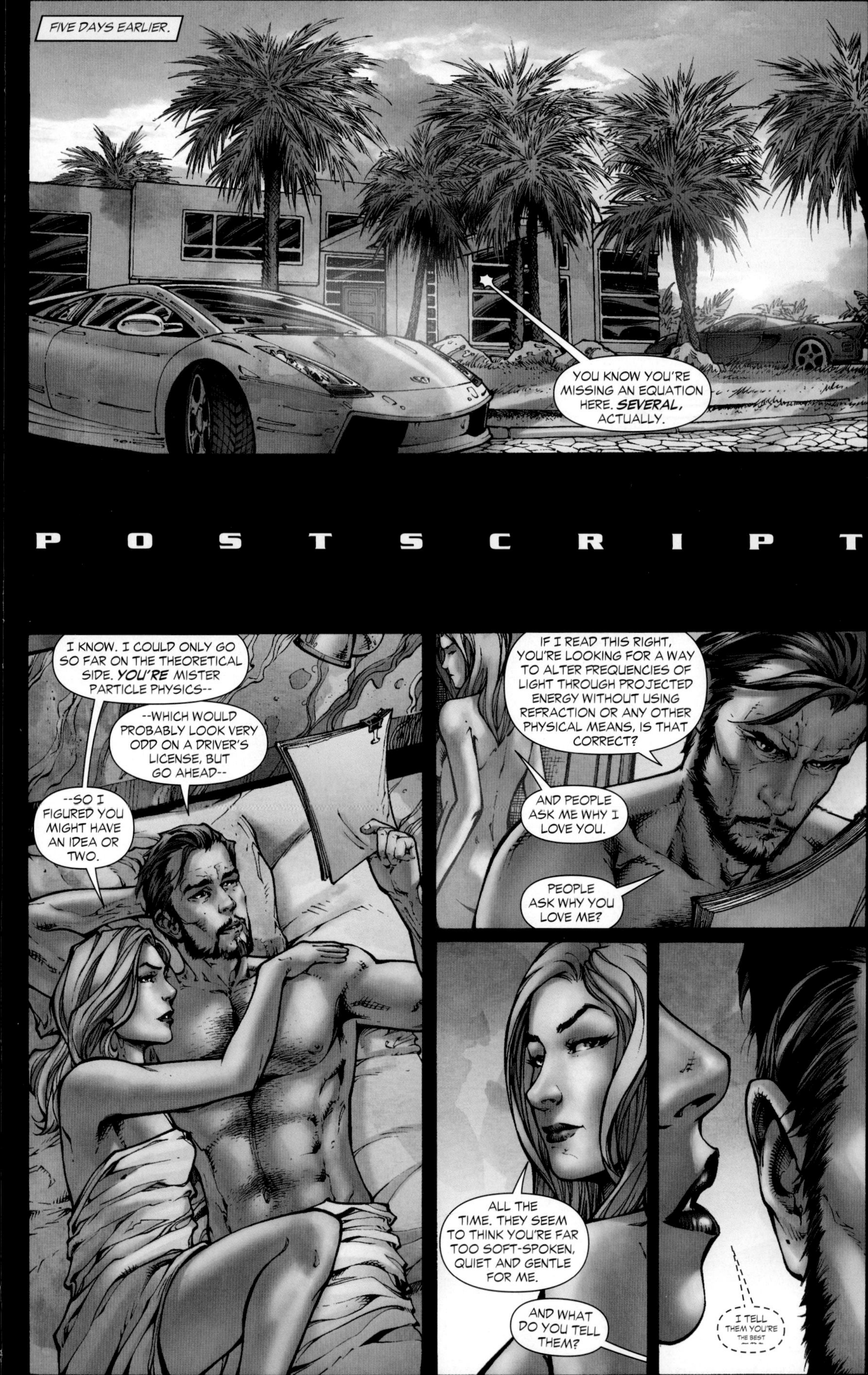

FIVE DAYS EARLIER.
YOU KNOW YOU'RE MISSING AN EQUATION HERE. SEVERAL, ACTUALLY.
POSTSCRIPT
I KNOW. I COULD ONLY GO SO FAR ON THE THEORETICAL SIDE. YOU'RE MISTER PARTICLE PHYSICS--
--WHICH WOULD PROBABLY LOOK VERY ODD ON A DRIVER'S LICENSE, BUT GO AHEAD--
--SO I FIGURED YOU MIGHT HAVE AN IDEA OR TWO.
IF I READ THIS RIGHT, YOU'RE LOOKING FOR A WAY TO ALTER FREQUENCIES OF LIGHT THROUGH PROJECTED ENERGY WITHOUT USING REFRACTION OR ANY OTHER PHYSICAL MEANS, IS THAT CORRECT?
AND PEOPLE ASK ME WHY I LOVE YOU.
PEOPLE ASK WHY YOU LOVE ME?
ALL THE TIME. THEY SEEM TO THINK YOU'RE FAR TOO SOFT-SPOKEN, QUIET AND GENTLE FOR ME.
AND WHAT DO YOU TELL THEM?
I TELL THEM YOU'RE THE BEST

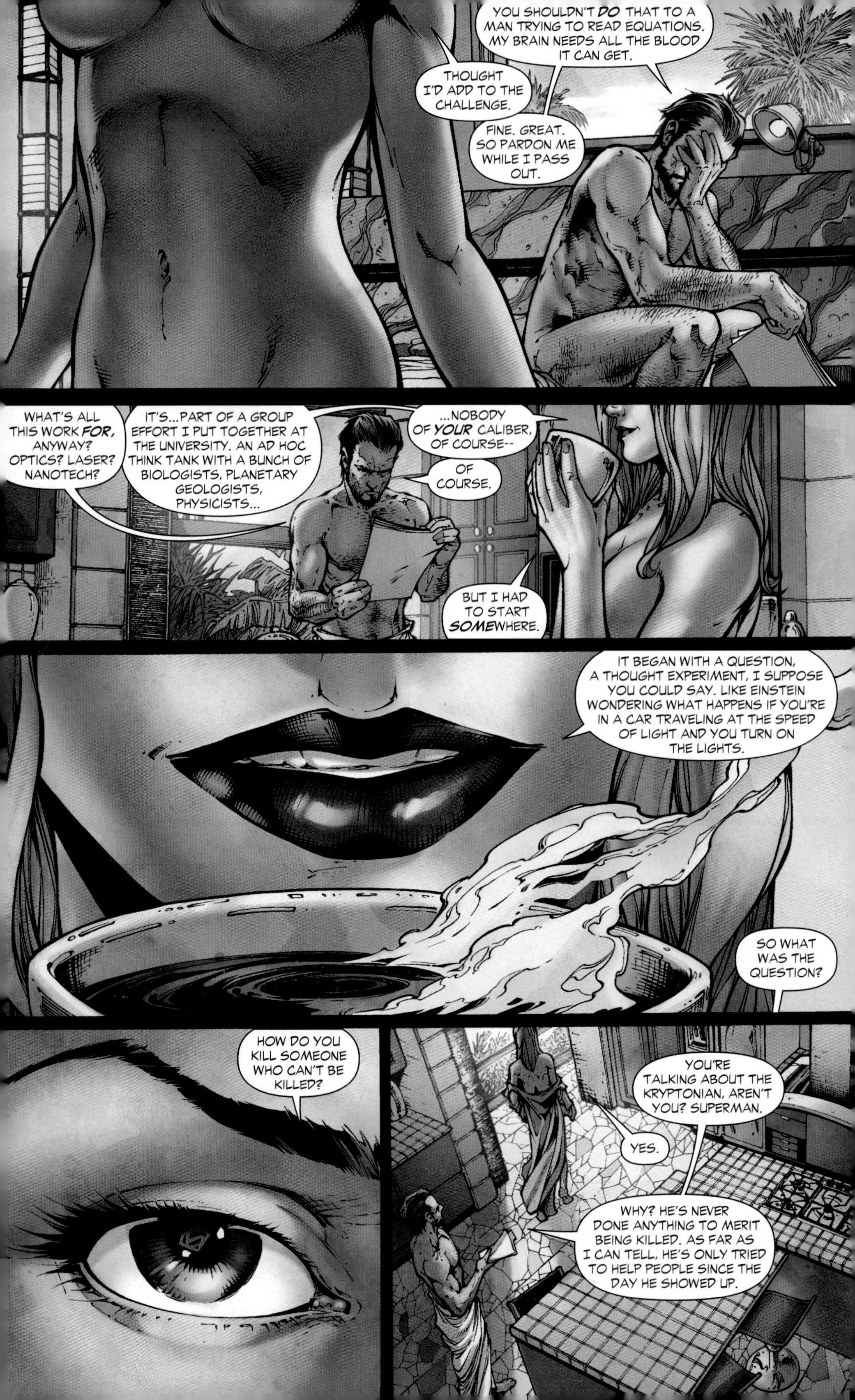
THOUGHT I'D ADD TO THE CHALLENGE.
YOU SHOULDN'T DO THAT TO A MAN TRYING TO READ EQUATIONS. MY BRAIN NEEDS ALL THE BLOOD IT CAN GET.
FINE. GREAT. SO PARDON ME WHILE I PASS OUT.
WHAT'S ALL THIS WORK FOR, ANYWAY? OPTICS? LASER? NANOTECH?
IT'S...PART OF A GROUP EFFORT I PUT TOGETHER AT THE UNIVERSITY. AN AD HOC THINK TANK WITH A BUNCH OF BIOLOGISTS, PLANETARY GEOLOGISTS, PHYSICISTS...
...NOBODY OF YOUR CALIBER, OF COURSE--
OF COURSE.
BUT I HAD TO START SOMEWHERE.
IT BEGAN WITH A QUESTION, A THOUGHT EXPERIMENT, I SUPPOSE YOU COULD SAY. LIKE EINSTEIN WONDERING WHAT HAPPENS IF YOU'RE IN A CAR TRAVELING AT THE SPEED OF LIGHT AND YOU TURN ON THE LIGHTS.
SO WHAT WAS THE QUESTION?
HOW DO YOU KILL SOMEONE WHO CAN'T BE KILLED?
YOU'RE TALKING ABOUT THE KRYPTONIAN, AREN'T YOU? SUPERMAN.
YES.
WHY? HE'S NEVER DONE ANYTHING TO MERIT BEING KILLED. AS FAR AS I CAN TELL, HE'S ONLY TRIED TO HELP PEOPLE SINCE THE DAY HE SHOWED UP.

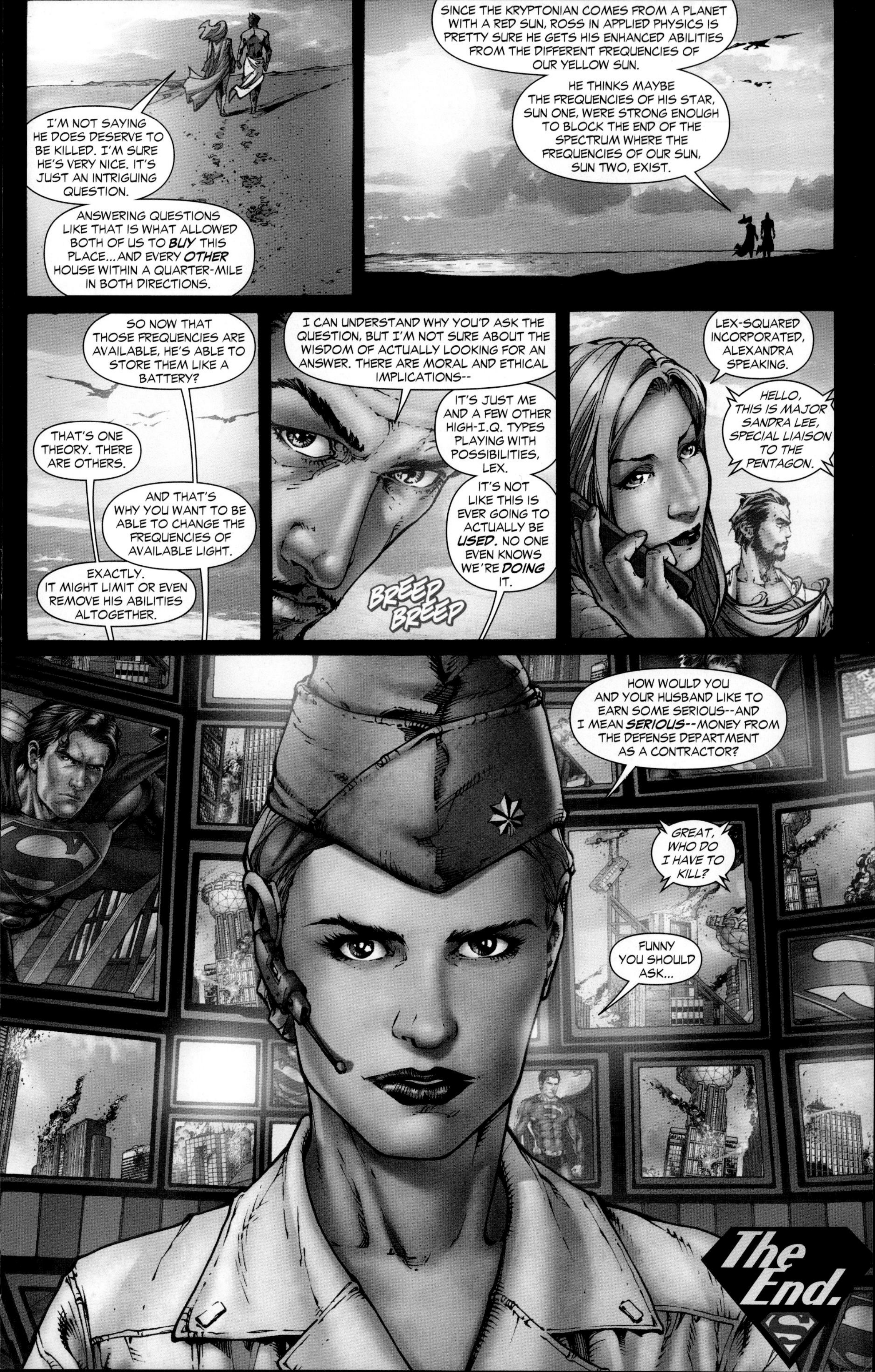
I'M NOT SAYING HE DOES DESERVE TO BE KILLED. I'M SURE HE'S VERY NICE. IT'S JUST AN INTRIGUING QUESTION.
ANSWERING QUESTIONS LIKE THAT IS WHAT ALLOWED BOTH OF US TO *BUY* THIS PLACE...AND EVERY *OTHER* HOUSE WITHIN A QUARTER-MILE IN BOTH DIRECTIONS.
SINCE THE KRYPTONIAN COMES FROM A PLANET WITH A RED SUN, ROSS IN APPLIED PHYSICS IS PRETTY SURE HE GETS HIS ENHANCED ABILITIES FROM THE DIFFERENT FREQUENCIES OF OUR YELLOW SUN.
HE THINKS MAYBE THE FREQUENCIES OF HIS STAR, SUN ONE, WERE STRONG ENOUGH TO BLOCK THE END OF THE SPECTRUM WHERE THE FREQUENCIES OF OUR SUN, SUN TWO, EXIST.
SO NOW THAT THOSE FREQUENCIES ARE AVAILABLE, HE'S ABLE TO STORE THEM LIKE A BATTERY?
THAT'S ONE THEORY. THERE ARE OTHERS.
AND THAT'S WHY YOU WANT TO BE ABLE TO CHANGE THE FREQUENCIES OF AVAILABLE LIGHT.
EXACTLY. IT MIGHT LIMIT OR EVEN REMOVE HIS ABILITIES ALTOGETHER.
I CAN UNDERSTAND WHY YOU'D ASK THE QUESTION, BUT I'M NOT SURE ABOUT THE WISDOM OF ACTUALLY LOOKING FOR AN ANSWER. THERE ARE MORAL AND ETHICAL IMPLICATIONS--
IT'S JUST ME AND A FEW OTHER HIGH-I.Q. TYPES PLAYING WITH POSSIBILITIES, LEX.
IT'S NOT LIKE THIS IS EVER GOING TO ACTUALLY BE *USED.* NO ONE EVEN KNOWS WE'RE *DOING* IT.
BREEP BREEP
LEX-SQUARED INCORPORATED, ALEXANDRA SPEAKING.
HELLO, THIS IS MAJOR SANDRA LEE, SPECIAL LIAISON TO THE PENTAGON.
HOW WOULD YOU AND YOUR HUSBAND LIKE TO EARN SOME SERIOUS--AND I MEAN *SERIOUS*--MONEY FROM THE DEFENSE DEPARTMENT AS A CONTRACTOR?
GREAT, WHO DO I HAVE TO KILL?
FUNNY YOU SHOULD ASK...
The End.

DAILY PLANET

★★★★ City Extra   "A Great Metropolitan Newspaper"   75¢

PARASITE REVEALED AS SERIAL KILLER

Murders Began Long Before Killer Reached Metropolis

By LOIS LANE
Metro Desk

Raymond Maxwell Jensen, 31, liked to keep a low profile. He paid for nearly everything in cash (obtained through means he never explained), and stayed with friends rather than renting or buying property (during which time many of these "friends" disappeared). He had one credit card tied to a mail box in Philadelphia rented under a different name. Several intensive web searches resulted in just one hit, a group photo of his high school graduating class. At every step he was careful to erase his footprints, eradicating anything – and anyone – that might be used to follow him.

His only point of contact with the rest of the world was his sister, Theresa, who believed her brother to be a consultant with a real estate company with holdings around the country, thus explaining his constant travel. He was brilliant, charismatic, personable and charming when he chose to be.

He was also one of the most successful and methodical serial killers in American history, even before the accident at S.T.A.R. Labs that transformed him into something even more dangerous, culminating in a series of deadly massacres.

That campaign of terror came to an abrupt end in the hours immediately after Jensen – dubbed the Parasite for his

(DAILY PLANET photo by James Olsen)

newfound ability to consume energy – was defeated by Metropolis's resident guardian, Superman. According to one Pentagon source, Jensen "died of coronary infarction shortly after his capture, an event likely triggered by energy deprivation. He didn't even live long enough for us to put him into a cell."

When asked about eyewitness reports suggesting that a still-living Jensen was seen being loaded into a military ambulance and driven away under police escort, the source said only, "They're mistaken."

The Pentagon has not yet responded to the Daily Planet's request for a copy of Jensen's autopsy.

KILLER STARTED YOUNG

A preliminary investigation into Jensen's background reveals a

troubling pattern of incidents that began at a young age and worsened over time. As with most nascent serial killers, he started with small animals and

IN TODAY'S LIFESTYLE SECTION

- **Fall Fashions Arrive on New York Runways**
- **New TV Series Retells Vlad Dracula Story**
- **Speculation Abounds Regarding Gotham's Mysterious Bat-Man**

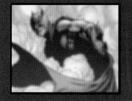

Coverage continues on page 7

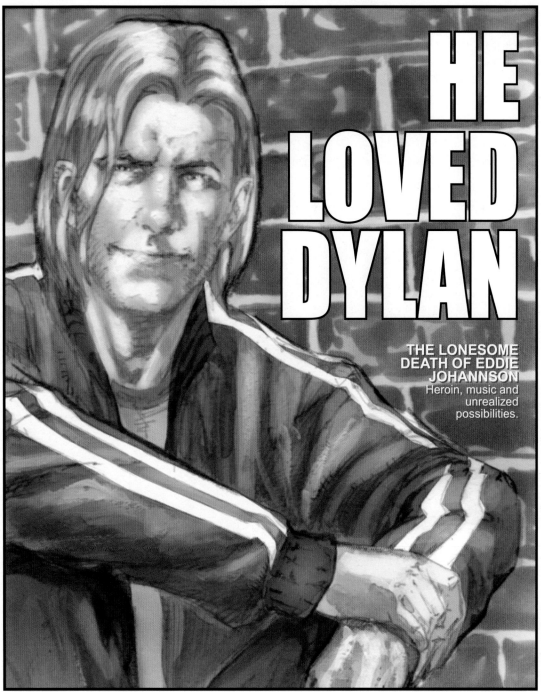

HE LOVED DYLAN

THE LONESOME DEATH OF EDDIE JOHANNSON
Heroin, music and unrealized possibilities.

(Photo courtesy of the Johannson family)

Eddie Johannson loved to listen to Bob Dylan. His neighbors said he would play his CDs late into the night, but rarely too loud. He didn't want to attract attention or bother anybody, at least not until three nights ago – the night he died from an injection of heroin.

Heroin's scientific name is diacetyl-morphine. Somehow that doesn't sound as bad as saying heroin. It sounds almost like a new diet drug. In fact, for over twenty years, ending in 1910, heroin was marketed by the Bayer Pharmaceutical Corporation as a cough suppressant. Heroin was the name they trademarked to make it easier to say, like aspirin. Heroin: Ask for it by name.

"Any man not busy being born is busy dying." That was the favorite reprise of Eddie's favorite Dylan song. I don't think he really knew what he was singing along with. Or maybe he did. Maybe he was playing a call for help. And maybe he just really liked the song.

Eddie lived in a small apartment just off the main lobby of a building on the south side. He greeted everyone coming in, and told everyone leaving to have a good day. Everybody knew his name. Well, everybody knew Eddie.

Nobody knew his last name, or that he was the oldest of four children, or that he attended Carnegie Mellon for two years before quitting so he could travel and see the world. He had a guitar in the closet. No one knows if he could play. No one ever heard him play. If he couldn't, then why was the guitar in his closet in the first place?

Feature Article by CLARK KENT

Maybe he could play. Maybe he was going to learn, one of these days. Maybe he had plans. Big plans.

Dead people are infinities of maybes.

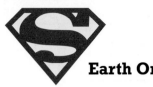

Earth One Sketch Book

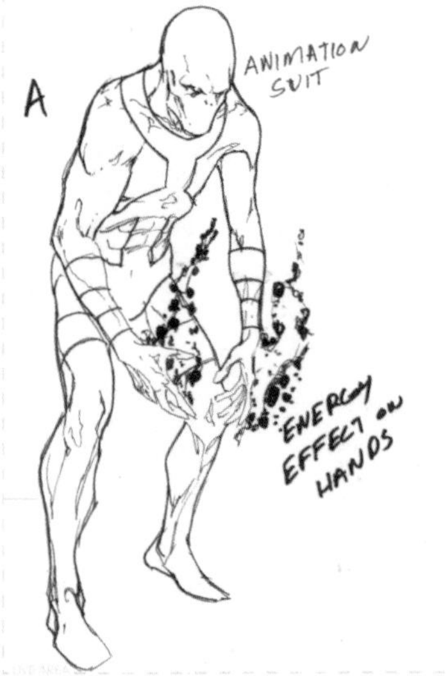
A
ANIMATION SUIT
ENERGY EFFECT ON HANDS

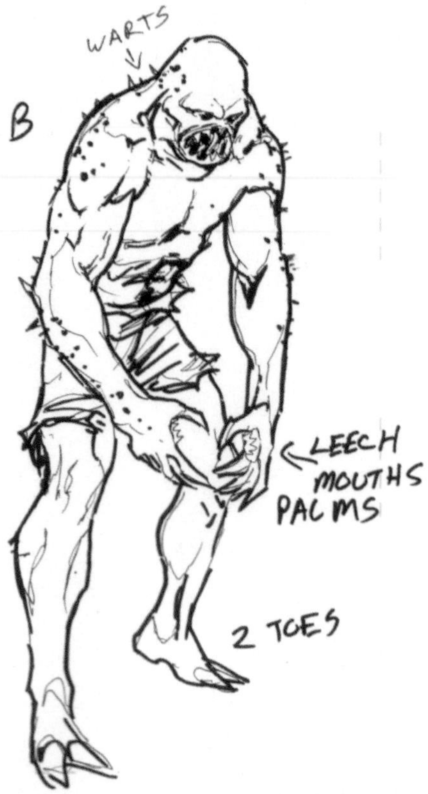
B
WARTS
LEECH MOUTHS PALMS
2 TOES

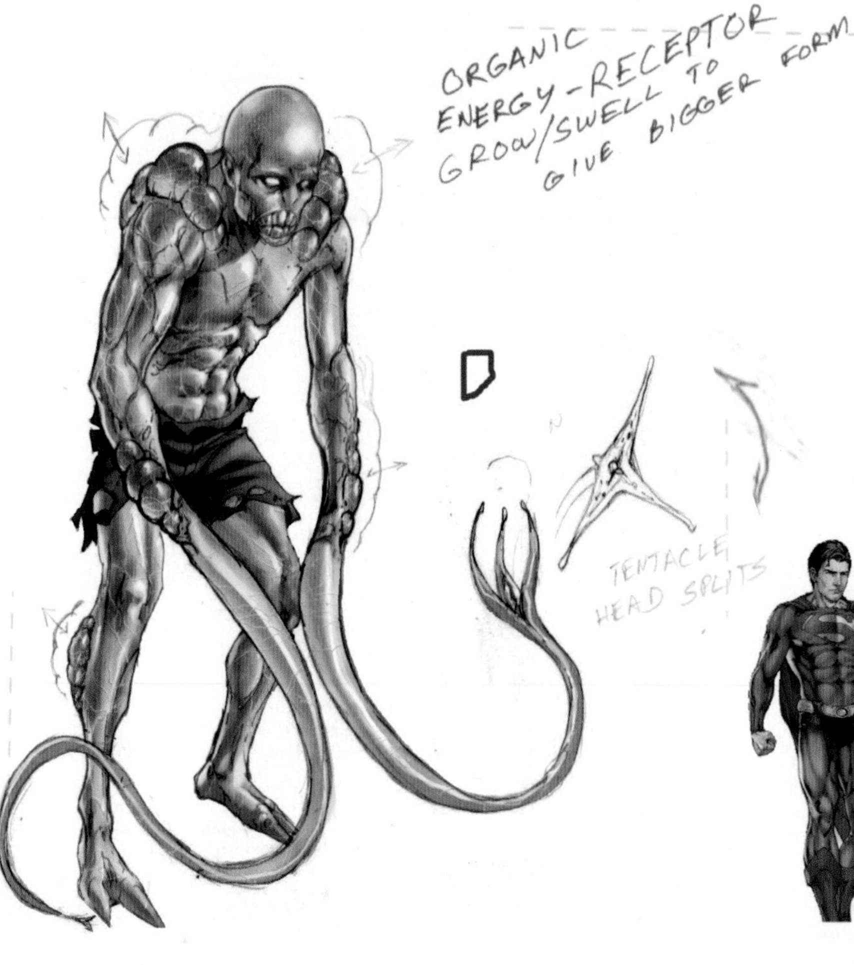
ORGANIC ENERGY-RECEPTOR GROW/SWELL TO GIVE BIGGER FORM.
D
TENTACLE HEAD SPLITS

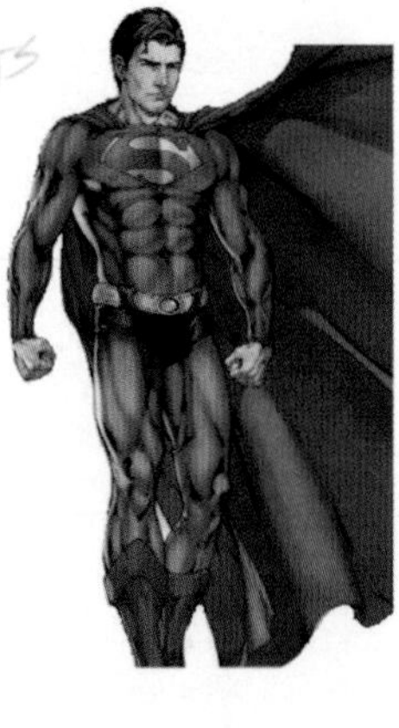

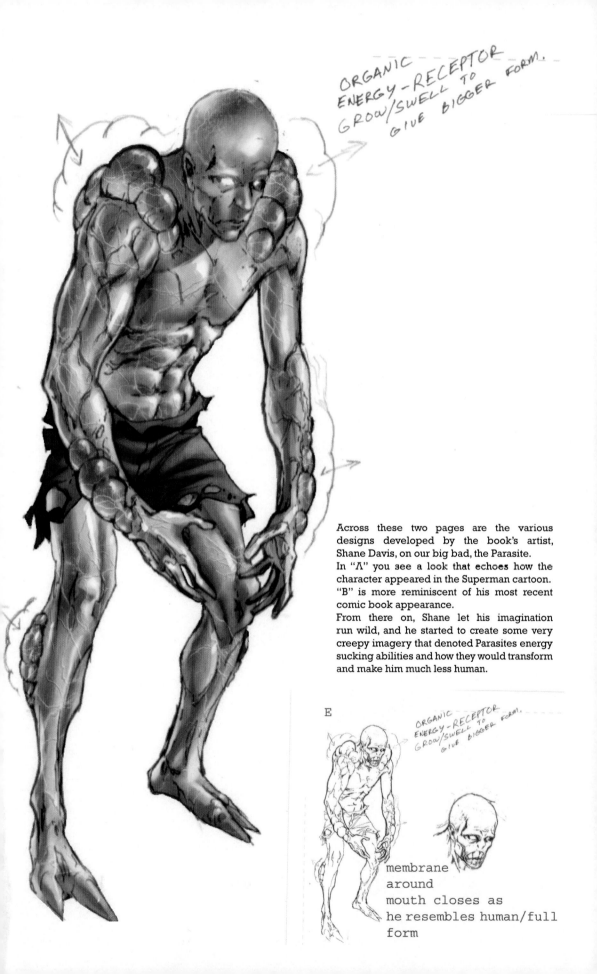

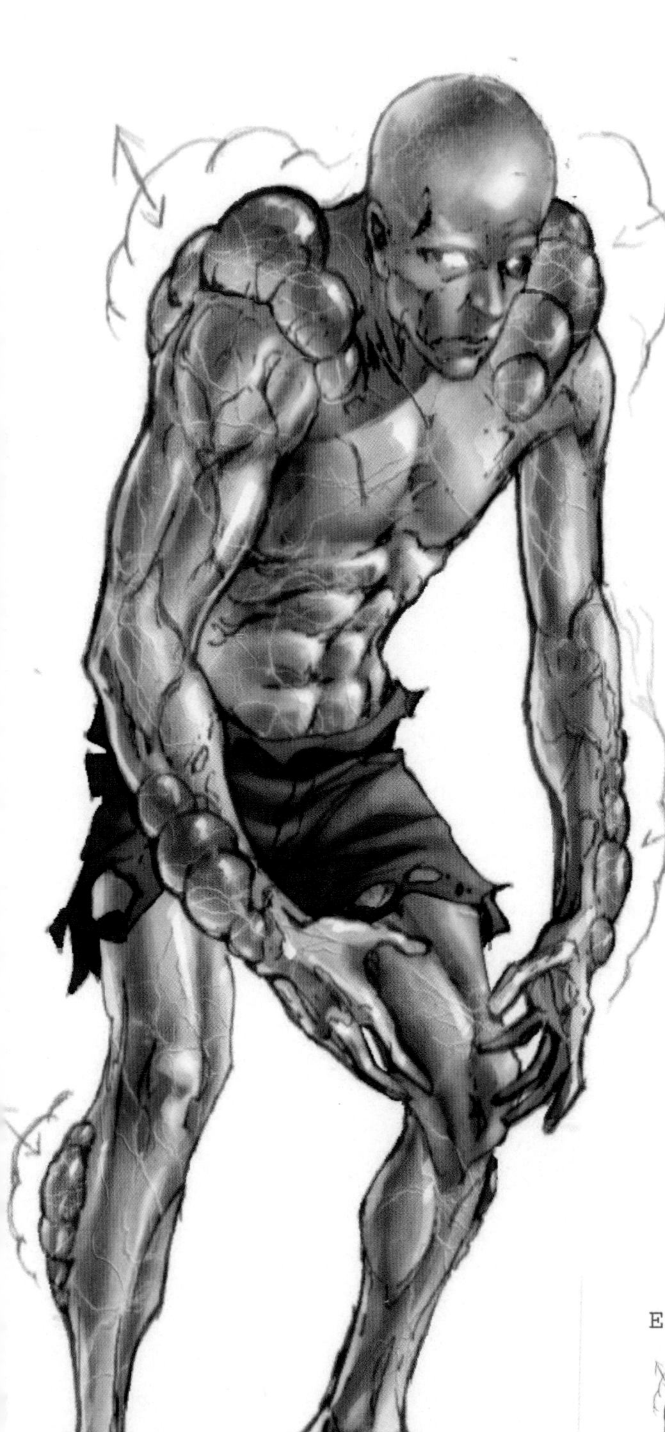
ORGANIC
ENERGY-RECEPTOR
GROW/SWELL TO
GIVE BIGGER FORM.

Across these two pages are the various designs developed by the book's artist, Shane Davis, on our big bad, the Parasite.
In "A" you see a look that echoes how the character appeared in the Superman cartoon.
"B" is more reminiscent of his most recent comic book appearance.
From there on, Shane let his imagination run wild, and he started to create some very creepy imagery that denoted Parasites energy sucking abilities and how they would transform and make him much less human.

E

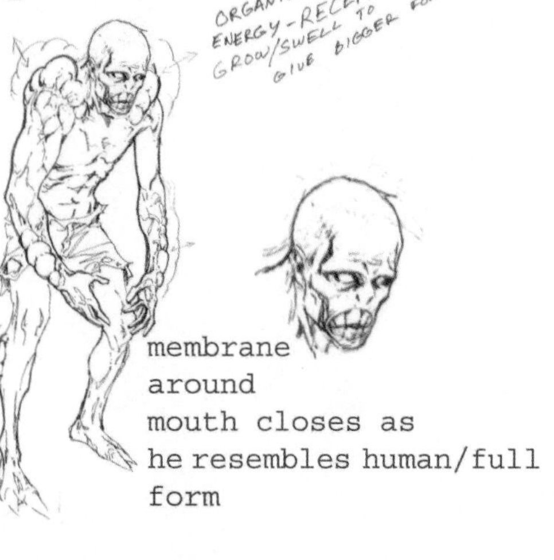
ORGANIC
ENERGY-RECEPTOR
GROW/SWELL TO
GIVE BIGGER FORM.
membrane
around
mouth closes as
he resembles human/full
form

J. MICHAEL STRACZYNSKI is an award-winning writer for film, television and comics. A former journalist for the Los Angeles Times and TIME Inc., he has worked on such series as *The Twilight Zone* and *Murder She Wrote*, and created *Jeremiah, Crusade* and *Babylon 5*, for which he may be best known. He penned the screenplay for Clint Eastwood's *Changeling*, for which he received a British Academy Award nomination, and *Ninja Assassin* for the Wachowskis. His work has earned him two Hugo Awards, as well as the Saturn, the Eisner, the Inkpot and the Ray Bradbury Award, among many others. His comics work includes *Rising Stars* and *Midnight Nation* for Top Cow/Image, *The Amazing Spider-Man*, *Supreme Power*, and *Thor* for Marvel, and he now writes both BEFORE WATCHMEN: NITE OWL and BEFORE WATCHMEN: DR. MANHATTAN for DC Comics.

SHANE DAVIS is an award-winning American comic book artist. Shane's pencils have appeared in JUSTICE LEAGUE OF AMERICA: THE LIGHTNING SAGA, MYSTERY IN SPACE and SUPERMAN/BATMAN: THE SEARCH FOR KRYPTONITE.